A Deeper Shade of Red

Loving United...Living with Liverpool

Mark Nevin

'Enjoyed it thoroughly...a darn good read'

http://manchesterunitedmemories.wordpress.com

Published in 2013 by Nevin Publishing/Unwashed Territories.
Copyright: Mark Nevin, 2013

ISBN-13: 978-1484856383
ISBN-10: 1484856384

This book is dedicated to those supporters in IMUSA and others who fought so staunchly to keep ownership of the club from Rupert Murdoch in the late nineties. All United supporters owe you a massive debt of gratitude. You harnessed the true spirit of radicalism within our football club and won, not just for United but for the game of football.

About the author

Mark Nevin was born in Prescot, Lancashire to Liverpool-supporting parents and grew up in Widnes, chiefly among Liverpool supporters. Soon after Prescot was taken from Lancashire and dragged rudely into Merseyside which, to Mark, seemed just part of an encroaching Merseyside influence over his life that he happily rebelled against, flying in the face of enormous peer pressure by becoming a Manchester United supporter. He once earned a precarious living writing articles on local football for a newspaper and, among other things, has his own United blog, which shares the title of this book, and regularly writes articles for the www.redmancunian.com website. He now lives in Cheshire with his wife and two children, one of whom now regularly accompanies him to Old Trafford. He doesn't, so far as he knows, live among Liverpool fans any longer, although he's not entirely certain about the cat's footballing allegiances.

Table of Contents

Acknowledgements

First of all, thanks should go to my mum and dad, Liverpool supporters through and through, who didn't attempt to influence or dissuade me from following a very different path in life. Our relationship has survived despite the rivalry of our clubs and this is pretty much exclusively down to them for being so damn reasonable about it. I'd also like to thank my son Tim for accompanying me to United games for the last half a dozen years or so and for allowing me to share some of the history contained in this book with him during walks to the ground across Trafford Bridge, half-times at Old Trafford or waiting for the reserves to kick off at Altrincham. Inevitably, a number of books on the subject of United, Manchester and football in general have been crucial in putting this book together. A full bibliography can be found at the back of the book which includes a range of books on both United and football in general; especially valuable have been Dave Hill's brilliant dissection of racism in football and on Merseyside *Out of his Skin* and city fan Dave Conn's two brilliant books on the state of the game in the modern age, *The Beautiful Game?* and *The Football Business*. Thanks to the *United We Stand. Red Issue* and *Red News* fanzines and to http://www.redmancunian.com and http://thebusbyway.com for consistently enjoyable and inspirational United-related reading and also to Dandelion Radio for providing musical inspiration during and indeed beyond the writing period.

Introduction

It's become a cliché to say that Manchester United are more than a football club and the problem with clichés is that people eventually stop thinking about them seriously and lose sight of what caused them to exist in the first place. It can be forgotten, even among some United fans, just what their club stands for, where it came from and how it got to be what it now is.

It's similarly the case with the United-Liverpool rivalry It becomes such a part of everyday life for fans of both teams that we can convince ourselves without much effort that our kids are born with it in their DNA, that it's persistently there, like a mathematical truth or a Roy Keane grudge, that it doesn't have a history of how and why it came into being, a reason for being there and an impetus that sustains it while other footballing rivalries grow and subside according to the fluctuating fortunes of the teams concerned.

The truth is that both the phenomenon of Manchester United and the rivalry with Liverpool have a history *and* a reason for being there, and the two are closely connected. While the rivalry is a more recent phenomenon than is often acknowledged, its roots are long, reaching back into economic tensions between the two great industrial centres of north-west England, through the two cities' very different social and political histories, even in their unrelated accents and dialects. For centuries there have simmered tensions, feuds, jealousy and envy all of which came together in a heady brew that nurtured the animosities between the two clubs that came to fruition many decades, even centuries later.

That the tensions and feuds pretty much all had Manchester on the right side and Liverpool as the unmitigated villains is important to the context of this book. You can interpret this in one of two ways. One, it's an accurate account of how things are, or two, this is the work of an extremely biased and partisan Manchester United supporter who would see things that way, wouldn't he. I would claim, actually, that both statements are true.

I am a biased and partisan Manchester United supporter, but I also believe I've produced an accurate account of how things are. It just turned out to be favourable to Manchester and United because that's the way things are too.

Another thing that informs the writing of this book is the fact that I'm not simply a Manchester United supporter, but one who grew up in fairly unusual circumstances, circumstances that gave me a particular perspective on the matter. I'm the son not only of one but of two avid Liverpool supporters. I went to primary school only a few miles from Merseyside, a school in which there were no other United fans and where nine out of ten supported Liverpool, including the teachers. During that time Liverpool were winning everything in sight. They were still winning pretty much everything in sight over a decade later when I decided to go to University of Liverpool to study for my degree. I've frequently watched footie games in pubs where the balance was heavily in favour of Liverpool supporters. Oh, and on one occasion I nearly got my head kicked in while queuing outside Goodison Park for a ticket to the Merseyside derby.

All of which tends to affect the development of your character a bit. I've learned to stand my ground and support my club in hostile circumstances which, I hope, may provide a view from close to enemy lines that that inevitably will be different from those in the many very good books about Manchester United in circulation.

This isn't, however, a straightforward autobiography. I can't imagine anyone would be interested in reading a purely autobiographical study of me so, although there are some autobiographical details in here (rows with Liverpool fans, gloating, that sort of thing), this is more about my emerging discovery of the nature of Manchester United and that rivalry with Liverpool. Fans of the two clubs do, it seemed to me from a very early age, tend to have a very different way of seeing the world and of seeing football. This inevitably brought me into conflict with almost everyone around me and has probably made me the awkward, blood-minded bastard I am today.

What also emerged in my life was a realisation that, not only was it impossible to understand all this without considering wider cultural elements in the city of Manchester and the place of Manchester United within this broader context Thus, Factory Records, the Peterloo massacre Madchester, the rise of The Smiths, , the Manchester Ship Canal, *Coronation Street*, the plays of Shelagh Delaney and even the paintings of L.S. Lowry all form part of a rich radical Mancunian culture that has, at least since the fifties, had Manchester United at its heart. I say 'even' L.S. Lowry because he was a city fan.

It will be a significant challenge to keep together the relatively small but very good circle of friends I've build up over the years once they've read this book. I'm already viewed as an intensely partisan supporter (is there any other kind, really?) of my club by the Liverpool FC supporters who already hold a natural majority in my family and seem, somehow, to have retained a rump of support among the steadily changing group of friends who've managed to endure my company over the years.

Incidentally, I've chosen, where relevant, to include references in the text. This might give the book an academic appearance, and if that puts you off I would invite you to ignore the little numbers in brackets, or even cross them out if it makes you feel better. I've included them because, occasionally, my opinions do have some basis in factual evidence and are not always merely the fevered rants of a partisan supporter. In other words, United rule Liverpool and I can prove it. Not only that but there's so much rubbish talked about United by rival supporters that it's important to me to be able to demonstrate that I'm right and they're wrong. There are also some very good books out there that you might wish to consider for further reading, which strikes me as a good enough reason in itself for including the references.

Anyway, I don't like over-long introductions, so I'm going to leave it there. I hope you enjoy the book although, if you're not a Manchester United fan, I'd warn you that this is very unlikely.

Mark Nevin, Widnes/Chester, March 2013

Prologue

The Boleyn Ground, 2 April 2011. West Ham United 2 Manchester United 4

The Ball Public House, Liverpool Rd, Widnes, 2 April 2011

It was a locality selected for its big screen and geographical proximity rather than its beer, the quality of which would put it well down any league you care to mention, including financial fair play. Despite the brew's lack of potency, at half-time the Liverpool fans who'd been imbibing the stuff were already celebrating in a manner that, to the untutored eye, might have indicated they were either rolling drunk or had won something important.

In fact, their own club was so far out of the running for the Premiership that they were, as my granddad used to say, 'nearly in the Scottish'. The reason for their giddy excitement was simply that the score at this point (2-0 to the Hammers) threatened to deliver a fatal blow to United's attempt to secure a record nineteenth English title, thwarting our bid to erase Liverpool's name from another of their diminishing places in the record books. The vicarious thrill of watching Chelsea walk to the title instead of us was revealingly indicative of the psychological impact on them of their own club's decline from dominant force in English football to ignominious also-rans harbouring only the vain hope that fourth place might allow them the occasional brief run in Europe.

United were by now seasoned veterans at shoving such hopes where the sun didn't shine. Even later in the season of 2006-07, with the league title still very much up for grabs, we'd been two goals down at Everton while Chelsea appeared to be heading to a routine home victory against an already pretty ordinary Bolton side missing more than half their outfield regulars. In the event, Bolton snatched an unlikely equaliser, United ran out 4-2 winners and we went on to recover the premiership trophy from its only three year holiday in London since the thirties.

Now, at half-time, as ludicrously premature celebrations went on around me, I went to the bar and pondered the options available to Ferguson in his efforts to pull off something similar. He'd been playing Rooney as a lone striker in the first half. This being a game we had to win, there had to be a strong argument for getting that season's revelation Chicharito on in the second half. Ferguson duly obliged, but, in a manner that had also become exhilaratingly familiar, also did something that no one, not me, not anybody in the pub, nor the pundits on the telly had come even close to predicting. He took off Evra to bring on the free-scoring Mexican and then, as the second half kicked off, it became apparent that Ryan Giggs was now playing at left-back.

Giggs, despite a career of Sinatra-length proportions (not to mention other off-pitch social activities comparable with those of Old Blue Eyes), had never before played in this position. It was a completely unexpected move and one that began to work straight away. While those around me speculated about whether Evra had picked up an injury (surely that had to be the only logical explanation?), Giggs continued to be an attacking threat on the left side while working to cover the left-back slot, and dropping back deep into that slot to thread through the most breath-taking left-footed passes both up the wing and diagonally through midfield. It had seemed to me, as it seemed all the other United fans in the pub, that there'd been nothing especially wrong with our first half play that the addition of a second striker wouldn't put right, but as the second half advanced it became clear that we'd now taken our domination of the game to a further, and irresistible, level. After twenty minutes of this, Rooney scored and the floodgates, as they say, were barged open by his freshly liberated and bullish physique. He went on to score a hat-trick and Chicharito added another for us to run out 4-2 winners once again.

The Liverpool fans in the pub had become increasingly pissed off as the half went on, spitting beer at the award of a soft United penalty (no softer than one that West Ham had got in the first half, but they were in no mood to admit this), frothing at the mouth at the failure to send off Vidic after a supposedly indisputable second yellow and going so red in the face as United seized the game by the scruff of its neck to leave West Ham's defenders breathing through their arses, that it seemed flames might be about to sprout from all their upper orifices, and probably their concealed lower ones too. Even before Chicharito's final goal most of them had stamped off home, complaining that life had dealt them another shitty hand, their hopes dashed in a maddeningly familiar way and by maddeningly familiar rivals.

This area of north-west England remains largely disputed territory between Liverpool and Manchester United supporters. And even here, with the managers of the pub confirmed United fans and the bulk of the blokes in the bar that day sharing their allegiance, many of an age that harked back to Busby and beyond, in what, you might say, could even be called a United pub – certainly in comparison with the Sporting Ford, Sundowner and Hammer & Pincers which remained a distinct shade of Liverpool red – there would always be enough Liverpool fans knocking about to retain the unique flavour of the rivalry that pervaded this and other towns in what used to be called south Lancashire. Not much more than twenty years previously I'd have been in there, cheering the other team, in the usually vain hope that someone else other than Liverpool would win something. Now, whoever you supported, it was a Manchester United world we lived in.

I went for a double Jameson's to celebrate.

Even here, where the oval ball had historically held sway, with home town Widnes ascending frequently to the national championship in a period of domination that ended roughly parallel to that of Liverpool, the round ball (while never completely replacing its misshapen cousin) had an appeal it couldn't match. The great thinkers, such as they were, had always hailed the superiority of association football, and rightly so. In 1933 Giraudoux, with the magnificent style of the great Argentinian and Uruguayan sides from that era in mind, talked of the ball as something that was characterised by a tendency to escape and defy physical laws, hence the magical, unique appeal of the game of football. [1] Lest rugby fans should feel accommodated by his musings, he added that only man and monkey had hands and they were so endowed by the almighty because both animals were, by nature, cheats. Thus, any game that chiefly depended on these appendages was necessarily flawed. Camus concurred, identifying the game's inherent unpredictability as the source of its unique appeal [2] and thus it became a subject representative of the existential nature of life itself. The elusiveness of the ball and how to combat it: therein lay the magic of football and, inextricably linked, the magic of Manchester United.

Those other powers of English football in my lifetime – and particularly those dominant Liverpool sides – sought to tame the game, to reduce control of that ball to a scientific system. I speculated, as I took the umpteenth piss of the day in the pub's grimy bogs (which looked and felt like a back yard with some enamel thrown up, a throwback to the great open-plan toilets of seventies football grounds, although admittedly an improvement on the likes of Queen of the South and Northwich Vics' now abandoned Drill Field, among other classic open sewers) that it was perhaps uniquely United in the English game who celebrated the very lawlessness and spontaneity of football in the manner of the two thinkers above. 'Liverpool would never have had George Best in the side,' a Liverpool-supporting friend had told me, for some reason seeing this as something to be pleased about. The same friend had had a good laugh, he presumed at our expense, when we'd signed Cantona. The laughs had ceased many years ago, their hollow echoes carried in the faces of those who'd vacated the pub early that day, their raddled countenances reflecting the inevitable misery of those who seek to tame reality rather than dare to dream.

I returned to the bar and got another pint. It was crap but I enjoyed it anyway.

[1] From 'La Gloire Du Football' in Glanville, B. (ed) *The Joy of Football*, p206.

[2] From 'France Football' 1958, ibid p143.

Chapter One: Three Minutes from Merseyside

All Saints CofE Primary School Playground, Hough Green, Widnes
Some time in 1975

It was cats versus dogs. The dogs were winning, easily. And I was a cat.

As something like the fiftieth punch rained down and an Airwear-cushioned boot was jabbed with some force into my ribcage, I pondered the wisdom of my decision. There was, I concluded quickly, essentially no logic at all underpinning my choice of allegiance any more than there was a detectable way out. Around fifteen sweaty boys barking like demented Alsatians clambered over the top of the three of us who affected to be cats. Bite, on this occasion, duly followed bark and the punching, kicking, butting, gouging and the occasional thrusting of handful of grass up nostril showed little sign of abating any time soon.

There was little excuse for my predicament. When I'd thrown my hand up and volunteered to join the cats I'd known there were only two of them, a couple of emaciated kids who looked like they'd been accosted by a gang of things with sharp teeth and claws even before battle (if it can be called that) commenced. The charge of the shite brigade. The phrase ricocheted through my mind as the attacks continued. Meanwhile the dogs – a grinning horde of seasoned campaigners in the field of playground warfare – leered at the easy pickings before them, smacking their chops like Billy Bremner and Norman Hunter lining up against a midfield possessing the physique of four Jesper Olsens and none of the guile.

After about twenty minutes of this, the dogs got bored and walked away. There were, after all, restricted levels of satisfaction to be had from such a one-sided contest. The tears that rolled down my cheeks were of rage at the injustice of it all rather than any of the many pains inflicted on my skinny frame. Why couldn't just some of the dogs have sided with the cats? Why did everyone who joined in automatically side with the ones with the greater numbers? Why didn't someone stick up for the underdogs? And whatever the reasons, why couldn't somebody tell me so that I could avoid falling victim to regular pastings like this?

There's a character played by Jack Warden in Sidney Lumet's film *Twelve Angry Men* who personifies the image many other fans have of the Manchester United supporter. Warden's character is keen to get a quick resolution to the jury's deliberations so he can get away quickly to the ball game, so much so that, when Henry Fonda tips the balance towards a 'no' vote, he changes sides, desiring only to be with the winners and untroubled by any concerns of conscience or personal loyalty, interested only in expedience and seeking the quickest route to success, whether earned or not. And when the nervous guy in the ill-fitting suit from the wrong side of the tracks played by Jack Klugman tells him he doesn't support the Yankees, but rather the ailing Baltimore, the character becomes animated in a way he never does during the rest of the film, genuinely amazed that anyone can support a bunch of losers, mystified that loyalty can be anything more than the desire to be on the side of perpetual victors, an unquestioning disciple of the view that allegiance can only be motivated by an amoral desire for success.

Those who hold such a view about United are often far more like Warden's juror themselves, distressed by the consequences of their own allegiances and so seeking demonization of United purely for the purposes of self-appeasement, pretending that support for United has no real depth, is purely there for the gratification of those who seek an easy route to success. I suspect deep down they know this isn't really why they hate us. Keith Dewhurst has identified the true source of such animosity better than anyone else, identifying United as the only true and consistent representatives of the spirit of heroism of the English game because historically we've striven most earnestly for stylistic perfection – Dewhurst claims that this, and not for any success on the field, is why United are so detested by other supporters.[1] And true heroism, of course, means sometimes standing out from the crowd;

some fuzzy sense of which may or may not be why I decided to throw my lot in with the cats.

In truth, at school I felt far more like the Henry Fonda figure, except I never managed to convince anyone else over to my side of the argument.

Conformity to rigid and unquestioning codes of behaviour is as much the scourge of the English schools system as it is to English football. I don't just mean the nurturing of subservience to unblinking authority as administered by teachers, but also that doled out by the pupils themselves. In fact, I mean *especially* that doled out by the kids. My school life reads back to me like a re-enactment of *Lord of the Flies* with not enough Ralphs and too many Jacks. Although I recall occasional pretensions to nobility among the scabby masses at senior school, my four years at junior school frequently yielded skirmishes like the one described above whereby open warfare was only ever declared by the many against the few. It wasn't as if the few were conscripts, as it was left entirely open to you which side you joined, which may raise questions as to how the side of the few managed to exist at all. The answer, I suppose, was they managed to exist because of people like me, my default tendency throughout my school life being quite consciously to choose the side with the odds stacked against them. 'Only dead fish swim with the tide,' said Malcolm Muggeridge, though I suppose the cynical might ask how they got to be dead in the first place.

There was nothing especially deliberate or high-handedly moral about my position. Looking back, I can only put it down to either an unfocused and often debilitating masochistic streak or something far more psychologically complex understandable only, perhaps, through the twin obsessions of football and music that appear to have underpinned my life and that seem to me, rightly or wrongly, to offer a way of understanding most things.

There will, I'm sure, be some who are now flicking from this page and back to the cover in puzzlement that what they thought was a book about Manchester United now appears to concern the reminiscences of someone imperilled by an attraction to minority causes, no less, and thus could scarcely have anything to do with a club enjoying levels of support that these days usually gets put at a worldwide figure that, it sometimes seems, exceeds the number of people in existence on the planet. Let me assure you that in the period to which I refer, and in my geographical position, supporting United was a most conspicuously marginal choice and one that in time would be highly likely to see me on the receiving end of many more of the kinds of beatings meted out to the unfortunate cats. And even before the perilous era of maximum hatred of United dawned, you were at best likely to have the most askance of askance looks delivered in your direction at the sheer oddness of your choice and this, in an institution hell-bent on conformity, was arguably far more dangerous.

It was 1975. The season before that United had come up from the second division. The school was All Saints CofE Primary School and it was, and still is, situated in the extreme north-west corner of Widnes, a part of the world that remained defiantly Lancastrian, though by then its decaying industrial corpse had been crudely shoehorned into leafy Cheshire when the counties were stripped from their tradition geographical identities and reconfigured the previous year. More significantly this was the area of Hough Green, to give that north-west corner its name, which has a sign at its most western point that reads 'MERSEYSIDE' in big unfriendly letters. The area surrounding All Saints was, as it is now, 90% 'scouse overspill' as the local Widnesian vernacular had it.

There are similar areas all over north Cheshire and what was once west Lancashire, filled with populations who were either ousted from Liverpool when they set about destroying city centre tenements, back-to-backs and near-slums during the sixties, and who – although they continued to bleat allegiance to the scouse cause – went comparatively upmarket and moved to spanking new council estates in Kirkby, Skelmersdale, Runcorn, Widnes and elsewhere – all towns to which the word 'upmarket' could scarcely be applied in any other circumstances. Because of a desire on my parents' part, for no discernable faith-based reasons, that I should go to a 'church' school, and because All Saints was only one of two such choices to CofE kids available in the town, I found myself schooled in an area whose contrasts with the rest of Widnes remain marked to this day. Not only were there no United fans in the school, I very much doubt that the possibility of supporting United crossed the mind of anyone there except me. In fact, it was three years after declaring my support that I even got to really know another United supporter.

Widnes was and still is, on the face of it, territory barren of professional or even senior amateur football and where the prevailing wind blows very firmly in the direction travelled by the oval-shaped ball of rugby league, as indeed was the case in much of what had the previous year still been known as south Lancashire. Try it yourself. Find Bolton on the map and draw a line horizontally west from it. Then draw vertical lines down both sides through the eastern edges of Liverpool and Salford. Then at the bottom draw another horizontal line across from Chester. As the period of which I currently write is prior to Wigan Athletic being elected to the football league, you then have a box 27 miles wide and 34 miles deep with no professional football clubs in it at all. While the north-west of England was one of the original hotbeds of the professional game, such hotbeddery (if that's even a word, which it clearly isn't) occurred to the north, west and east of this box and, within it, you found the ancient and modern strongholds of Lancastrian rugby league – Wigan, St Helens, Warrington and of course Widnes. With the exception of the modern Wigan Athletic, the football teams in these towns continue to play at a level of the game disproportionately small for the size of their populations. Few towns of Warrington's size (42nd largest urban centre in Britain) can support nothing bigger than a semi-professional football team, and the same is true on a slightly smaller scale of St Helens and Leigh. Widnes is the 130th biggest town in Britain and, come census time, does battle with Dewsbury to secure the status of the largest town in the country without a football club senior enough to compete in the FA Cup (a tussle it won with ease in the most recent census). And even towns without a rich rugby league heritage – Skelmersdale , Kirkby, Maghull, Prescot, Chorley, Ormskirk and others – have never been able to sustain a football club above the level of the conference. Runcorn had a team at the birth of Rugby League (Highfield), but it folded and a later attempt to resurrect it ended in serious levels of embarrassment to a town that could really do without such things.

Highfield managed to lose every game they played in a full season (1989-90) and soon bit the dust again, an embarrassing footnote in the history of the sport.

The concept of the thwarted development of football in rugby league territory seems logical enough, but why those non-rugby playing towns? In the skewed environs of All Saints (that only recognised Liverpool and Everton as forces of any note in the round ball game, with some acknowledgement of the existence of the then notorious, high profile and infamously villainous Leeds United) it wasn't apparent to me then; but the parallelogram within which sat the Lancashire rugby league belt was a no man's land of contested footballing loyalties every bit as fierce as within the major footballing centres themselves where allegiance to the four major (a word that may be contested when applied to some of these teams, and one in particular) Merseyside and Manchester teams, rather than to the oval ball, is what has stunted the potential growth of other clubs.

While Liverpool and Manchester United have by far the largest reservoirs of support across the area, there is more support for Everton and Manchester City outside their own immediate localities than is commonly acknowledged. For instance, though it defies conventional assumptions put about in recent times, over 50% of city's season ticket holders come from somewhere either in this geographical zone, slightly to the north of it in Oldham or in the south easterly light blue stronghold of Stockport). [2] While this hasn't stopped these towns supporting football league clubs, the case to the west is very different, and consistently so, suggesting a level of support for the Merseyside and Manchester teams that is fierce, uncompromised and historically well-established, not merely an aspect of recent trends towards non-localised support.

When looking at the 'out of town' element of support, there's no evidence whatsoever to support the conventional view that city fans come from Manchester and United fans come from anywhere but. The same is true on Merseyside, where Everton fans frequently make the same claims, largely due to feelings of inadequacy and a desperate desire to lay claim to *some* sort of significance, rather than any basis in fact. There are differences in the make-up of the support of these four teams but these are, rather, differences of scale, so that the further west you go the more support for city thins out, and similarly so in the opposite direction for Everton. Within that sizeable expanse of land, all of these clubs have meaning for some proportion of the footballing public, but the United and Liverpool support is vastly more prominent and the battleground between the two rival clubs more pronounced here than anywhere else in the world so that, to watch a Manchester United-Liverpool game in Warrington, for example, is to observe the fervent nature of the bitter rivalry in its most naked form.

In fact, all those people from around the world who pay up good money to visit Anfield or Old Trafford via Thomas Cook's in search of true north-west footballing passion would, i'd contend, be far better shelling out their euros, dollars or yen on a few pints in front of the telly at The White Hart when United v Liverpool is on, and a room at the local Travelodge, as opposed to the anodyne and over-priced arrangements the tour operators have arranged on their behalf. As you go further east, you then find United v city games have something like the same fervour while to the west some of the spark remains in Liverpool-Everton games despite Liverpool fans' gradual historical march away from their ancient rivalry, just one of the many things that have, over the years, brought about the self-marginalisation of Liverpool FC. But more of that later.

While you'll struggle to find many Liverpool fans at the very east of this quadrangle in the city of Salford, you'll find plenty of support for United in areas like St Helens and my home town of Widnes, both of which bank right up on to the eastern suburbs of

Liverpool, support that's been there for generations, long before St Helens was dragged out of Lancashire by municipal county boundary changes and into Merseyside, where few St Helens residents, possessors of one of the richest south Lancastrian dialects of all (for outsiders , consider if you will the cases of Colin Welland and, even more so, Johnny Vegas) feel they belong. The writer of the entry on St Helens on The Knowhere Guide names the made-up county 'Miseryside' and says he continues defiantly to use Lancashire rather than Merseyside in his postal address. [3] Such a staunch position is not unrepresentative of attitudes within the town.

There are reasons why United have resonance for football supporters in these areas that go well beyond this resistance to creeping municipal boundaries and which will be explored in more detail in the book. In time, when I moved to senior school in the thoroughgoing Widnesian enclave of Ditton, I would find that, while still very much in the minority, I wasn't anywhere near as alone as I'd presumed. But at All Saints I cut literally a solitary figure, standing alone while 90% of the school swore allegiance to Liverpool FC, by far the most successful club of the era, a small number expressed loyalty to an Everton side that had last won the league only five years previously and a bunch of avid Widnesians stood out against the whole business, lampooned the footie fans as lesser men, and professed love only for rugby.

I stood, my United scarf in one hand and some bizarre fantasy in my head that fed off a rich ore of misunderstanding and nurtured the ludicrous possibility that, despite my obvious shortcomings on the football field, I was a Gordon Hill, that final piece of the Docherty jigsaw that had created the unique mid-seventies Manchester United side, in waiting. That Hill had gone from playing for Millwall to a starring role for United in an extremely short space of time provided a vague sense of hope that such a transformation was possible, but my young mind was sorely underestimating the kind of leap in status it would take even to render me not one of those who, at the end of picking sides for a game of footie at dinner time, would be subjected to the crushing phrase, almost always enunciated in disparaging scouse tones, 'youse can have them'.

At All Saints the majority of the school population and their parents were displaced Liverpudlians and, in what may well be my first experience of the peculiar kind of doublethink that is very much a hallmark of Liverpool FC support, imagined themselves not even to be displaced. Hough Green Railway station just up the road was then regarded by British Rail as lying within the Merseyside boundary which enabled the use of Merseyrail saver tickets for cheap rides into Liverpool (or 'town', as they called it, many referring to Widnes, disparagingly, as 'the village'). One day, the headteacher Mr Binnall had used the traditional Monday morning assembly – a horrific ritual which every week entailed singing hymns and listening to bible readings for about three hours with crossed legs to the accompaniment of children screaming as they were carried out with cramp – to show off the cup won by our victorious institution's football team and proudly pointed out that its crest revealed that we'd won it for around two-thirds of its existence. Not quite the achievement his boasts made it out to be. Practically all schools in Widnes were obsessed with playing rugby while at ours, so close to that Merseyside boundary, we never played with anything other than a round ball in my four years there, something that made me deeply unprepared for the violence of the other game when first exposed to it at my senior school, Bankfield, where they played little else (I still recall with some terror my first flimsy attempt at the act of advanced GBH that rugby classifies as a tackle being met by a 'hand off' that felt like it had dislodged part of my brain and which I, having experienced only the somewhat less pugilistic rules of association football, immediately appealed to the referee about, not imagining such an assault could possibly be legal). So beating those other schools to win the local junior league was a bit like defeating a dyslexic in a spelling bee.

Few at the school weren't football daft, and the Liverpool fans were contemptuous of the rugby supporters, almost universally feigning to support the other team on the frequent occasions that Widnes were at Wembley and three-quarters of residents of non-scouse territories of the town decamped there with them, leaving shops closed and tumbleweed a-blowing. Well, this being Widnes it was more discarded chip papers, cider bottles or the occasional unidentifiable piece of chemical refuse from the tip at the back of my parents' house that was a-blowing. Forced to spend my school days in the one area untouched by the rugby league team's exploits, as Liverpool's league title and UEFA Cup in 1973 was followed by FA Cup in 1974 I found around me a deafening cacophony of triumphalism as many of those who I like to think had rather less fortitude than me deserted whatever half-hearted allegiance they'd professed to the blue side of Merseyside and became sudden converts to the sweet promise of success offered by Shankly's team. Although my uncle took me to a few Everton games throughout 1974-75 the only long-term thing he really achieved by this was the nurturing of a lifelong hatred of Liverpool FC, for which I am eternally grateful and which may have, along with the aforementioned tendency to find myself in the position of one of those kids on Mike Reid's Runaround left behind after the rest, seeing the number who'd picked the other option, had transferred sides in a frenzy of peer pressure, helped to provide me with the defiance required to resist the pull of the Red & Shite Kop. If the idea was to make me an Everton supporter, then I fear I was left only with the memory that keeper David Lawson always seemed to save with his legs and that the match day programme always seemed to show them either one place above or below Sheffield United in the table. At the time, of course, United weren't even on the same page, imbuing them with an enticing mystery which, when exposed to highlights of their second division games on Granada TV, I was to find irresistible.

Despite the melting pot of rivalries across Old South Lancashire, it's curious that at that point the United-Liverpool hostility was still largely under-developed. Circumstances, however, were to ensure that the dormant volcano that was Red-on-red animosity wasn't going to remain so for long. At my school, given the rather fickle level of attachment of most of the kids to their football teams and their scouse or pseudo-scouse heritage, few had an interest in the game that even extended to knowledge of who United were, let alone seeing them as something that, in their adult years, they'd become very agitated about to the point of obsession. For the rest, their interest reached really only as far as Tommy Doc and the Lou Macari saga of 1972/73. Regarding the former, Docherty's public image stood in stark contrast to the restrained demeanour of Liverpool's Bob Paisley or the egregious countenance of his predecessor Bill Shankly, from under whose nose Macari had been rudely snatched, and these miniature Kop-ites got from their dads the general idea that the Doc was little more than a rent-a-gob in charge of a fly-by-night footie team who were too big for their boots and going nowhere fast.

The battle over Macari's signature, however, provided the first real stirring of the United/Liverpool rivalry that would, within a decade, grow to become the most fervent in English football. Celtic's young star Macari had gone to Anfield to watch a game with the full intention of signing for Liverpool afterwards. But the Doc and then-assistant Pat Crerand happened to be sitting near him in the crowd and smartly offered him the chance to join United instead. With United careering towards relegation and Liverpool heading for the championship, it shouldn't have been much of a contest. However, a mixture of Caledonian allegiance (United at that time sometimes fielded as many as eight Scots in their first team) and what appeared a genuine desire on the part of Macari to be part of a building process as opposed to joining a club that, like Celtic, was pretty much the finished article in terms of winning trophies, as well as – even at their lowest point – that magic United undeniably had, swung the deal and Macari came to Old Trafford for a then enormous fee of £200,000. To be surrounded by Liverpool fans at that time was to see what a massive kick in the teeth this was to their previously untainted assumptions of superiority, and the ensuing resentment contained much anti-Italian (citing Macari's ancestry and an unwillingness, given that Shankly was their manager at the time, to count him as a Scot) invective. And it wouldn't be forgotten.

The first time I became aware that I wasn't completely alone, stuck between the two vast and unrelenting land masses of Liverpool FC and Rugby League, was also the first time I began to become fully aware of the particular passion associated with support for my club. I don't know, and I presume never will know, the identity of the individual who was the catalyst. The occasion was sparked by a pre-emptive anti-sectarian initiative on half of my CofE primary school and St Basils, the RC school a couple of hundred yards up the road. With the atrocities being committed on both sides of the Northern Ireland divide being played out regularly on everyone's TV screens, it isn't far off the mark to say that, in those days of very little live football, we saw more action from that than we did of any of the hostilities being enacted on the football terraces, and there were enough violent skirmishes between the Rugby League 'Widdies' and the Scousers in the town to be going on with, without national and religious divisions getting added to the cocktail. So, in a seemingly honourable outbreak of community spirit, the two schools decided to run as many joint activities as the educational authority and archdiocese could come up with to snuff out any potential religious tension before it took root in our unformed and vulnerable young minds. Such ventures might, I think, have had more success had not our headmaster not called the other school's teachers 'left footers' behind their backs or constantly referred to the Liverpool Roman Catholic cathedral as 'Paddy's Wigwam'. It was, however, in this spirit that the whole school was duly trooped up to St Basils to hear a talk to pupils from both schools from the popular football writer Michael Hardcastle.

In a move that was indicative of the rather half-hearted aim of the exercise, the school hall was divided into two halves, Basils to the left and us on the right, with a chain of teachers from both sides in between. In what turned out to be more an exercise of anodyne suffusion of young spirits than anything else, the writer's first questions to his young audience were stultifying and predictable, as was the response. 'Who supports Liverpool?' he asked, and so many hands went up it was almost impossible to detect the few dissenting bodies scattered among them. 'And Everton?' Another, much smaller, bunch of hands. 'Anyone support anyone else?' A few hands shot up. 'Leeds,' said one scrawny lad with gnarled features a few rows in front of me. 'Widnes,' shouted out one of the rugby-league-first-and-last community in a large, typically defiant voice, far too deep, it seemed, for the tender years of its owner.

This left me and one lad amid the Basils contingent to declare our support for United, a couple of pariah-like hands with the eyes on us a mixture of curiosity, mirth and a fair bit of simmering Macari-inspired contempt. When Hardcastle got to the end of his talk and asked for any questions, there was silence, generated by a general apathy that flourished in the fake bonhomie of the occasion. The only hand to go up, its passion unsuppressed, was that of my unknown fellow United fan. 'Have you written any books about United?' he asked. The author shook his head, saying that, although he'd written a book called 'United', this related to the fictional Bank Vale United. He only wrote fictional books and hadn't written any about real football teams. Any more questions? Nothing, and then the United lad stuck his hand up again. 'Do you know anyone who's written any books about United?' Despite another negative answer, the lad was persistent, following this with a barrage of at least a dozen more United-related questions, uninterrupted by anyone else in the hall. By the end, the hapless author seemed mildly irritated by his persistent interrogator, few of whose questions he could answer positively or in any depth. 'Anyone else got a question?' he'd ask, to be met with no response until the United fan put his hand up again.

The unknown supporter that day provided me with nothing less than a moment of epiphany, reflecting back to me what it was like to be a lone United fan in that area and also the level of passion and commitment to the cause that went with it and that lay at the heart of our mutual obsession. In the true spirit of his club, he injected vibrancy into an occasion where there was clearly intended only to be room for the controlled and artificial, the school hall a sterile microcosm of English football of the seventies and eighties, and his a defiant burst of flowering life and energy amid the cold stones of my youth, a benign and yet provocative two fingers raised to the dumbing efforts of the day, time and place. Our love for United, alone, could not be snuffed out, could indeed survive in any circumstances, whether hostile or inert, and in ground however inhospitable and barren. My sole regret is that I sat there like a forlorn Paddy Roche in a muddy six yard area, with no questions of my own to offer. I ought to have joined him in his solitary crusade and helped him crush the tide of conformists that sat to the left, right, front and back of us that day and throughout our primary school lives. I'd spend the rest of my school life, it seemed, seeking earnestly to right this wrong.

[1] Dewhurst, K. *When You Pull On A Red Shirt,* p21
[2] Brown, A. *Do You Come From Manchester?* pp10-15
[3] http://www.knowhere.co.uk/St-Helens/Merseyside/Northern-England/info/worstthings

Chapter Two: Isolation

22 August 1953, Anfield – Liverpool 4 Manchester United 4

While the rivalry between the two clubs would take another two decades to flower into the outright hostility we know today, history records this match as the forum for the first stirring of any outright animosity in a match between the sides, at least from the Liverpool end.

It's not the only precursor of the future in evidence that day. Liverpool's most successful manager, Bob Paisley, was in their side, while United's line-up illustrates the transition period between the first great post-war team (Jack Rowley and Allenby Chilton both featured) and the emerging 'babes' (represented by Roger Byrne, Tommy Taylor, Johnny Berry and David Pegg). Byrne, Rowley and Taylor were among the scorers for United; some reports claim Billy Liddell opened the scoring for Liverpool, while Louis Bimpson grabbed a brace early in the second half, but others don't have Liddell among the scorers at all and report Bimpson scoring a hat-trick. Scott Murray, reporting on 'great Liverpool-United derbies', in *The Guardian* in 2008 concurs with this latter analysis [1]

Understandably, however, Murray and other observers devote more newsprint to what happened towards the end of the game. Seven minutes from time, with Liverpool leading 4-3, Taylor grabbed an equaliser by crashing the ball, and keeper Charlie Ashcroft, into the net. It was, we're often led to believe, the kind of goal you saw all the time in the fifties and, as my granddad would have had it, it's only the balloon-kicking softies of today who have a problem with it. The Kop didn't see it that way and there was practically a riot, only quelled when a police cordon formed across the whole of the Liverpool end to prevent them spilling onto the pitch, with the ref and Taylor the undisputed targets of their ire. My dad, like my mum a Liverpool supporter, would have been seventeen at the time and I try to imagine him, prior to the development of the sub-Elvis quiff I've seen in photos of him later in the decade, standing there among the cloth caps and rattles, but fail: I can only picture him as he is now, his only accessory a piss-soaked rolled up Liverpool Echo in his back pocket. Or perhaps it's the bloke in front of him who has the gradually dampening Echo and my dad is standing behind him with a suspicious grin. Apparently the river of urine that lay at the foot of the Kop in those days did a passable impression of the Mersey at full tide, complete with floating garbage and the occasional dead fish, I like to think.

By the time the sides met again at Old Trafford in December, the emerging thrust of that young United side was evident, in contrast with a Liverpool team now entering its most significant winter of discontent for many years, brought about by a miserable run after which a late rally in the spring was insufficient to prevent them from falling out of the first division for the first time in the twentieth century. The 5-1 score line mirrored their result against Portsmouth seven days earlier and was followed by a 5-2 reverse at the hands of West Brom on Christmas Day. It would be a further eleven games before Liverpool's dismal run came to an end, by which point it was much too late.

By this point, Bill Foulkes and Duncan Edwards had now joined those involved for United while, aside from Liddell, the Liverpool team reads like the bunch of forgotten non-entities it unquestionably was, to be ranked alongside Souness's spice boys in the nineties or the dismal side of 2002-03 that recorded the longest interrupted series of Liverpool defeats since this side dragged its murky snail-like trail down and out of the first division.

Unfortunately, such stuff was all buried in the history books by the time I knew anything about it; by this point the Liverpool side of 24 years later that had wrecked my childhood was rampant, its trail more reminiscent of the recently developed Concorde ripping apart the sky than the aforementioned snail, its sonic boom still smashing apart what remained of my childhood.

You'd think, given the current rivalry between United and Liverpool, that my mum and dad might have cast me out into the street, arranged for therapy, or maybe even attempted something not unlike an exorcism when I informed them, out of the blue one Sunday afternoon, that I'd found the team for me. Yet when anyone else in our extended family or neighbourhood questioned how such an abomination could be visited upon the family, my dad defended me stoutly. 'He had me and his mum going on about Liverpool,' he'd say, 'and his granddad and his uncle trying to get him to support Everton, and he said "bugger the bloody lot of you"'. It was a highly prescient and accurate observation.

In fact, there was a strange but very real commonality between us. Both of my parents had grown up in predominantly Everton-supporting families within which high levels of hostility towards the Anfield club ran rampant and so their decision to adopt Liverpool – in pre-Shankly days no less – did represent some kind of momentous two fingers of its own. I simply continued the tradition with an even more defiant salute and a baring of both cheeks to Merseyside into the bargain. And while other Liverpool fans I knew have ploughed ever deeper into their trough of hatred towards the beast from down the East Lancs Road, my mum and dad continue to represent an uncommon yet still persistent strain of northern supporter who takes the view that 'no matter what, when it comes to north against south, you always want the northern team to win'. They aren't completely alone in this, although the species is now a severely endangered one. Forced to bite my nails in the pub during United's game with Spurs in 1999 that would be the final step to the league title, I was dismayed that the space I'd found in the bar placed me next to a Liverpool supporter. He proved, I was pleased to note, to be another of this rare type and, whatever consequences it had for the treble and opportunity for United to make history in what turned out to be the most dramatic way possible, he expressed a preference for United 'over Arsenal any day' and we spent the duration of the game in unlikely mutual celebration with most of his comments centring around how great Beckham was (remembering of course that this was the widely demonized 1998 World Cup Beckham model and not the soon to emerge cuddly national media personality) . I admire my mum and dad for their lack of animosity towards my team, especially as I can see they've regularly been required to defend their position among their increasingly vehement and self-righteous fellow supporters. In some ways I wish I could be like them and return the favour, but I can't. My detestation of Liverpool FC is ingrained and irremovable. Years later, with United fully established in our position of top dogs, I tried to talk myself into it, tried to say to myself, 'Come on, if Liverpool win this game it doesn't matter to us anyway because they're so far off the pace, and it'll make my mum and dad happy.' I might even have persuaded myself to go through with it prior to the game starting, but as soon as it kicked off and I saw the all-red strip in what for them amounted to full flow, I instantly reverted to the default position of wanting to see the bastards getting their arses kicked more than anything else in the world.

It was my dad, despite his very different loyalties, who filled me in on the history of United and gave me an idea of the depth of what I'd got into. While I indulged my newly discovered love of the game and the thrill of watching Docherty's young team, it was he who told me of United's great tradition of celebrated creativity on the football pitch, inevitably of the Babes of the fifties, the incomparable Best, the mercurial Law and the brilliant Charlton. He told me of the great national mourning at the time of the Munich disaster and the astonishing re-birth of the club to win the European Cup just ten years later. United, he confirmed, were once the nation's team, but their decline after Busby's retirement had been swift and devastating and now, he told me without any pleasure, they were struggling to get out of their period of ignominy. Whatever I felt about the current generation of players, United were, he told me bluntly, not the club they once were, and Docherty was certainly no Busby.

Strange that a lifelong Liverpool supporter should help along my initial impetus in this way, but it fed oxygen to a spark that continues to burn with sustained ferocity to this day. One thing I've learned about myself is I don't do things by half measures and can't get an interest in something without it turning very quickly into an obsession, so I longed to find out more, to head full-on into research of the Busby years and then to discover as much as possible about the origins of the club with whose fortunes my life had already, I knew, begun to be inextricably bound up. I started to perceive the paucity of knowledge among many of the self-proclaimed pre-teen experts who surrounded me and, due to the solitude of my pursuit, my understanding of United was untainted by any of the idiotic half-truths (at best) of the playground. I duly discovered a club who, far from the Disneyfied concept of United so prevalent today, had far greater meaning for me as the ultimate outsiders, with the added bonus of an identity about as far from the Liverpool FC model it was possible to get.

I found a club that had emerged in the forties without a trophy to its name in the years between the wars, had almost gone out of business in 1931 and emerged blinking in the post-war years with a bombed ground that was clearly going to be out of use until close until at least the end of the decade and with no money to speak of to repair it. Even when the war started, United had been in debt to the tune of £70,000 [2] After it, they had to recover from this position and spend pretty much every penny brought into the club on getting Old Trafford operational again; the amount they'd received from the FA yielded only a very small proportion of what was needed to do the job and it took four years even to get permission from the Ministry of Works to carry out the necessary repairs [3]. Even then the amount released, £17,478, was nowhere near what was needed to get the job done. [4] Much is understandably made of the lack of a financial level playing football nowadays, but never forget that United were far from being able to compete with much bigger clubs in that era and that we only survived then, and thrived eventually, due to the astonishing loyalty of our supporters matched with the acumen of men like James Gibson, Walter Crickmer and Busby who somehow got the club punching well above its weight. Despite such unpromising prospects, United won the cup in 1948 and the league in 1952 and it was only through increases in club revenue via the big crowds they attracted to their exiled games at Maine Road that United pulled themselves away from financial danger.

By 1951, following six consecutive years of profit, United had finally paid off their debts [5]. A rare club in English football who don't need to answer the question 'where did all that money go in the days of the maximum wage?', United now ploughed it all into ground rebuilding, having to put a roof on the main stand before they could even think about investing in the floodlights everyone else was getting and emerging with a side that, bereft of money for transfer fees, was largely developed via a brilliantly conceived youth policy and which, playing with a flair unmatched by their contemporaries, captured the imagination of the country. Having established this great team, the club was then hit by Munich and, once again, the very real possibility that it might cease to exist, before recovering again in the sixties to win two more league titles and the European Cup with, despite the loss of such an remarkable generation of players, a side that included no less than nine players who'd been at the club since they were teenagers, a feat that, even in the seventies, seemed unlikely ever to be repeated and which now looks an even more remote possibility. It's something that's conveniently ignored now by our enemies, but it's a remarkable thing that United made it as far as the sixties at all.

Admittedly, when you're nine or ten years old, past history means a lot less to you than what's happening at the time. The histories of United and football I read in books inevitably provided a pretty dry experience set against football that you could see, hear and absorb through your match-day pores. And it seemed a very different time to the one my dad talked of anyway, so the football of even ten years earlier had a sepia tinted quality that crumbled quickly in a period that was suddenly obsessed so much with the now, whether that involved the collapsing post-war socio-economic consensus or the year zero attitude of punk.

As I moved into senior school, all of this was coalescing not into the every-bastard-for-himself consumerism that would emerge in the eighties, but a much rawer, more nihilistic period that would make the even-handed fairness of my mum and dad far more difficult to achieve, something that was graphically reflected in the terrace warfare of football and the senior school to which I progressed, which was essentially dominated by gangsters (the kids rather than the staff, although in some cases...) and proto-fascists.

The values of the time were confused to say the least, and navigating a course through them was precarious if you were going to emerge with any shred of your own identity intact. So many of the Factory bands in Manchester that would begin to attain such fascination during my teenage years (not only Joy Division and New Order, but the likes of Durutti Column and A Certain Ratio) had Nazi-inspired names, all of which was nothing to do with far right extremism and everything to do with putting the biggest possible barrier between theirs and previous generations, emphasising difference rather than continuity in the crudest but most emphatic way. Probably this was part of the reason why so many of my peers daubed swastikas on every possible wall or desk, but I sensed in many cases this was due to rather deeper and more worrying character flaws, personified by one lad in my school year who wore swastika earrings and would subject anyone who refused to address him as 'Adolf' to a rigorously administered 's'apelle' (which involved getting your nipples in a bull clip-like grip and sharply twisting). And, though I draw no conclusions from this other than to note the preponderance of both, swastikas and NF signs scratched into desks usually sat alongside an LFC, scratched by a similarly belligerent hand. Again, I opted to buck the trend, my less than artistic use of hammer and sickle alongside MUFC gaining in increasingly unwelcome notoriety as I progressed (if you can call it that) through senior school. Not only was I now in the small minority of United fans, as Reagan was elected and the cold war attained an even deeper chill, I was also the school's token commie.

None of this was going to endear me to my peers, and it provided me with yet another masochistic opportunity to parade my differences in an arena that's culturally obsessed with uniformity: the school playground. Monday 23 May 1977 was unique in my school life and would provide a similarly unique opportunity to celebrate my outsider status rather than zealously defend it. On the Saturday, we'd beaten Liverpool 2-1 to secure the FA Cup and it was the first and, it would sadly prove, last time that I could walk into school with a spring in my step that arose from United winning a trophy. Jimmy Greenhoff had gone down in history as probably the first player to score a winning goal in the FA Cup Final without even knowing it; the United defence, marshalled by the imperious Buchan, so effectively nullified the threat of the celebrated Keegan, in his last domestic game for Liverpool; the young Arthur Albiston's stunning full-back display at Wembley is so inexorably etched in my memory that, when asked many years later to nominate my favourite United full-back of all time I ignored the highly respectable claims of Gary Neville, Dennis Irwin and Patrice Evra and went for Arthur.

When I mention this to people now, I can see them pondering whether this could possibly be correct – did Manchester United really win only one trophy between my entry to school in 1970 and my gleeful departure from it in 1981? The answer is of course yes, but it was a big one and had an importance that has resonated in the years since.

Despite skirmishes like the Macari episode, the United-Liverpool rivalry, so strong today, still hadn't really taken hold for many fans on both sides, however much retrospective reinterpretation has gone on since. While it's incorrect to say that no animosity at all existed, the events of August 1953 and the Macari transfer can be said only to be precursors of the mutual hatred that would later emerge. That day at Wembley, a lot of United fans joined in the applause of Liverpool's players as they went around the pitch, vociferously wishing them the best in their forthcoming European Cup final against Borussia Moenchengladbach, an especially noble act given that the event would rob us of our claim to be the only English club to have won it. United/Liverpool tensions are not something you can trace through the decades, and claims to the contrary represent nothing more than retrospective garnishing of facts to suit the argument.

It's different with the city and Leeds rivalries. While there would be fans right up to the sixties who would merrily shake their rattles at Old Trafford one week and city the next, tension between the two clubs goes back easily as early as the enforced city player auction and subsequent plundering of their playing assets by United in the early years of the twentieth century; when United fans organised a boycott of the Arsenal match at Old Trafford in 1930 its failure was down, substantially if not wholly, to the provocative action of city fans mischievously attending the ground in their stead, an invasion that was roundly encouraged by the journalist Burnage in the Manchester Evening News. [6] Of United's game at Leeds in 1925-26, another journalist H.P.R. wrote that he couldn't recall at any other football match the level of bitterness shown towards the United team by Leeds supporters. [7] In contrast, the most disreputable episode involving United and Liverpool players in the first half of the century was one that involved collusion rather than conflict, the match where players on both sides were found guilty of contriving to produce a result that would keep United up, leading to the banning of several players including United's Enoch 'Knocker' West, the only one of them to fail to get it lifted during his career because of his refusal to declare anything other than his innocence, which he continued to proclaim right up to his death. I suspect we'll never know the truth about Knocker, or even if there's any more to know, but his lone stance would endow him with a small part in establishing what is now more generally acknowledged as the Cantona template, a peculiarly United phenomenon, where a player is willing to stick to his guns whatever the authorities think and whatever it denies him in terms of career advancement. Indeed, the template, as we'll see later, pre-dates even Knocker.

On a personal level, however, the rivalry had been there pretty much from day one, because for me the bastards were in my face to a degree that neither city nor Leeds could match. When Liverpool secured the league title of 1976, with the defeat of an ordinary Wolves side to win the title ahead of QPR, my parents were in an animated state of pre-championship nerves that I could feel no part of, and wouldn't experience for many years, as they listened on the radio to their side coming from behind to steal the title with a Toshack goal five minutes from time. The game is understandably one that has attained legendary status among Liverpool fans, with the official website claiming that 20,000

Liverpool supporters made the trip with more than 7,000 of them unable to get into the ground. [8] Which is interesting when you consider that Liverpool's average home match day crowd had significantly declined that year, by almost 10%, to over 13,000 less than the average crowd at Old Trafford. Either the website, not for the first time, has been somewhat generous in estimating the number of Liverpool fans at the game – it was after all an important one for Wolves fans too, as they were relegated following the defeat, so a big home crowd was expected – or fans who hadn't exactly frequented Anfield in droves that season to watch the cold science of Liverpool victories being ground out via pass after pass back to Ray Clemence found the prospect of imminent glory rather more of a desirable proposition. Understandably, the taste for victory, once savoured, led to high expectations, so the occasional high profile defeat such as that inflicted by United at Wembley the following year rankled more than it perhaps had a few years earlier. 'Don't bring the subject up,' a Liverpool fan at school beseeched me, sympathetic to the misery of one of his less hardy colleagues after our Cup win. 'He takes his football seriously'. So, as Blackadder later put it, I didn't mention it to him. Well, not very often.

Looking back, the event brought to life what was a nascent, undeveloped yet I think inevitable tension between the two clubs. It's as if some pre-existing form of the rivalry, in what I would now term the the Platonic sense, was already there and we simply needed the historical circumstances to bring it into material existence. Missing out on the treble stung Liverpool fans pretty badly, perhaps more than they'd realised it would. When they went on, four days later, to lift their first European Cup, that event, rather than rendering the lost FA Cup an event of minimal significance, served only to further stoke the resentment unleashed towards the United fans who understandably had the temerity to go berserk with pleasure at the sight of our first trophy for nine years (excluding the second division championship, which didn't count, as Buchan, Macari and other United players have confirmed by declaring themselves too embarrassed even to celebrate the achievement) [9]. Those United well-wishers at Wembley forgotten, Liverpool fans were determined to parade the European Cup as a measure of their new superiority. And when they won it again the following year but saw crowds at Old Trafford still dwarfing those at Anfield and the hordes following United still throbbing in allegiance to our cause despite the evident gulf in quality between the two sides, I think something broke in them. Something that would mean so many of them wasted their years wallowing in their growing hatred of United rather than gathering their bountiful rosebuds while they may. I grew up in close proximity to all this and, as my years at Bankfield High School rolled on, the attitude of Liverpool fans towards the few United supporters now turned, over a period of no more than two or three years, from lethargic opposition to teeth-grinding hostility.

And it wasn't just the kids. I recall a Maths teacher, a pedagogic Neanderthal of scouse origin, taking time out from expressing his irritation at our failure to produce the next Pythagoras or Leibniz to warn us of the moral dangers of not following the wholesome cause of supporting Liverpool. He did so not in the zealous manner of a partisan fan, but in the measured, cautioning way of a crusading redeemer, a kind of Ned Flanders with a slide rule. There was, he entreated us to believe, something essentially wrong in the character of these United supporters who were all over the newspapers after their involvement in some terrace battle or other, and the good-natured fans of Liverpool were the ones we ought to join were we to follow the path of righteousness and avoid finding ourselves on the slippery slope to damnation. 'But isn't that just the way the papers present it sir?' asked a United fan from somewhere at the back as some of the Liverpool fans sniggered behind their hands, the train ride to Lime Street to 'greet' opposing fans in what had become the established manner both a recent and regular memory. Rather than seize the educational opportunity this presented, he merely carried on with his tirade. We were, it seemed, bound for hell and only by switching allegiance to the cause of LFC could we hope for any salvation. I wondered, years later, how he reacted to the events at

Heysel. Presumably by taking a similar moral mace to fictional Chelsea fans.

We lived in a world of folk devils back then. The seventies were a violent time. Football hooliganism was a very real part of life, whether we indulged in it ourselves or simply witnessed the events at close hand, on the telly or second-hand via those accounts of the Lime Street Saturday boys. And these regular weekend battles took place within a society into which the even more serious levels of violence over in Northern Ireland were piped via our television screens. When punk reared its head just as I was making the transition from primary to secondary school, its aggressive strains inevitably struck a chord with a wider range of individuals than might normally be expected for what was, at heart, outsider music. That many ascribed to it some greater tribal significance is a hallmark of the age in which it emerged. For me, by then and by choice an outsider and a loner, its true and lasting significance couldn't be more obvious and, as with United and the cause of the ill-fated cats, I jumped in with both feet.

Although my social isolation remained pronounced throughout those secondary school years, my mum and dad were often regaled at parents' evenings with teachers' bemusement that this didn't lead to me, generally speaking, getting the crap beaten out of me. I put this down to three things. One, the only other kids I found interesting at school tended to be rough bastards, villains, social outcasts, many of whom went on to establish long criminal careers in their later lives while some lived and died by the sword, almost literally so in the case of one lad in my year who as a young adult got axed to death over a game of cards. Although I didn't choose them as mates for the cynical reason of securing their protection during violent times, good fortune decreed that they filled this role adequately enough. I suspect many would-be tormentors left me alone simply because of some of the big, smelly uncouth bastards I hung round with, which kind of came home to me the day I saw a lad who'd had the temerity merely to make a mildly confrontational remark in my direction being crudely sat on by the biggest, smelliest lad of the lot, taunted by voracious insults incurred through foul smelling breath, flakes of dirt cascading from louse-infested hair into his terrified face.

Two, the school itself had such a hard reputation it was regarded as 'not done' for the tough lads to pick on anyone other than those of a certain level of violent pedigree, pedigree which I certainly didn't possess. Those who broke this rule would quickly find themselves subjected to brutal vigilante attacks from the large gangs that thronged the streets on the way home down Blundell Road. I witnessed enough of them to be aware of the level of savagery involved. They weren't pretty, and nor were the scrum-worn features of the rugby lads administering them. Thankfully, the nearest I got to being on the wrong end of this was during games of rugby itself in which, because of my height and nuisance value at line-outs, I generally found myself ordered into the second row of the scrum. It wasn't a pleasant place to be. 'Get yer head down. Do you like the smell of sweaty armpits?' yelled the games teacher. No I didn't, but I didn't much like the strange odours that lurked down below either.

And three, while my football affiliations didn't find too much commonality among these oval-ball loving thugs, my musical tastes did. Punk complemented their uncompromisingly violent ways like a Cole-Yorke one-two. Unwittingly, the situation granted me a freedom to pursue my outsider proclivities in a manner that, for other lads like me in different circumstances, would surely have culminated in being on the shitty end of the stick both figuratively and literally (a stick with a dog turd on the end being the weapon of choice among my less delicately fragranced peers).

At All Saints, I'd specialised in quirky, one-off remarks that would either be greeted with tides of belly laughter or derisory hoots but rarely with indifference, and whose downfall was frequently an attempt to try to drag out rather more humour from a situation than was actually there, such as when someone told a joke in Miss Ogden's class and the whole class laughed, including the teacher, but after a few seconds of this I injected a ridiculous guffaw that dwarfed every other sound in the room and, in a pure instance of Humean coincidental connexion, appeared to set the school bell off. This brought a second wave of laughter, but this time Miss Ogden didn't join in and, as this wave subsided, simply said, 'The Headmaster's office. Now.' It was a familiar instruction in those days. The other class clowns, members of the scouse brigade to a man (there were no female jokers and no rugby-playing jokers, for some reason – make of that what you will), trod much safer territory, not in the sense that they escaped Miss Ogden's wrath but that their line of jokes tended to be of the tried and trusted variety, plundering the rich stereotype that decreed that anyone with a Liverpudlian accent (even a faked one) was bound to be funny anyway. While I wouldn't proclaim myself any sort of Pythonesque innovator, the rest of them brandished an asinine non-humour that made Russ Abbot look like Groucho Marx and, at worst, consisted of a series of inane grunts that could only generate laughs in the minds of those who were troubled by the consequences of failing to get the joke, ie that they might find visited upon themselves the same wrath that afflicted supporters alighting at Lime Street or even the dreaded stick. Unable and unwilling to visit any such retribution on non-laughers myself, the only alternative was to try to say something that was actually funny. And, somehow, I managed this often enough to survive.

My support for United collided with all this to give me an outsider identity that, in primary school, saw me attain a kind of appealing (to me) and presumably irritating (to others) infamy. In secondary school, where such random outbursts were less tolerated by teachers and where the conformity factory really ground into gear, I simply opted out. Unwilling to lower myself to the level of those who conformed with the prevailing mood by adopting a whole armoury of fitting-in techniques, only one of which was allegiance to Liverpool FC whether you had any interest in football or not, it brought almost unanimous derision, but to me that was preferable to joining the conformist masses on their patch. I couldn't see any difference between what they peddled and the petty rules that informed what passed for secondary education in my benighted school, other than the difference between the cane and the aforementioned stick full of shit.

There was certainly no method in my apparent madness. But being a school that served a particularly poor area of an already severely socially disadvantaged urban community, there were inevitably many socially disadvantaged types to rub flaky shoulders with. Tough bastards to a man; many of them smelling of grease, oil and God knew what else, and some dragged out to the front by overtly vindictive teachers who would verbally dress them down in front of the class for coming to school in such a state, while completely overlooking (gratuitously, surely, because they must have known) the extreme poverty many of them lived in. Given the appalling nature of these humiliating rituals, it was little surprise that these kids brandished the only genuinely anti-authoritarian stances on display at the school. When the Queen was visiting Widnes and we got a day off, one such lad was asked by the teacher whether he would be going to see her. 'Why should I?' he replied. 'She wouldn't fuckin' come and see me.' When the same lad bunked off class once, I was walking alongside him the following day on the way into school when the teacher wound down his car window and asked him why he'd missed his lesson. 'Because I fuckin' 'ate yer,' came the instant answer.

Having such characters as my only friends in the school inevitably made me even more unpopular with everyone else. I was told by other kids they'd have nothing to do me if I carried on hanging around with such social detritus, which suited me just fine. Similar threats would be made regarding my refusal to join the faceless regime that gathered around Liverpool FC, which saw many a prospective United fan, to his shame, buckle under and go with the flow. I could never understand the relentless desire to 'prove you're normal' that is such a pervasive concern of youth and instead chose the old 'path less travelled' whether or not it led me into the undergrowth, which it invariably did. I found it hard to accept the number of kids I knew who were determined to sacrifice as much of their individualism as possible just to keep in with their peer group, and I know it's no different today. And it seemed to me that the whole idea of Liverpool FC was tied up with it, something which I now realise was far more than simply coincidence via an accident of geography.

Dave Hill, whose book *Out Of His Skin* has rightly gained acclaim as a brilliant study of racism in football and is a strong contender for the title of most important football book ever written, also has much to say on the subject of how conformity to group norms, suspicion of individualism and pressure to submit to the suffocating group identity lie especially at the heart of Liverpool FC. [10] [11] In contrast my club, it seemed to me, were the only non-musical thing in life that went against the whole concept of stultifying conformity. Teachers were similarly disposed to see my tendencies as something to be actively discouraged. I was frequently separated from the rough, proto-criminal fraternity in class and, on one particularly memorable occasion, received a caning for no reason that I can see other than the fact that I was perceived to be hanging round with a known trouble-maker. Perversely, the day was my solitary day of popularity in the five entirely useless years I spent at Bankfield High.

Theirs was a world where adherence to what everyone else in the playground knew to be true (however inaccurate) was everything and where, I kid you not, such was the assumption that Liverpool FC's dominance ran through everything, and that it was important that it *had* to run through everything that – for example - it quickly became the established opinion among my peers that 'We Are The Champions' by Queen was in fact written on the Kop. I waited for the day when someone would inform me, quite seriously, that Terry McDermott was carrying Britain's hopes in that year's Tour De France, Emlyn Hughes had romped to victory in the Eurovision song contest and Tommy Smith had saddled up John Toshack the previous weekend and won the Grand National.

The aforementioned was only one facet of a mythology gaining impetus down our way that pretty much anything related to football was initiated at Anfield, something else that made it inevitable that United and Liverpool would have to be natural enemies because those same supporters would be forced at some point to confront the fact that it is, after all, United who historically are the English game's foremost innovators. The response among Liverpool fans to this has either been belligerent denial or a laughable attempt to create an alternative footballing universe within which their own claims could be held to be true. Thus the claim to 'We Are The Champions', which just seemed foolish to anyone outside this community of Liverpool supporters, grew to achieve the status of a truth the kinds around me held to be self-evident. This may have been a phenomenon unique to our school, but it was within such a contrived set of beliefs that powerful myths surrounding Liverpool FC began to take root, there and elsewhere.

The claim would, indeed, quickly expand into a proclamation that the Kop was the place where singing at football grounds began in the first place. While Celtic supporters claimed 'You'll Never Walk Alone' as their own long before Liverpool did, the song had also been sung at Old Trafford in the aftermath of Munich a good six years before Anfield fans first claimed it. Significantly, it didn't catch on at Old Trafford. Although United were, at that time, cast in the now unfamiliar position of every other supporter's second favourite team, United fans rejected the schmaltzy, glib anthem and trite sense of finger-down-the-throat faux community it evoked. Nowadays, a popular T-shirt available on the unofficial merchandise stalls outside Old Trafford depicts a Red Devil beating up a Liver Bird under the slogan 'I'd Rather Walk Alone' and it is this pariah status, along with a sense of doing it for United and United only that was, by the seventies, firmly established within the identity of the club's fans and that chimed powerfully with my own experiences. Liverpool fans embraced such trite, vacuous nonsense much more readily, but being Liverpool they also had to ignore the history of the song and claim they'd thought of it first. Nor did terrace singing in general, contrary to the almost unanimous proclamations of my peers, begin on the Kop. Norwich City can date the signing of 'On The Ball City' at Carrow Road back to the 1890s.

In truth, the only things that the Kop can genuinely claim credit for originating are such rich cultural activities as pissing in each other's pockets and throwing human excrement at United fans in the Anfield Road end. Regarding 'You'll Never Walk Alone', most Liverpool fans I encountered held the mistaken belief that one of their own (Gerry Marsden) had even written the thing, when in fact it was the American duo Rodgers and Hammerstein. The fact that it first saw the light of day in their musical *Carousel* back in 1945 gives some credence to the claims of Fulham fans that the song goes was in fact first sung by them not long after the second world war, almost two decades before these Liverpool fans apparently even knew of its existence. [12] Whoever first introduced this appalling mantra into the footballing songbook, we have here a body of people who are willing to claim sole rights to a song that was clearly sung by others on multiple occasions before them, and attribute songwriting credits to a scouser over the undeniable copyright of a couple of Americans. Against such a cultural context, the claim that they collectively wrote a song first sung by a gay Welshman which also had nothing whatsoever to do with football is perhaps less remarkable.

In any case, Queen and Rodgers and Hammerstein songs were never going to get close to my personal playlist, whether in a footballing context or otherwise. I was more than happy to walk alone, no matter how many dead ends it led me into.

Punk conveniently arrived at around the same time to provide a soundtrack that resonated completely with my experiences, where the whole notion of conformity was treated with deserved contempt and where it was beneath contempt to lay claim to any sort of historical context to your ideas. It was also crucial to my developing cultural awareness that its throbbing pulse within a rebellious heart should reverberate most lastingly in and around Manchester in a music scene where, in the wake of Buzzcocks' 'Boredom' complete with its two-chord guitar solo, vibrant originality, individuality and innovation would spring because, as both Pete Shelley and Mancunian journalist Paul Morley recognised, being neglected by the mainstream was always a source of creativity rather than a barrier to it. [13] Was it just the coinage of my young mind, or was I beginning to sense something similar afoot in football too? It's hard to talk of the two separately, so enmeshed were the two cultural forces in my consciousness. June 1974, which still producing little of interest to me musically, offered a resonance I didn't then appreciate, setting in place events in football that would later begin to run parallel to the culture shocks being delivered by punk. Two things happened that month. The magnificent Holland team made their glorious, though ultimately failed, bid to win the World Cup in West Germany. The other event of importance wouldn't yield benefits for many years; but my god in time would they be worth it. Because it was in June 1974 that a Scottish journeyman footballer called Alex Ferguson was appointed to his first managerial position – as boss of East Stirlingshire.

Nostalgia can do funny things to you, and very often when you see replays of games from long ago they aren't quite the momentous occasions your under-nourished noggin made them out to be, but whenever I see footage of that Dutch side in action their magnificence is as pronounced as my recollections always suggested they were. There was an extraordinary fluidity and inventiveness in their play that no one, not even the great Brazilian sides or the magnificent Spanish teams of recent years, has quite been able to match.

I hear people talk of total football now like it's a bit of a myth, or at least an exaggeration, but that 1974 footage is there to be observed by anyone who cares to take a look and it continuously reminds me that this is no fabrication of an idealised memory. Their failure to win the thing didn't matter. Many have sought to identity precursors of total football, and the direction most fingers point in is towards the Manchester United team of the 1950s. But there was a fascinating irreverence about those Dutch players too, which is why, whatever their legendary merits, those precursors from the fifties could be no more than just that. The total football side of 1974 was very much of the seventies, both in terms of liberation from the strictures of previous conventions and its lack of cap-doffing to established values. The philosophy of that Dutch team was built around the incredible Ajax side which had won the European Cup three times in the early seventies. After their first, onlookers were astonished to see one of the players walking to the team bus with the European Cup being carried as if it were a bag of groceries; then, when the boot on the coach was opened, the player in question simply threw the cup in along with the rest of the luggage. These were players who added careless abandon to breathtaking style. Add to this not just Cruyff's ability to tie defenders' intestines in reef knots, but his refusal to don that most essential of seventies footballing accessories, the shinpad, and you have a model for footballing irreverence that wouldn't be replicated again until Cantona tore up the rulebooks in different, but similarly intoxicating, style.

Whatever differences have become apparent to me now, it seemed to me back then that the United team emerging from the second division in 1975 were the closest an English team has ever got to reflecting the style of those Dutch masters. Both were originals and therefore imitators neither of each other nor of anyone else. While the Holland 1974 team has been duly recognised and celebrated as such, I don't think the unique character of Docherty's mid-seventies team has ever been fully appreciated. They played not 4-4-2 but 4-2-4, an attacking line-up that was more akin to the great Brazilian teams of the fifties and sixties, a radical design worlds away from Ramsey's World Cup winning England side or the mechanical, precise football of Liverpool FC or the turgid, rugged fare that passed for football on offer from Leeds United, the two accepted powerhouses of my early years. Not only did the sides from 1975 through to Docherty's departure in 1977 play with two out and out wingers (Hill and Coppell), they did so without the established figure in the English game of the tall target man that, it was conventionally assumed, two wide men required – instead, the nippy, stylish Pearson held sway. There was no holding player in midfield, as a gradual evolution was underway that ultimately led to two reformed strikers – Macari and McIlroy – filling the central midfield berths. At the back were two ball-playing central defenders of a kind barely known in the English game at that time, with both Buchan and Greenhoff standing at less than 5'10" and both comfortable with the ball at their feet. As with the Dutch, the thrilling brilliance of the side failed to bear fruit in terms of trophies in the 1975/76 championship and Cup Final. United would, indeed, only win three FA Cups between then and 1989 so that my youth and early adult years were riddled with long periods of coping with disappointment punctuated with occasional exhilarating success while the massed Liverpool support around me won everything in sight. However, what we experienced in terms of exhilaration on the football field was something that somehow wasn't measurable in trophies and that's why, to this day and after many years of watching more successful United sides, that mid-seventies model remains close to the hearts of all United fans who experienced the thrill of being a part of it.

This is not to say that making a connection between what I'd seen of the Dutch side and what I was now seeing with United was the only thing that drew me to the Red Devils. It needs, rather, to be seen in the context of the rest of that primordial soup of individualism and outsider status from which my youthful existence was emerging. As punk began to invigorate my life and with it draw out the endless possibilities that lay beyond the restrictions of conformity, so the many facets of United – its associations with hooliganism, even, as well as the unmatched quality of their football – attained a rich cultural resonance within the melting pot of life. The image of United was, like punk, simultaneously exciting and dangerous, energising and mysterious, welcoming and forbidden.

The path set ablaze by Cruyff didn't catch fire across the dour post-Ramsey state of English football, only in the unrestrained and almost perverse attacking verve and individuality of United under Docherty. I encountered punk at just the right age, and it was through this music, through Manchester as its emerging focal point and through Manchester United that I understood that I wasn't as alone as I'd presumed in my contempt for the formulaic and contrived. The emphasis on cold practicality and reasoned strategy imposed by Liverpool on the beautiful game [14] seemed to me as enticing a prospect as David Soul replacing Howard Devoto as the singer in Buzzcocks. The machine-like, empirical philosophy of English football was inherently stifling and everything that Dutch team and punk rock weren't; so it was with some inevitability, I realise now, that I found what I was truly looking for in Docherty's Manchester United, with the fact that they were in Division Two at the time absolutely irrelevant, and indeed in many ways part of the appeal. They were, so to speak, off the map, at least the one the All Saints kids read from, in so many ways that counted. Just as punk emerged from the low-rent pub rock scene to crash impudently into the mainstream, so United, it seemed to me, emerged from the second division to crash into the dull world of the top tier of English football with impetuous brashness and creativity.

That so much of the music that comes out of Manchester and its surrounding areas deals with a sense of isolation and lone-ness (as opposed to loneliness), and that the city's music picked up most fruitfully on this rich stream that emerged from punk was something that only struck me gradually. While I was absorbed with so much of what was happening in punk in the late seventies, the music of Buzzcocks was something that resonated with me far more than anything else. At first I don't think I even consciously connected them with Manchester, or even knew where they came from, but the celebratory introspection present in songs of both the Devoto and post-Devoto era was something that later seemed to fit perfectly with a great musical lineage that over the new few years came to include The Fall, Joy Division, The Passage, The Chameleons, A Certain Ratio, that paradigm for musical introspection The Durutti Column and many more, all very different but all characterised by a similarly defiant idiosyncratic approach as important to music as Cruyff had been to football.

The raw proclamations of 'Boredom' rang through a series of declarations of emotional devastation like 'What Do I Get' and 'Promises', the latter almost a manifesto of reasons for staying out of the whole business of emotional relationships before it even really occurred to me to get involved in any. 'Orgasm Addict' was an early addition to the fine punk sub-genre of celebratory odes to Onanism, and you can't get a more defiant or asocial statement than what Onan did in one of the earliest and most graphic, if somewhat messy, contraventions of the word of God. '16 Again' and 'Fast Cars' took conventional rock and roll ideals and turned them on their heads: being sixteen again would be the worst thing that could happen to anyone (which was largely borne out by my own experience) and fast cars were pointless and despised false gods of material existence. Even the band's existence resonates with a sense of idiosyncrasy, with Devoto's departure after the first EP for no other reason than he wanted to move onto something else a decision made from a pure sense of existential freedom and defiance of the commercial rewards that sticking with Buzzcocks were clearly already promising. A few years on Joy Division came along and subverted the Buzzcocks musical template to strip out the jangly guitars and offer a deeper view into the essential isolation at the core of the human condition. And while it might be somewhat trite to label the act of suicide as an act by its nature even more individualistic than that of Onan, it'd be no less true for all that, and certainly no more defiantly experimental 'career move' has occurred in music than the transition from the band that was Joy Division becoming New Order.

For me, the individualist spirit of punk, Cruyff and Docherty's United threw a Molotov cocktail into the already violent circumstances of life in the 1970s. In football generally, younger supporters had begun to experience the game very differently from previous generations While there was nothing new about footballing rivalries as such, the animosity that was at play in the seventies was of a level alien to fans from previous decades, as the somewhat more reasonable approach of my own parents demonstrated. Bobby Charlton, though an avowed Newcastle fan in his younger years, has talked of going to both Newcastle and Sunderland games as a child [14] and the same was true of many supporters in Merseyside and indeed Manchester. Charlton also speaks of the famous 5-4 win at Arsenal in the weekend before the fatal trip to Belgrade in 1958, identifying it as perhaps the greatest game of football ever played and noting that everyone in the ground, despite Arsenal's defeat, stayed and applauded for five minutes after the players had left the pitch, and goes on to talk of the enjoyment that he and other United players derived from trips to watch Liverpool at Anfield in the sixties. They were times, it seemed, when the need to be entertained at a football ground had precedence over demonstrations of loyalty and rivalry. But I knew nothing of these times, growing up instead in a 1970s Britain where there were bomb attacks across Northern Ireland and Britain, where there were National Front rallies drawing uncompromising responses from the Anti-Nazi League, where spitting and ripping each other's earrings out while jumping up and down were all part of the entertainment at gigs, where football hooliganism mirrored this at footie grounds and where, wherever you looked, confrontation and violence seemed never very far away.

In retrospect, I can see that the passion for violence among football fans in the seventies was both generational and symptomatic of social and economic patterns of the period, although for United I think it was about far more than that. The post-war communities' love of football as entertainment spectacle was founded largely on relief from wartime austerity further developed upon by a new breed of players and occasionally clubs, of which United emerged as easily the most notable, who played football with a skill and verve that was a million miles from the tactical stranglehold of Chapman's Arsenal in the pre-war years. In that post-war period, it's easy to detect a keen identification with the Busby Babes as the most exhilarating confirmation of a more hopeful future firmly based on youth and positive, attacking play. This was reflected elsewhere both in the wing play of Matthews and Finney and the no-holds-barred passion of forwards like Lofthouse and Milburn. Unfortunately, glorious though it may have appeared to some, the England World Cup victory of 1966 was based not on the youthful abandon of the United side of the fifties or the liberated wing play of Matthews and Finney, but on dogged pragmatism as old as the English game itself.

United and Busby's self-defining obsession with the European Cup led to the creation of a team that achieved the goal, as well as showing a way forward for the game that was far more enticing than the Ramsey model. During this era United set themselves apart from the prevailing model in more ways than are commonly acknowledged, and within this lay the seeds for United's status as both the most forward-thinking and individualistic of all clubs and as pariahs within the English game that for me made the intoxicating parallels with punk so enticing. Given the unmistakeable trends of that seventies era, I reckon I wasn't as alone as I thought

Although it would be some years before English footballers entered the realms of the super-rich, there was a steady increase in both transfer fees and wages across the English game, a development that United remained aloof from for years. For several years after the war, United were a club dependent on an overdraft to survive [15], but Busby had always refused to be involved in the culture of backhanders that supplemented the maximum wage in the fifties [16] United lost the services of the brilliant John Connelly over a refusal to match what Blackburn offered him in the mid-sixties and, in 1966, almost lost Denis Law for the same reasons. Eamon Dunphy notes that, back then, United's top earners were still only getting half of the £100 a week Fulham had begun paying Johnny Haynes five years earlier; indeed, United had, according to Dunphy, the lowest wage bill in the first division at the time.[17] Even at the end of the seventies, with the club's owners growing fat on the controversial rights issue sale, Dave Sexton was being told by the board he couldn't have Ray Wilkins without making up the money by selling players, which he managed to do via the sale of Brian Greenhoff, David McCreery and Stuart Pearson. [18]

Contrary to popular and convenient belief, for the majority of its history United have been run on strong principles of thrift; it was among the rest of English football that the rich gravy train was being followed so resolutely. Ultimately, the fact that United would latch onto it to overtake everybody else is held up as evidence that we instigated the process in the first place, but that couldn't be further from the truth. At the same time, a steady swelling of the rivalries between clubs that had always existed in a less clearly defined form was now rising to the surface so that it was simply no longer possible or desirable to do what Bobby Charlton and his brother Jack had done as kids growing up between Newcastle and Sunderland. By the time I was that age, club loyalty had become the defining feature of the game and it was a short step from this to the football-related violence that arrived in the early seventies. And it was at that point, simply through historical coincidence, that my obsession began and saw United in all their confrontational glory, scarfs tied around wrists and in pitched battle with everyone and anyone, that pariah status now graphically defined in terms that were emblematic of the time.

Throughout this generally difficult period, and despite the fact that declining attendances across football grounds were blamed on the advance of the hooligans, despite the fact that success for the club was, when it happened at all, fleeting, United established themselves as easily the best-supported team in English football, achieving permanently a status that had only been held onto for short spells in the fifties and sixties   Between 1973 and 1987 – a period that brought only three trophies and even a season in the second division – United had the highest average attendance in English football in every one of those fifteen seasons despite the tally of championships during that time showing a 9-0 victory for Liverpool. During that period, the average attendance at English first division grounds fell from 31,323 – when Liverpool had the highest average gate in 1972 - to 19,273 when the same club acquired the mantle, again briefly, in 1988. During these years, while United's attendances experienced ups and downs, the average remained persistently above the 40,000 mark and saw conspicuous rises in a time when most other clubs were struggling to get people into their grounds.

It was as if, in United's darkest period for around forty years in terms of success on the field, the unique nature of United's support was being emphasised more defiantly than ever before, and that therefore the nature of that support had far more to do with allegiance to a stylistic model deemed unconventional and outmoded by the rest of the game and United's already fully fledged outsider status than any kind of material success. Although the kids at my Liverpool-obsessed school didn't seem remotely aware of it, United were reversing patterns of match attendance to an extent that is difficult to comprehend for supporters of any other clubs, which I suppose is the reason why so many enemy fans nowadays cling to the myth that the size of United's support is due to the club winning trophies and nothing else. While the values of football supporters were changing along with other social values in the post-consensus years, the rich swell of support that had emerged during the game in the fifties had subsided across the country, except among United supporters. By 1980, with attendances collapsing all around them, United boasted an average attendance more than 12,000 above what it had been in their championship winning year of 1956. Of the ten most supported teams that year, only United and Liverpool – the latter in the middle of an era of unprecedented success – had experienced any sort of improvement in attendance during the period, while other clubs all showed declines in attendance upwards of 6000 per game. Newcastle United, so often held up by elements of the British media as a paradigm of loyal support, lost well over a third of its fan-base during the period. It was clear that every other club in the higher echelons of the English game experienced their attendances ups and downs according to whether or not they were successful on the pitch. Despite an identity rich with outsider status and defiance of stultifying rules and conventions, or perhaps because of it, only United had the long-term loyalty among supporters to buck this trend and, even more than that, the ability to continue to attract many new supporters along the way.

United were, and remain, the only objects of mass support I've ever felt drawn to. And it seemed to me that the club's appeal in the seventies was burgeoning because, and not despite, the adverse circumstances around us. Just as Barcelona developed into the great footballing institution it became via the melting pot of outsider status that was post-Spanish civil war Catalonia, so United, in very different circumstances, and without the bonding factor of conventional nationalism, have a similarly defiant sustenance. It was an appeal to me that, given my own pariah status, now seems inevitable. We are, against all odds, United.

[1] http://www.guardian.co.uk/football/2008/mar/20/sport.comment3

[2] Crick,M. & Smith, D. *Manchester United: The Betrayal of a Legend,* pp12-13

[3] ibid, p21

[4] Dunphy, E. *A Strange Kind of Glory,* p126

[5] Crick, M. & Smith, D. op cit pp21-22

[6] Blundell, J. *Back From The Brink,* p350

[7] ibid, p181

[8] http://www.liverpoolfc.com/news/features/wolves-classic-match-may-1976

[9] Egan,S. *The Doc's Devils,* p220

[10] Hill, D. *Out Of His Skin,* p176

[11] ibid, p46

[12] Worrall, F. *Celtic United,* p21

[13] Hill, D. op cit p46

[14] Charlton, Sir B. *The Autobiography – My Manchester United Years,* p27

[15] Dewhurst, K. When You Pull on a Red Shirt, p98

[16] Worrall, F. op cit p130

[17] Dunphy, E. op cit p30

[18] Crick, M. & Smith, D. op cit pp118-119

Chapter Three: Feed the Enemy

17 August 1974, Brisbane Rd. Orient 0 Manchester United 2

It was the best of times; it was the worst of times. The first twelve words of Dickens' most over-rated novel could be applied to United's experience of playing in the second division in 1974-75. In one sense it was easily the club's lowest point for four decades, just seven years after we'd triumphed in Europe; but for the rest of English football's second tier times had never been better. In those days there still existed the spirit of even-handedness in the distribution of gate money so, while many of the local shopkeepers might have feared for both their insurance premiums and their premises when United's fans came to town, it was ching, ching, ching all the way for the clubs themselves.

United's first opponents in the second division for thirty-six years were an Orient team on an equally rare high. The previous season they surprised just about everybody by putting three seasons of flirting masochistically with the cruel mistress relegation behind them to finish fourth in the division, just one place off promotion. In doing so they'd turned their six and a half thousand average gate into a ten year high average of 11,793. Orient have never again finished in the top half of the second division, and the Orient board might well have supposed that things would never get that good again.

Then, on 17 August 1974, at least in home attendance terms, they did. All the recently established records were smashed when Manchester United arrived in east London. It's widely assumed that, the 17,772 crowd that day was made up of many thousands of reds, many of whom filed into the Orient end more for the fleeting thrill of seeing Tommy Docherty's new reds in action than out of interest in the home team's fortunes. United duly romped to a 2-0 victory courtesy of goals from Willie Morgan and Stewart Houston and would never look back on the way to an instant promotion that looked already a foregone conclusion when the Reds secured a fourth straight win at Cardiff fourteen days later. Orient's Brisbane Road ground would be relatively barren for the rest of the campaign, their average crowd easily less than half of their peak in that first game of the season. Cardiff would follow a similar pattern, welcoming more than 22,000 to the United match, easily exceeding any other attendance during the season and almost 9000 more than turned up for the home match against Sporting Lisbon in the European Cup-Winners' Cup. In the twenty-one away games United played in the second division, nineteen would provide their opponents with their best or second best attendance of the season.[1]

I watched from a distance. In a family with its eyes purely focused on the first division, I caught glimpses of United only when Granada TV deigned to show highlights, usually placed way down the programme's schedule, on a Sunday afternoon. It was literally like something from another world. Although this was second division football, the raw footballing thrill was on a higher level than anything I'd watched elsewhere, and it was played out against a backdrop of the most raucous, passionate support imaginable and always in packed stadia. What peculiar footballing universe was this that could harbour such magnificence in its second tier? As the three minutes or so of highlights ended and I returned to earth with a bump as Gerald Sinstadt's mug filled the screen, I craved the next instalment with a hunger that seemed incompatible with the rest of the dull, staid and mechanically obvious footballing world around me.

There are certain English football teams who are regularly praised in the media for the loyalty of their support and others who are renowned for its comparative fickleness. Carry out a straw poll among footie fans and I'm willing to bet most would put Newcastle and city somewhere near the top of the list when it comes to club loyalty. Asked whether, on balance, smaller clubs have more loyal fans than clubs like United, my prediction would be that the majority would answer yes. And asked a question about whose fans are the most fickle and success-oriented, those same fans would put United at or near the top of this list. If we went a bit further to look for evidence to justify these responses, we would perhaps be asked to consider the fact that Newcastle and city, when relegated into the second tier of English football, invariably continue to attract crowds of 20,000+, far in excess of any other clubs in the same division.

It's true there are clubs with remarkable numbers of loyal fans, but it ain't them. The most notable of these clubs is the subject of this book. In 1974-75, after United had become the first side since the war to achieve the highest average attendance in the country despite being relegated from division one, the club's supporters went on to attain a double distinction by securing the accolade of best supported side in the country despite being in the second division, the only club to achieve this in the last sixty years. Not only that, but our average attendance rose not just slightly, but by more than 13% during that season in the second tier of English football and was 1.7 times better than the average attendance for the season's first division games [2]. This is extraordinary, but no less remarkable than the widespread conviction that United's support is of the fair-weather nature that flies so wildly in the face of all factual evidence.

Incidents of a team increasing attendance in the season after being relegated from the top division have occurred only 20 times since the war (less than 14%) and for a club to experience a rise of 13% or greater in its support during an ordeal of this nature is much, much rarer. I take my hat off to the clubs who have achieved it: along with United, this very short list comprises only Sunderland (1997), Sheffield Wednesday (in both 1958 and 1990) and Leicester City (2002). Not, note, city or Newcastle.

While United's is a conspicuously astonishing case when it comes to club loyalty, and completely contradicts the view most opposing fans have of the nature of United fandom, it's not entirely unique. Curiously, in measuring the persistence of support among different clubs, we can often draw a very neat distinction between local rivals. Just as, in spite of the protests of conventional wisdom, there is simply no contest when it comes to comparing city's fans' response to fickle fortune with that of United, a similarly straightforward distinction can be made when it comes to comparing Sheffield United and Sheffield Wednesday. You can pretty much set your watch by Sheffield United's support. It's up and down like a whore's draws depending on the club's position in the league and the division they're in. Purveyors of over-simplified logic among Sheffield United's support might make a claim for the season the club spent riding high in division four in 1982, when support rose to an average of over 14,000, but this is only a small recovery when you consider the fall from an average attendance of over 33,000 just ten years earlier, when the club were in division one. Although there are dips in the support for Wednesday, there is a general consistency about it that is largely resistant to adversity. Wednesday's support rose despite the club dropping a division in 1952, 1956 and 2004 (the latter a drop from the recently re-named division two to division three), something that neither their city rivals nor ours have ever been able to claim. What's baffling is how city and Newcastle fans can receive such widespread acclaim for retaining support through difficult times. If you want a club that consistently does this, Wednesday are it.

Consider also Aston Villa and Birmingham City. At a rare high point in the late fifties, the blues' average support exceeded 33,000 as the team reached the nosebleed-inducing high of sixth in the table. The two second city rivals then weren't far apart in terms of home attendances. Normal service at St Andrews was resumed in the mid-sixties when frequent relegation skirmishes saw a dip to the low 20,000s, before promotion in 1972 brought a sudden leap again, this time to over 36,000, only for the club just six years later again to struggle to get 20,000 into the ground as relegation loomed once more. By 1989, admittedly at a low point for the game as a whole, Birmingham's average crowd was down to 6,265. Villa, though subject to ups and downs in support as well as status, have consistently retained the bulk of their match-going fans, their support rising during relegation in 1960 and climbing up to over 31,000 when they found themselves in division three in 1972, their highest level of support for nine years. Although they suffered the kind of decline in match day support during the eighties that prevailed across the English game, attendances then picked up significantly during the season in which the club were briefly relegated in 1988, climbing still further during their season in division two; at that point they were again in the same division as Birmingham but more than doubling their city rivals' average gates.

Although United, like Villa, admittedly experienced their rising crowds in the second division during a season that went well and resulted in promotion, even so this remains an unusual achievement and something most other clubs in the same situation can't match. If we restrict ourselves not just to those clubs in the post-war period who experienced promotion at the first time of asking, and add those who were at least in with a shout for promotion right up to the end of the season, we find that 44 clubs have been in this position since the war, and yet only 15 of them increased their support (and most of them only by a very small margin). The vast majority of clubs not only fail to improve their attendance in such situations, but more commonly experience a significant slump that's usually reversed on returning to the top division and which shows, incontrovertibly, that a large proportion of their match-going support aren't interested in supporting the club unless they're in the big time.

United continued to attract massive support both as relegation loomed and from the very beginning of their sole period in the second division. We also put thousands on the attendance figures in away matches during that period too. Far from United's received reputation of having only glory-hunting supporters, we are in fact among a very small minority of clubs whose support endures at high levels during hard times and in a class of one in terms of the scale of durability of our support over any length of time. In addition to Villa (who were relegated three times from the first division during this period and whose support went up on two of those occasions) and Sheffield Wednesday (who've had six relegations and improved their attendance after four of them), the only other clubs who might lay claim to membership of the elite group are Spurs (whose single relegation season in 1977 brought a rise in support) and to some extent Wolves, who've been relegated five times and managed an increase in attendances on two of those occasions.

There are a lot of names missing from that list, many of whom receive acclaim, with no credibility whatsoever, for the supposed thick and thin loyalty of their support, one of many triumphs for conventional wisdom in football over the truth. The only big club we can't really comment on is Arsenal, alone in not having been out of the top division during that period, although it's worth noting that during the difficult years they experienced in the sixties their crowd went down to a mere 4554 at one point. At which point we see perhaps something significant emerging. Although the post-Wenger Arsenal have injected a much needed flair and style into their game, for much of their history the general supremacy of Arsenal over Spurs – interrupted only very occasionally by successful Tottenham sides – relied on a dour commitment to throttling every bit of entertainment out of the games and almost boring rivals into submission of art being ground down by bludgeoning efficiency.[3] It can scarcely be argued that Spurs have been the club whose supporters have demanded that the game be played with a certain style - Danny Blanchflower's famous 'glory' standard - and that successive Tottenham sides have adhered to this model, while the Arsenal fans' chant of '1-0 to the Arsenal' is just as revealing – historically, their ethos has been one that has demanded success and results whatever it takes.

Danny Kelly's identification of Spurs as a 'rock and roll' team set against the establishment appeal of Arsenal has sustained their rivalry, and it is this, I believe, that has led to Spurs' fans greater resilience in the face of adverse fortune. [4] Similarly, it's no accident that Sheffield Wednesday have a more loyal support than their United rivals: they have a similar historical commitment in style, clearly illustrated when they kicked up a hell of a fuss when Jack Charlton tried to impose a long-ball game on them, something which the Blades were all too happy to accept years of. While nothing comparable to the aura of United, Villa do have a certain definable charisma, developed over decades, that Birmingham have never got anywhere near to emulating, nor really tried to. It's instructive that, when Alex McLeish joined Villa from the blues, Villa fans' protests were less to do with where he came from and more to do with the sterile, over-physical garbage Birmingham had been serving up while he was there. It's not an easy thing sometimes to explain why some clubs have greater levels of support than others, but style and clubs that stand for a certain approach to the game clearly have an edge in retaining their supporters through bad times as well as good. It's more important to their fans, it seems, that the club stays true to its ideals rather than that it necessarily enjoys success.

In the case of our historic rivals, it scarcely needs pointing out that while we stand for something in the game, their levels of support experience the kind of fluctuations of other run of the mill clubs that essentially stand for nothing at all beyond trying to win football games, and when that stops, large numbers of their supporters stop too. Our close neighbours city have of course enjoyed a lot of yo-yoing during the period in question; in fact, they've been relegated from the top division on six occasions, and despite their reputation for resilient loyalty among their supporters, on all of those occasions their average attendance declined while they were in the second tier. This is despite the fact that twice they followed this up with a quick promotion and on one other occasion (1983) only just missed out. Leeds United, it's true, experienced the drop in 1948 and responded with an improved average attendance despite a pretty awful season in the second division, but attendances soon after the war were affected by a range of factors and could be very volatile and in many cases bore little relation to the level a club played at. That changed from the fifties onwards and, on the three occasions they've been relegated from the top division since then, their support has plummeted. They lost more than seven thousand, over a third of their fans, from their average attendance when going down in 1960, almost a third in 1982 and over seven thousand again in 2004.

And what of that other team so often held up by the media as a paradigm for fan loyalty – Newcastle United? As we've seen, their close neighbours Sunderland at least bucked the trend in one season, so surely this bastion of supporting commitment, not to mention a single-club town with the biggest uncontested catchment area in the country, would be able to top this? After all, if you travel directly north from Newcastle the first senior club you get to plays in the Scottish League, so the area is absolutely ripe for the picking when it comes to recruitment of football fans. Unfortunately, as is so often the case, we find that media representation and conventional wisdom don't tie in with reality. Newcastle have suffered the drop four times since the war, and, only on one occasion – in 1961 – did their average attendance show a very small increase. In the three relegation seasons since then, they've consistently seen mass evacuation of St James' Park that would only be reversed on return to the top division; over 20% deserted them in 1978, there was a small but notable decrease in 1989 and a fall of over five thousand in 2009, despite their team winning the Championship that year.

When Liverpool endured relegation in 1954, they managed to shave over 10% off their support during their first season in the second tier. And in case you're thinking that smaller teams who pay a brief visit to the top division fare better, given their supporters' familiarity with rougher times and thus what is again generally assumed by so many to be a greater resilience among them, think again. The evidence suggests that these clubs tend to pull a load of supporters out of the closet during their brief encounter with the big time who quickly depart when relegation occurs and mundane reality kicks in again. Consider the cases of Bradford City in 1995 (14% of their support didn't return the next season), Burnley in 2010 (over a quarter of their support deserted them on return to the championship) and Northampton in 1966 (in the year following their single season in the top division, a third of their fans found other things to do on Saturday afternoons). Oldham Athletic also shed a third of its support when dropping down a division in 1994, while Swindon lost over 40% when returning from whence they came in 1994, and Carlisle said farewell to a similar number after their excursion to the top division in 1975. And the most fickle of the lot? Bristol City, who in 1980 were relegated from the top division and lost a mammoth 52% of their average crowd in the process.

The romantic image of the support of small clubs remaining resolutely with them through thick and thin is nonsense. United's fans are conspicuous in the strength of their support whatever fortunes befall their team, something that only clubs with a certain defined aura and comparable attachment to style can get close to emulating. It's often been said by United fans that the true intensity of our support comes out in times of difficulty and I believe that's true, tying it as it does with the peculiar attachment to pariah status we so enjoy. Amid the disappointment of a defeat, I always experience a peculiar sensation of my attachment to the reds strengthening even further and it also seems to me that, when making my way along with thousands of others across Trafford Bridge and into Salford following a disappointing outcome, there's a conscious swell of increased devotion to the club hanging in the air around us. This is one reason why, if we're going to have a bad result, I'd rather be there at the ground rather than watching it on the telly. The communality of the experience is overwhelming and in its own very singular way uplifting.

While it's also true that these days our home support could be a lot more vocal than it is, in times of difficulty Old Trafford can be a hell of a place to be. I doubt if any club in the world could have replicated the atmosphere in the ground during the Champions League game at home to Bursaspor in 2010. The game itself was pretty bog-standard, and ended in a routine and unspectacular 1-0 win. But it happened during the week when we learned that Wayne Rooney's departure was apparently imminent and, indeed, on the radio driving to the ground that evening the statement came through from his agent with Rooney's spurious reasons for wanting to depart. The sense of togetherness in Old Trafford that night was tangible, as Rooney's statement – clearly an attempt to curry favour and link to the anti-Glazier sentiments prevalent among United fans at the time – was digested and spat out with the player roundly identified as the villain of the piece. Every time Alex Ferguson got up from his seat that night a goose-bump generated wave of support and applause went around the stadium. The United family had come together at a time of crisis, and it was melancholy and yet wonderful to be a part of. Rooney of course changed his mind, and I'm not kidding myself it was because of our reaction rather than the money, but what it did show was that the imminence of potential bad times ahead had a demonstrably positive effect on the allegiance of United fans, providing a glimpse into the psychology of the loyal core of United's support and their remarkable persistence. Of course, it's great when we win things, but even the experience of a title-winning game or a trophy presentation doesn't come close to matching Old Trafford when the need for genuine supporters to rally together presents itself.

Those attendance statistics – which can be sourced very easily – rarely get referred to in the media, much of which seems happy to present United as a bloated commercial monstrosity, successful on the field only through having greater resources and with a group of fans only tagging along for the ride as long as the ride's a good 'un. Particularly prevalent are not only references to United's non-Mancunian support but the unchallenged assumption that such support by its very nature must be fickle. Despite two-thirds of Manchester postcode areas containing more United than city fans [5], it's long been depicted as part of the identity of Manchester United that the club has an appeal only to non-Mancunians. In a thorough study, published in 2002, Dr Adam Brown of Manchester Metropolitan University investigates these widespread assumptions. [6] It's barely surprising to a United fan that Dr Brown finds these stereotypical notions not to be supported by fact and he inevitably concludes that 'a Season Ticket holder in the M postal area (ie in Manchester) is more likely to be a Manchester United fan. [7]

I think it's the sheer scale of United's support that makes it difficult for some elements among the media and supporters of rival clubs to understand this: the truth is we have both massive international *and* local support, but, given the enormous size of United's fan base, it seems the feat to grasp that the two can co-exist is akin to the challenge of understanding certain propositions from quantum mechanics. Perhaps if the teacher recalled in the previous chapter had spent more time teaching my peers maths than conscripting them to the Liverpool FC cause there might have been more, at least in my locality, who can manage the fairly straightforward arithmetical feat involved in comprehending this obvious truth.

Of course, among supporters of all sides there are many individuals who, I don't doubt for a moment, feel every bit as intensely towards their club as I do towards United. However, the sheer size of United's match-going support, certainly since the sixties, has remained solid in a way that just doesn't happen with any other club in England. It hasn't always been thus. In the years after the first world war, while United's support could even then reach heights beyond those of any other club in what were boom years for first division football, it was notoriously volatile. In 1921, 70,504 fans filed into Old Trafford to watch a game against Villa, establishing a record that would stand for 85 years, yet in the same season a mere 10,000 drifted through the turnstiles to see United play Derby. However, at some point after that, United's support attained fortitude in the face of whatever fortune threw up that is unmatched in the English game.

United fan and self-styled Mr Manchester, the late Tony Wilson, advanced the theory that United's astonishing levels of support from across the country are due largely to three factors. 1. The Munich Tragedy, where large swathes of the population not only grieved with the club but also admired their incredible resilience: the club moved from a position where it appeared even closure was on the cards to participation in that year's FA Cup Final and eventually to becoming European champions just ten years later. 2. The mesmerising trinity of Best, Law and Charlton in the sixties. 3. The level of football violence and the infamy United gained from the resulting publicity, far from putting off would-be supporters, actually enticed young males to Old Trafford and brought a new generation of fans in, more than enough to compensate for those who might find the new atmosphere in the ground a bit too much of an adventure on a Saturday afternoon. [8]

When Wilson wore an FC Bruges rosette to present Granada Reports on the night Liverpool faced the Belgian club in the European Cup Final, it was the first time I'd seen my own feelings towards Liverpool reflected so staunchly by a high profile figure. It couldn't have been better that it was Wilson, who until that point I hadn't even realised was a United fan, who was responsible for this display of anti-Liverpool sentiment. What I did know him for was presenting Granada's Friday night *So It Goes* and *What's On* programmes that followed Sinstadt's preview programme *Kick Off* and did so much to bring to my attention some of the great music of the era, both from within Manchester and outside. It was the first place I got to see the Sex Pistols, sitting on a couch next to my parents who sat open-mouthed, clearly unable to believe the generational stake that was simultaneously being driven between us and into the heart of English values and traditions. His Factory label would soon introduce Joy Division to the world, a band who would speak to parts of me the Pistols couldn't reach. Both bands were short-lived, and always seemed somehow destined to be so – brief shocks of the new that stunned the world like sharply delivered electric currents after which it would never be quite the same again, whether it liked it or not. I was already an avid listener to the John Peel show on Radio One and had had to accommodate the disappointment that he was not only a Liverpool supporter but a particularly obsessive one who'd even given his kids middle names like Dalglish and Anfield. It was great to discover that Wilson, that other filter of life-changing music, was one of us.

Wilson has a prominent place in the line of great Mancunian individualists and his grasp of the deep meaning and significance attached to United, Manchester and Mancunian music is undeniable, but his statements are characteristically designed to be epigrammatic and punchy – relying as they do on that politicians' rhetorical trick of 'the power of three' - rather than necessarily on the mark. He ignores, for instance, that the great swell of appreciation for United in the fifties actually preceded the Munich disaster, United having tapped into the post-war mood by nurturing a new generation of young men playing the game with skill, verve, imagination and in the right spirit despite financial destitution. Busby's Manchester United struck a chord with a post-war footballing public in a way that no other sides (including the 'Bank of England' club Sunderland, Matthews' Blackpool, the established 'glamour club' of the pre-war era, Arsenal, and the then massively supported Newcastle United, Everton and Spurs) could match. The Munich disaster didn't kick start the mass appeal of Manchester United – rather, it drew together in one terrible, tragic and collective moment something that was there already. But this was not the resolute, partisan support of today; rather a symptom of a national bond formed with the club that went across and beyond supporters' existing loyalties.

Wilson does, however, take us a few steps in the right direction in understanding that what United had, unlike any other club, was a multi-faceted identity that, while distinctively Mancunian, could pull in appeal from many disparate sections of the nation and, indeed, the world. Among United scribes, Keith Dewhurst has come closer to grasping it fully, delineating the complexity of what United represents across a whole book 'When You Pull On A Red Shirt' without feeling the need to over-sanctify the Busby years or neatly bundle them into a few sentences like Wilson. [9] What constitutes the appeal of United is impossible to simplify. Like Spurs, Villa and Sheffield Wednesday, that the club stands for a certain style, a certain accepted way of doing things is a good starting point in understanding our appeal, but a closer look reveals that the enormity of United makes these clubs' cases incomparable in terms of sheer scale and depth.

Like Joy Division and other genuinely important bands, elusiveness in pinpointing the source of the greatness of something plays a large part in establishing its magnitude. The actual components of United's style may be difficult and elusive to identify, but something about them makes the club unique in football, allowing it to build and retain a following that isn't prone to fluctuations according to the laws of success and failure, and that manages to attract even kids like me, knowing none of this history and arsing around on a school playing field less than a mile from Merseyside but gasping at the sight of the likes of Pearson and Coppell in full flow, the appeal and draw undeniable and the fact that they were playing in the second division completely irrelevant.

Like gravity, we only identify such a significant force not by observing it directly but by its effects on the world. In my case, I've always had a natural aversion to anything that involved mass participation, so the effect of such a popular phenomenon on me is highly unusual, if not unique, possessing a power that cuts through my normal tendencies and attitudes with an extremely sharp knife. In music, give me a small intimate gig over a stadium event any day. And give me a small to medium sized festival over a Glastonbury. The worst and least productive times in my life have always been occasions when my circle of close friends expanded to a point where the number of people I was trying to accommodate in my life had grown to a level I was unwilling to try to manage. I found myself in danger of sacrificing my identity to the crowd and recoiled, cutting them out of my life. In my twenties, sitting in a local pub one night in a crowd of about thirty people, they all burst into 'Hi-Ho Silver Lining' along with some awful singer with a tape machine behind him while some woman next to me talked about how great Jimmy Nail was live in concert; I excused myself to go to the bog, walked straight out of the door and went home. At around the same time I had my own flat. One or two people around having some cans and putting the world to rights I could enjoy – as long as they broadly agreed with me - but occasionally the numbers would grow and I'd suddenly find myself in the midst of what was dangerously close to becoming a party, at which point I'd invariably get fed up and chuck them all out, quite prepared to insult and threaten them if they refused to budge, the impetus for such an outburst anything from someone taking a chocolate éclair out of my fridge or mocking the soundtrack of surf guitar instrumentals I'd so lovingly provided for their visit. I am, you might think, an anti-social bastard, and you could be right. Before you judge me, however, I would ask you to build into your calculation the proportion of arseholes involved in the aforementioned situations which, believe me, reached tipping point at a fairly low threshold. Not only that, but my Sartrean 'hell is other people' tendencies have never dimished a life-long socialism: it's a combination that in itself marked me out at an early age as distinctly pro-Mancunian. The city has always resonated with the spirit of individualism that has never tempered for a moment its long-standing commitment to fairness and social equality. The city that gave us entrepreneurial industrials not only became the unquestioned centre of political dissent in Britain, but there was even a time – during the mid-nineteenth century – when these two groups with apparently contrary objectives were joined together at the forefront of the political challenge to the forces of privilege and inherited wealth in Britain.

Perhaps somewhere within here lies the reason why I can sit among 70,000 plus people at Old Trafford and feel utterly and completely at home. This seems to me to say something about the peculiar nature of United's appeal and its intrinsically Mancunian nature as well getting close to the reasons for it. The club can attract people, such as me, in both the most unlikely places geographically and for whom the default social position is one of contented solitude. The reason it can do that, I suggest, is because the identity of Manchester United is not, whatever their recent owners or the rest of football might want to believe, anything like the brand identity of Coca-Cola or Nike, who build up a consumer image that, at its rawest level, draws people in via promoting conformity and group identity. Its power is such that it can accommodate so wide a spectrum it can even touch those who would rather die than buy anything with a Nike label on it; a significant, and possibility crucial, element in the power of Manchester United is that all you have to do to belong is carry on being yourself. If I had to sit in the pub next to some of the tossers I've found myself next to at United, I'd have walked out. Yet sitting at United behind that couple in the north-west quadrant who tut every time I indulge in my customary unbridled goal celebrations, or next to that guy in K-Stand who's always farting and talking loudly and disparagingly about his wife, or even in the family stand behind the family who sit munching hot dogs, belching and apparently paying little attention to the match are all something I can go along with. The connection with United is enough, so powerful that I'm willing to tolerate and even on one level enjoy the company of people I'd otherwise not be able to stand the sight of.

Perhaps this is why, while other clubs rely on on-field success to keep their support close to maximum capacity, United have a far greater hardcore following, one that's remained attached to the club during the long period between 1968 and 1990 during which only three trophies were won. It's often scornfully noted that United draw their fans from everywhere in the country, as if diluting the power of that support, but I'm willing to bet that all of those out of town United fans are in the minority in their own areas. Perhaps not as extreme a minority as I was in at All Saints School, but nonetheless outnumbered, their devotion to the reds as kids tested every day by the ultra-conformist kids who borrow the League Of Gentlemen mantra that this is a local team for local people, and in many cases end up just as emotionally mutated because of it. These kids not only become seduced by the overwhelming power of the United image; it gives them the strength to revel in their own minority status and in turn keeps that spirit and that identity moving forward into future generations. It's a bit like what Timothy Leary said about self-selected elites, only without the LSD (although there's that gang of lads from Collyhurst in the Scoreboard End...). Any club could actually achieve this with a bit of imagination and long-term thinking. In doing so to any more than a limited extent, United are alone.

[1] Egan, S. op cit p160
[2] Crick, M. & Smith, D. op cit p228
[3] Mitten, A. *Mad For It*, p142
[4] ibid, p145
[5] Brown, Dr A. op cit, p4
[6] ibid, p2

[7] ibid, p3

[8] White, J. *Manchester United: The Biography* p8

[9] Dewhurst, K. op cit pp21-22

Chapter Four: The March from Peterloo

Old Trafford, 13 April 2008 – Manchester United 2 Arsenal 1

Arsenal, for so long our closest challengers, suffered their third consecutive trophy-less season having succumbed to a Cristiano Ronaldo penalty and an Owen Hargreaves free kick which will always remain his most significant contribution to the United cause. The two goalscorers went on to play little part in United's immediate future as, at the end of the season, Ronaldo would bluntly reveal his desire to join Real Madrid. After one further season, United would accede to his request, pocketing £80 million which the debt-laden Glazer regime would conspicuously fail to re-invest. Hargreaves would suffer horrendous injury problems before eventually departing the club to join city, publicly blaming United's medical staff for his lack of games before featuring only five times for his new club, who released him after one season. Also on his way to city, but much sooner, was Carlos Tevez. That day a shot from distance following his arrival from a substitute's bench that would ultimately stand as a symbol of his combination of Jon Stark-like quality and restlessness (for the uninitiated, Jon Stark was a character in the Scoop sports comic of the late seventies, a 'gun for hire' who swore no allegiance to one club and sold his services on a temporary basis to whoever would pay his going rate), was a typically vigorous injection of energy from this paradigm case of the age of the footballing mercenary.

That night, I went to see Elbow at Manchester Academy. Very much a homecoming gig, lead singer Guy Garvey perfectly understood and expertly toyed with the Mancunian energies of the crowd. Bringing up the matter of football, Garvey skilfully left a pause following his opening reference to the beautiful game before simply saying 'United won', leading to inevitable cheers and boos in roughly equal measure from the audience. Garvey talked warmly about his Manchester upbringing and ruminated on the reasons why Manchester produced so many great bands. 'In Manchester,' he told the crowd, 'when you're in a band, nobody looks at you as if you've got two heads'. In Manchester, perhaps uniquely, you've always been able somehow simultaneously to both stand out and fit in, a major determining influence on its musical and footballing power and magnetism.

Elbow were actually formed in Ramsbottom, to the north-west of Manchester, and yet, clearly, Garvey (born in Bury) sees himself as heavily connected to and indeed essentially 'from' the city. There is no doubt that, to him, Elbow are a Manchester band and understandably have no reservations about seeking a place within that rich cultural heritage that places them among Joy Division, New Order, The Fall, The Smiths, Happy Mondays, Stone Roses and many more.

They are very much part of a post-punk Manchester lineage that has generated easily more ground-breaking and innovative bands than any other area of the country, And yet, if you dissect the membership of the bands mentioned in the paragraph above, barely 10% of them actually hail from the city of Manchester itself. More are from Salford, a city in its own right which clings to Manchester like a vital organ pulsing away at its side, its starkest and most lasting contribution coming in the shape of The Fall, whose origins and character are very much Salfordian although leader and permanent fixture Mark E. Smith has been for the bulk of his life a resident of Prestwich, in the borough of Bury. Half of Joy Division came from Salford, with the other half hailing from Macclesfield in east Cheshire. Ian Brown and John Squire met to form the Stone Roses in Timperley, south of Manchester, though Brown was actually a native of Warrington.

The twin forces of music and football have a kind of entwined power in the north-west of England, as a United fan like Brown would surely understand. [1]. But the nature of the pull from east and west Lancashire is very different. It's not merely my footballing allegiances that leads me to identify Manchester as the undisputed centre of it all, either; it's something which has more to do with the status and self-image of Manchester and Liverpool than a simple count of the number of bands from areas with an M postcode or the number of United supporters in east of Salford. Unlike other civic centres in the UK, Mancunian influence and identity stretch well beyond the boundaries of Manchester itself. The contrast with Liverpool is particularly striking. While you might get a band like Clinic (from Crosby) identified by outsiders as loosely 'from Liverpool', most towns within a comparable geographical distance – such as my home town of Widnes, or St Helens, Ormskirk or Warrington perhaps – would, unless they were second generation Liverpudlians, completely repudiate any suggestion that they had anything to do with the large metropolis to the west, and those scousers in exile themselves would recoil more than anyone at the suggestion that their new neighbours could be in any way part of their treasured Liverpudlian heritage.

They are, in their words, 'woolybacks'. The term has multiple origins and has referred at various times in history to (a) Liverpool dock workers, (b) medieval interlopers sneaking round the back into Liverpool to avoid being charged to go via the Chester city walls or (c) Liverpudlians moving out of the city to fill up 'overspill' areas like Hough Green. Now the term is most commonly employed to refer to those who live in towns geographically close to the city but culturally have no connection with it. There is no equivalent to the 'woolyback' in Manchester (the only other civic centre in England where the term has similar sociolinguistic origins and meaning is Newcastle) so those like Elbow clearly have no hesitation in identifying themselves as Mancunian, and nor is there any resistance to them doing so. It's an important defining factor in the civic identity of the two towns. While many Scousers like to think of themselves as essentially accommodating and friendly, and no doubt of many this is true, my youthful experiences of exiled scousers at my school cast them as peculiarly inclusive and clannish. On Sundays, my mum would have Radio Merseyside on in our house and when author Brian Jacques' 'Jacques' Town' programme (an enjoyable listen with children's author and poet Jacques evidently a genuine and likeable individual) came on, there was a line in his theme song that referred to how Liverpudlian culture meant responding to strangers with the invitation, 'See that open door.'. It's clear to me now that the goodhearted Jacques intended this to mean that strangers were always made welcome in the warm bosom of Liverpool households, but such was the experience I had with so many of the kids at school, who seemed to think – bizarrely - that proclaiming themselves as scousers gave them some easy route to social eminence, I honestly interpreted it to mean that strangers would literally be shown the open door and thrown out.

Those at All Saints who couldn't claim genuinely scouse ancestry often, curiously to outsiders, claimed some link into the bloodline, simply because they wanted to cement legitimacy as supporters of Liverpool FC and in deference to that scourge of young life, peer pressure. As the majority of my school colleagues fitted this category, that 'law of the playground' that, as Homer Simpson put it, means you never say anything without making sure that everybody else feels the same way, inevitably kicked in. To aid its application, and eliminate anyone making a dubious or invalid claim, a test was devised to determine whether you were a 'real' scouser or not. You were asked to say the word 'dickhead' and if, when pronouncing it, you gargled several litres of phlegm at the conclusion of the first syllable, you were accepted as a real Liverpudlian, as opposed to someone who was just trying to be one in a desperate attempt at credibility. Although my family history contained a decent proportion of Liverpudlians (and therefore was full of people who could easily gargle unseemly amounts of phlegm around a 'k' phoneme), I declined to take part in such ceremonies and instead distanced myself from the whole business by hanging around on my own or with a very tiny group of individuals happy to admit they were actually from Widnes, and, along with them, kept my phlegm pretty much where it was. As a result, I risked having the shit beaten out of me on those rare occasions that I wasn't accompanied by some hairy-backed Widnesian who, if anything, favoured the oval ball and could doubtless find far more unpleasant things to do with a throat full of phlegm should the situation warrant it.

Because of the cultural absence of the woolyback in Mancunian vernacular or lore, those who are touched by the city's civic spirit feel, and are welcomed in feeling, the full extent of an inclusiveness that co-exists because, not in spite of, its fiercely independent and brash nature. That is to say, although on first venturing into Manchester, a first impression might be to see its inhabitants as bullishly opinionated and socially unrefined, it's this very attitude that creates space for you to go in there and just be yourself, with no phlegm-gargling or any other retarded initiation required. You can see it in the stance and gait of self-confident young women and girls in the two cities: Liverpool girls have a way of walking around upright with their arms folded, indicating a psychological barrier to outsiders, while similarly self-confident Mancunian girls will walk with a brash openness, no less prepared to tell you to fuck off but approaching everything with an expansive, no-boundaries ambience that's up for taking on the world or embracing depending on the circumstances. It's the reason why, in and around Manchester, the spirit of individualism has always happily co-existed alongside the spirit of communality, where technological innovation and enterprise have thrived alongside the socialist spirit and developments like Chartism and the Co-operative Society.

Bobby Charlton, a native of a fiercely communal north-east, would come to find his whole life and identity bound up with both United and Manchester. As is illustrated by De Valera in Ireland, the Corsican Napoleon in France or Che Guevara in Cuba, allegiance to a place can be remarkably strong among those who are not natives to it. [2] Why is there an assumption that a native of a country has a stronger attachment to it than an immigrant? The first of these is there by simple accident of birth, the second by choice. That's not to say the former doesn't have a strong attachment to his or her place of birth, but the assumption that the latter cannot have a similarly strong attachment, if perhaps of a different kind, seems to me to be indulging in a spot of logical leap-frog. United players imported from elsewhere have a conspicuous tendency to remain in the area long after their playing careers have ended (the Glaswegian Pat Crerand is another notable example, one whose diehard commitment to United has few rivals despite his Celtic origins) [3]; despite many, like both Crerand and Charlton, originating from strong communities themselves, the pull to lay down new roots in Manchester is stronger than the desire to return home.

That's not to say that everyone arriving at the club acquires this sense of belonging. You only have to consider the cases of Tevez and Ronaldo, mentioned earlier, both of whom left the club in disappointing, if very different, circumstances. Yet even here, we find in Ronaldo's post-move pronouncements always a great love and respect for the club that grew during his six years at Old Trafford. Tevez's case is admittedly rather different, but even he made some crass attempts to ensure fans thought the better of him, vainly arguing that it was the club's refusal to offer him another contract, rather than his desire to strike it rich elsewhere, that was the motivating factor in his ignominious departure. To get to the bottom of this fully would require us to negotiate that particular conundrum known as the Tevez brain, and it would require a book of considerable length, plus a background in psychology I don't have, even to get started. But I recall being at Old Trafford, close to the front at the Scoreboard End, when Tevez made his first return as a city player and saw at close range his facial expression in response to the inevitable abuse he was receiving. He looked, frankly, confused and crestfallen at the vitriolic reception. Somewhere in there I sensed a genuine feeling of dismay at what his name now meant to United fans. Even in the heart of the perceived traitor, some strength of feeling apparently resided. And his actions in displaying that appalling and tasteless 'Fergie RIP' banner in 2012 seem to me to be the unthinking actions of an embittered man, whose jaundiced feelings couldn't even be shooed away by his new club winning the premiership. And while Owen Hargreaves eventually made the same journey to city, the eventual parting of the ways followed an offer to play for the club for nothing in order to prove both his fitness and usefulness to Alex Ferguson, his rejection by Ferguson again perhaps giving some context to those wounded and unnecessary criticisms of the United medical staff.

Not having the level of skill needed actually to play for United (or anyone else), my own strength of allegiance comes from a different place, one where the origins of the strangely intense feelings of loyalty of the football fan must to some extent, as David Hume might have said had he donned a Hearts or Hibs scarf and been around to write about it, remain a mystery to us. That uniquely harmonious positioning of both football and music at the heart of north-west culture seems to me to indicate the right place to look for potential answers to this question. The two are, admittedly, very different phenomena. Whenever I go back to Joy Division's *Unknown Pleasures*, The Smiths' *The Queen Is Dead*, Buzzcocks' *Another Music In A Different Kitchen*, or indeed any favoured album of Mancunian or non-Mancunian origin, I get essentially the same feelings from it. It doesn't let me down. It's always there for me and always yields positive feelings. Football lets you down. It's part of the game's nature and appeal that even the best player can fall on his arse, miss a sitter or hit it into Row Q. Mixed in with United's greatest triumphs in the nineties were 5-0 reverses at the hands of Chelsea and Newcastle, and the shipping of six on one all too memorable occasion at Southampton. In the seventies, this inconsistency was even more pronounced. My love for United could never be founded on anything reliable, especially as at the time it was subject to infrequent ups and spectacular downs. Supporting a club doesn't generate the same sense of fulfilment and celebration you get when listening to great music, and it can't be abandoned as soon as the great music stops. An avid collector of Smiths vinyl, this didn't stop me keeping my money in my pocket when they released their one duffer, the easily forgettable 'Shakespeare's Sister'. In football, love has to embrace defeat as well as victory, otherwise it ain't love.

Allegiance to a place clearly involves a more complicated bag of emotions still. Why should there be such a pronounced difference in attitudes towards neighbouring boroughs among inhabitants of the two metropolises of Liverpool and Manchester?

The reasons are rich and complex. Let's start with the geographical tension between Manchester and Liverpool that came with the opening of the Manchester Ship Canal in 1894. This thirty-six mile long waterway (the longest of its kind in the world at the time) was a direct, and ultimately successful, attempt by Manchester to recover its position as the industrial capital of the north by establishing itself as a successful port, by-passing the Liverpool docks and allowing ships direct access inland to the city. It was also Manchester's response to Liverpool holding the territorial advantage that allowed them to charge high rates for importing the raw cotton that Mancunian mill owners needed; [5] the canal was a development Manchester had been seeking for decades, plans which Liverpudlians had consistently resisted, protested about and even ridiculed in music hall routines, but which were eventually approved in 1885. Its arrival gave a massive two fingers to Merseyside, something that continues to have an effect on Liverpool's psyche today, despite the fact that both cities have long since lost their industrial eminence and have suffered very similar years of decline and impoverishment.

You can still see the hallmarks of the age now, framing the area in which I've spent so much of my life like two gigantic and immovable bookmarks – Ellesmere Port's Waterways Museum at the south of the Mersey still has buildings that were used as offices by the Ship Canal company as they snuck in goods via the Mersey's south side, while at the other end the immense Liverpool Warehousing Company building stands large and incongruous close to Old Trafford, its presence unavoidable to those who , like me, approach the ground via Salford and Trafford Bridge. The existence of the LWC goes back to 1846 in the Liverpool docks and their establishment of warehouses in Trafford Park was a direct result of this area's emergence as the world's first designated industrial site. It preceded, to Liverpudlians, the outright crime against nature that was the emergence of a successful port thirty miles inland.

As a symbol of the historic bitterness of Liverpudlians towards Manchester, the Ship Canal is a good place to start, while Mancunian resentment at the high rates charged for those cotton imports provoked much of the ill-feeling at the other end; but actually tensions go back a lot further. Liverpool's civic origins as a seat of power arise from its central role in the slave trade. In the city centre you'll still find many landmarks from the slave years (such as the Goree warehouses, named after an island near Dakar, from where many slave ships travelled) and many major streets that still carry the names of important slave-trading families, among them Earle Street, Gildart Street, Tarleton Street, Cunliffe Street and Bold Street. It might be asked why there hasn't been more pressure to change these names over the years, to help rid the city of its shameful past, but in the case of that last street in particular the reverse has been true. An important shopping area in the city centre, a suggestion to rename Bold Street Shankly Street after the death of the former Liverpool manager was strongly opposed by Liverpudlians who favoured retaining the name of a slave-trading banker. That's not to say that there was any particular affection for the banker in question, and it's entirely plausible that much of the support came from 'over my dead body' Everton fans, and understandably so, but it's also part of a general resistance to change and apparent unconcern about the city's past and what these street names denote among residents of the city.

That's not to say, of course, that Manchester has no unpleasant skeletons in its own closet: the odious twentieth century fascist Oswald Mosley was, after all, born in Ancoats. However, in the case of the city of Liverpool the street names are epitaphs to figures whose deeds stretch into the very roots of its civic identity and not merely to the occasional morally redundant political activist. Those who offer the counterclaim that Mosley St in Manchester was named after him overlook the fact that the street's been so named since the eighteenth century.

While poverty is nothing new to either city, socialism and left-wing political activism run far more deeply in the history and identity of Manchester, going back to the suffragettes in the early twentieth century, to the mid-nineteenth century Chartists and beyond all this to the 'Peterloo' massacre as St Peter's Field in 1819. Indeed, Peterloo – which gains its nickname from the contemporary bloody battlefield at Waterloo - as well as remaining the most savage act of violent repression by the authorities in British history, can be seen as the point at which Manchester established itself as the pulsing heart of socialism in Britain. A peaceful demonstration that descended into carnage after troops descended to break it up, it's an atrocity of a kind a city remembers through successive generations. From there, we can trace direct links to the massed crowd that gathered at Kersal Moor near Salford in 1838 that gave impetus to the nascent Chartist movement, and to the general strike of 1841-42 which Lancashire and Cheshire workers continued after the rest of the nation had accepted defeat and where the Manchester power-loom workers held out for a further month to stand as the last of the strikers to return to work. [4] The Manchester Radicals led by Richard Cobden and John Bright mobilized protests against the corn laws in the mid-nineteenth century and from their group arose arguably the most forthright voice of all for women's suffrage, the secular activist Elizabeth Wolstenholme-Ely. Though much is rightly made of the Moss Side origins of the Pankhursts, Wolstenholme-Ely - born in Eccles - has been vilified and largely air-brushed out of the history of the suffragette movement largely as a result of her militancy and willingness to denounce other members of the movement for their lack of radical fervour, not to mention her pariah status in Victorian society as an unmarried mother and outspoken non-Christian.[5]

Throughout the 1900s, Manchester was the heart of political dissent in Britain. Such an identity brought the city into direct conflict with Liverpool when Manchester supported Lincoln and the rights of slaves during the American civil war, while Liverpool, in defence of its economic interests, stood squarely behind the slave owners. Modern Liverpudlians that are predominantly left-wing by inclination and yet all too aware of the oppressive history of their city are fully aware that Manchester has the civic history it would desire for itself, although admitting this openly is rather less easy to bring about. The gulf between the two is mirrored in a footballing sense by the attempt to set up the first players union in Liverpool in 1899 failing pretty much before it even got off the ground, while a second attempt, in Manchester, was successful but ultimately saw only the group of Manchester United players led by Charlie Roberts and Billy Meredith stand firm against the FA when the authorities crushed it, leading to the club's nickname of 'outcasts' in the professional game in the earlier part of the century, a crucial episode in establishing the club's identity and singular, isolated niche in the English game. Unquestionably, whether the city of Manchester or Manchester United is being considered, the shade of red runs far deeper to the east end of Lancashire. In contrast, the radical waters of Liverpool run remarkably shallow. In contrast with all other major northern cities, Liverpool did not even have a Labour-run council until 1955. While the parlous economic conditions of the thirties and earlier had seen massive growth of socialism in Manchester, Newcastle and Sheffield, the movement remained highly underdeveloped on Merseyside until well after the Second World War. Equally, the earlier divisions in the trade union movement that had struggled to unite the common interests of 'skilled' and 'unskilled' labour forces had vastly diminished in most urban centres by this point, while in Liverpool they remained pronounced as the skilled workers looked out for their own priorities, stifling the rise of union activity in the city and ensuring that a culture of protecting vested interests prevailed instead. [6]

Such factors ensured Liverpool remained detached from the rest of the north-west which was, along with Manchester, deeply involved in the rise of left-wing activism in the country as Liverpool remained immersed in the old politics of the competing Tory and Liberal factions of the bourgeoisie and management classes. Throw in the ship canal and its direct threat to Liverpool's pre-eminence and you have a tangible symbol of this divide and a further reason for Liverpool's industrial elite embracing the stigma of victimhood, instigating in its population a conviction that their woes were all to do with competition from Mancunian aggressors and a framework within which the Roy Evans/Kenny Dalglish schools of management-by-pretending-the-whole-world's-against-us could flourish.

Liverpool's response to the ship canal was understandably to attempt to compete with the development, take the approach of the LWC and retain as much of its trade as it possibly could, which for many years it actually did very successfully. It's a strategy within which we can see the emergence of an 'if it goes anywhere other than Liverpool, it's a threat' attitude to the rest of the north-west – perhaps inevitable given Liverpool's history and geographical position. It bestowed on Liverpool an essentially insular civic outlook, a greater sense of its parameters and boundaries that persists to this day. In contrast, the ship canal – which fittingly came to feature on the Manchester United club crest – symbolised Manchester's links with its surrounding areas. Manchester could spread its territorial influence right across Lancashire and within this influence would its greater industrial power reside – through an expansionist mind-set, in contrast with the protectionist insularity of Liverpool. While other towns to the north unquestionably benefited from the establishment of Manchester as a powerful trade centre, the towns of South Lancashire who, unlike their neighbours to the north, hadn't developed a professional footballing culture of their own found connections with the city of Manchester were being nurtured just as the professional game was beginning to prosper, even among those towns directly in Liverpool's shadow.

Thus those from Bury, Stockport, Rochdale or Bolton, whatever their own particular local identities, happily felt at home on tentacles stretching out from Manchester to and beyond them; such tentacles spread right across South Lancashire from Salford in the east to Widnes in the west and south into Cheshire. Yet the ship canal really only cemented what had existed before it, with, for example, many individuals from these and other towns among the reported casualties and protesters at Peterloo, their fight for workers' rights and enfranchisement irrefutably connected to Manchester even in pre-chartist and suffragette times. While the lists of those killed or injured at Peterloo reveal that roughly half were from Manchester, a substantial number hailed from towns such as Oldham, Stockport, Bolton and Ashton-Under-Lyne, while smaller numbers are identified as having travelled in from places such as Warrington, Northwich, Macclesfield, Marple and Lancaster.

Michael Bush, in his excellent study of the massacre and its aftermath, notes with some surprise the absence of anyone in the casualty lists from Liverpool (or indeed certain other north-west towns like Blackburn or Wigan), concluding that it appears no one was present from these districts. [7] Perhaps it's reflective of the fact that, as we've seen, the fervour for political reform did not consistently embrace all areas of north-west England and that Liverpool was certainly among them. Certainly it's conspicuous for a city the size of Liverpool to be have been apparently entirely unrepresented at the Peterloo gathering.

More recent times have seen Liverpudlians claim for their city a reputation for political radicalism that historically it just doesn't have. While some might argue that the actions of the Militant-dominated council in the eighties secured for Liverpool a place in the vanguard of socialism, I beg to differ. Manchester's proud heritage of hundreds of years of left-leaning political activism and opposition to the status quo could not be matched in five minutes by the radical gestures of a population who, for a fair chunk of that time, had been growing fat off the gains of the slave trade. Rather than seeing any potential for collective political will in all this, scousers seemed to feel they had somehow to prove themselves more left-wing than anyone else, particularly the famed home of socialist activism thirty miles up the road and proceeded to embark on this pursuit with damaging results both for their city and for the English left.

The Militant Tendency had infiltrated the Labour Party on a significant level over the previous three decades and gained their firmest foothold on Liverpool City Council, unsurprisingly, as their origins in the Revolutionary Socialist League were largely Merseyside-based; their national secretary back in the sixties, Jimmy Deane, was a shop steward at Cammell Laird on the Wirral, and other prominent local members included Tommy Birchall from Bootle and Tony Mulhearn, who would become one of the leading Militant figures in the eighties. By 1982, Militant had taken control of Liverpool's ruling Labour group on the council, adopting the slogan 'Better to break the law than break the poor' and were hell-bent on a collision cause with Thatcherism, later defying the government's odious rate-capping policy to approve an illegal budget for the city. Although several councils initially adopted this defiant stance, only Lambeth joined Liverpool Council in following the fight through to the bitter end.

The problem was that the end was felt most bitterly by the council's workforce. After largely reversing the 1200 redundancies imposed by their Liberal predecessors on the council, in 1985 the Labour council, having battled a government only too happy to let it fight on to the point of self-destruction, found itself in the ludicrous situation of having to serve redundancy notices to all of its 30,000 employees. The following year, an investigation by the national Labour Party led to the expulsion of 40 members of Militant. There were many more to follow over the next few years. While it's true that Militant was undoubtedly active in Manchester too – they instigated repeated attempts to unseat prominent shadow cabinet member Gerald Kaufman – Fielding and Tanner, in their study of left-wing politics in Salford and Manchester show the role of Militant to be far less significant in those councils than was the influence of the traditional Labour Left at the time, [8] whose old-fashioned Bevanites and 'soft left' Kinnockites easily outnumbered the infiltrators and muck-stirrers. Understandably, civic centres that had large and influential socialist groups dating back well before the war were far more resistant to the activities of infiltrators than those, like Liverpool, who'd barely discovered socialism prior to the Revolutionary Socialist League gaining its foothold.

By this point in Liverpool, the council's deputy leader Derek Hatton had become a figure of national notoriety, not to say celebrity. A lifelong Everton supporter, Hatton was one of those members expelled in 1986, and had been very much the media face of Liverpool politics during the council's rebel period. Opinions remain split to this day in Liverpool on whether Hatton ought to be remembered as a heroic and vocal opponent against the destructive forces of Thatcherism, or a flash opportunist simply looking for a vehicle to further his own public profile. Those who take the latter view note that, after his political career, Hatton has been at various times a radio broadcaster, menswear model, motivational speaker and later media company chairman and property developer.

With the benefit of history, the whole period comes across as a rather embarrassing example of gesture politics, providing Thatcherism with a gift-wrapped opportunity to depict Labour as financially irresponsible and riddled with extremists in addition to leaving Liverpool itself in a far worse position as a result. The title of Militant members Peter Taaffe and Mulhearn's book – *Liverpool, A City That Dared to Fight* – is very telling, as if the chief aim was the attainment of a defiant and heroic left-wing image for itself and for Liverpool, whatever the consequences for the workforce and the broader needs of the city that the council represented. Contrast this with the approach of the more traditional Labour-dominated Manchester City Council of the time, where leader Graham Stringer brought stability in a difficult period from 1984 to 1996 while still playing a leading role in campaigns against the Tory government. Manchester became a prominent voice in the fight for equal rights and in particular against Section 28, that flagship for Victorian morality and the new right as, having suppressed the voices of left-wing economists, The Conservative administration aimed to do the same thing to the progressive tide of social liberalism. That they significantly failed to do so is due, not to the likes of Militant, but to the voices of an entirely different strand of political radicalism which found a more dependable platform on Manchester and other city councils.

While we had Militant councillors in Halton too, their power-base was the new town areas of Runcorn such as Murdishaw which, like Hough Green in Widnes, is a stronghold of the borough's scouse populations. Elsewhere, as in Manchester, the traditional Labour left held sway as the Halton constituency cemented its position as one of the safest Labour parliamentary seats in the country and the borough saw its last Tory councillor hanging on for grim life in (for Widnes) relatively leafy Farnworth.

Given the geographical proximity of Widnes to Liverpool, I've often encountered bemused reactions when exposing my dialect to other parts of the country. My reaction to the often heard comment 'you don't sound like a scouser' is identical to the one given by Steve Jones in the film *The Great Rock & Roll Swindle* when told 'you don't look like Johnny Rotten'. This is because the town in which I was born has, like many others in the twenty miles or so between it and Manchester, a deeply entrenched association that stretches way back even beyond the events outlined above which is reflected in dialects across the south Lancashire region. Alan Crosby, in *The Lancashire Dictionary of Dialect, Tradition and Folklore* notes a distinct geographical border between the 'Scouse' and 'Lancastrian' dialects and notes with interest how far west this border occurs. Anyone from outside the area might be surprised to hear, for instance, the difference in accents in only a few miles between Liverpool and St Helens and, indeed, between Liverpool and Widnes. The west Lancastrian dialects of Widnes and St Helens, although distinct in several respects from the more pronounced north Lancastrian dialect that predominates as far south as Wigan, have practically no discernable remnants of scouse whatsoever. Indeed, any differences among south and east Lancastrian dialects are thought to be remnants of Viking settlements in these areas. [9] It's still the source of much confusion among outsiders that the famous Spike Island Stone Roses gig didn't take place anywhere near Manchester, but in the West Bank area of Widnes, whose residents live in the shadow of the bridge over the Mersey and whose Lancastrian accents are as closely related to those of Mancunians as pretty much any other area of the north-west.

In short, there is no commonality in either culture or language between the South Lancastrian towns in what might be referred to as the 'Rugby League belt' and Liverpool. This is not to say that some sort of cultural magnetism doesn't pull from the west, but this is as a result of urban spread rather than any inherent historical or anthropological factors. During the fifties and sixties, a huge Liverpudlian exodus infiltrated west Lancashire from

Skelmersdale to the north-east of Liverpool right down to Runcorn in north Cheshire and gave all of the towns large second generation Scouse populations, including those whose offspring dominated All Saints School. These towns thus became cultural battlegrounds for the Liverpudlian identity and an old south Lancastrian post-industrial pride that defined itself equally proudly as non-Liverpudlian. Partly because of the events described above and partly because it's more productive to identify yourself with something as opposed to just against something, the allegiance of non-scousers to a sub-Mancunian identity grew and, in the post-sixties loyalty spiral of professional football and indeed much earlier times, found significant expression in support for United.

Why United rather than city? In a footballing sense, Manchester United had already, with remarkable foresight, placed itself in a position to benefit from these developments well ahead of the always less forward-thinking city, a club whose innovations during their existence are limited pretty much to the (thankfully rejected) proposal to merge with United in the sixties and inflatable bananas. City's bedrock of support comprised, and still very much includes, satellite towns like Bury, Oldham and Stockport (recent evidence shows higher concentrations of city than United support in the latter two towns [10] .[11]), simply accepted as 'Mancunian, as near as damn it' and substantiating the myth perpetuated to this day by the blues that their support resides solely within Manchester, while Manchester United's ground is not even based there. There is a peculiarly embittered logic at work here, which happily accepts east Lancastrian and east Cheshire acolytes as Mancunian, but sees the residents of Trafford Borough, with a Mancunian postmark, as somehow illegitimate. Not only is this self-serving and illogical, it is also non-Mancunian in character, removing from the Mancunian landscape a key element of Manchester's historical outlook and thus its very identity. By virtue of our expansionist and forward-thinking character, Manchester United have a far stronger Mancunian identity and thus simultaneously a much stronger link to potential support from the west purely because we represent what Manchester stands for so much more forcefully.

Within two decades of the ship canal opening, Manchester United, formerly the railway workers team Newton Heath, relocated to a new ground at Old Trafford, the first of many instances in history where the club's management was decades ahead of others in the game, with consequent benefits for the club still being reaped a century later. Fifty years on, when other clubs in the top division of English football wrestled with the problem of their grounds existing within large built-up urban areas, making expansion impossible, Manchester United were residing in an area close enough to the large populations of Manchester and Salford but sufficiently separated from these intensely urban areas to make increased stadium capacity a serious prospect when required, and with a stadium that was already big enough to accommodate the growing levels of support in the game. Although the otherwise excellent writer David Conn notes the 'accidental' benefits of Old Trafford finding itself situated in areas of car parks that meant an absence of planning problems for the club when the club needed to expand [12], this was actually more due to the foresight of United's owners in moving the ground away from an area where those issues would have given the club the same problems others - such as Liverpool - have experienced. And of course it's not as if those car parks were there when United moved into Old Trafford.

John Davies, who orchestrated the move, did so not just with these future aims in mind but also with a decree that the new ground should not just match but be better than any of the London stadiums. Even though United at that stage had not tasted anything like the success of later years, there was already a clear aim at the heart of the club to both have and be the best and to ensure the very heart of English football remained in the north of England. Any of the more successful clubs in the north at that time – Preston North End, Bolton Wanderers, Blackburn Rovers, Newcastle United or Everton (who for the first eleven years of league football had the biggest average attendances in the country) – would surely have noted the gaining of momentum among

London clubs during the era: in 1901 Spurs had become the first southern club in the professional era to win the cup and had done so in front of by far the biggest crowd ever to attend a club football match (over 110,000) while suddenly in 1908 Chelsea, albeit briefly, acquired Everton's mantle as the best supported team in England. Any of those bigger northern clubs of the period could have sniffed the wind and done something about it. It was United, the outcasts, who did. The failure of other clubs to match United's ambition is the source of their deep animosity now: northern clubs who resent the dominance of our club have only their own clubs' failure to seize such opportunities to blame, then and on many occasions in the future.

In a second major triumph of strategy, Manchester United, despite experiencing their most barren spell in the trophy-less period between the wars, began to expand rail links to the ground to ensure that those who lived outside Manchester and Salford, stretching right across Old South Lancashire and down into Cheshire, and wanted to see United play, could access the stadium more easily. In 1935, chairman James Gibson arranged for Midland Railway to put in a halt station for matchday specials, allowing access to visitors from as far away as Birmingham and London. The vision of Gibson, after he'd rescued the club from going out of business in the thirties, was to achieve something even greater for the city of Manchester: to make it into not merely a club for Manchester, but one that would be at the centre of the footballing world. [13] It was a statement recast from the height of the city's industrial heyday and the ship canal days: at the heart of Mancunian civic identity was an ambition never to be self-contained, but to reach out, encompass and have meaning well beyond the confines of Manchester itself. Those city fans who claim, inaccurately in any case, territorial priority and sole rights to Mancunian identity are guilty of ignoring the very essence of their own city. Manchester is at heart visionary and expansionist. Which is why United represent its civic identity in a way city have never come close to matching.

Gibson's plans went further, introducing an emphasis on youth development at United that, although not completely unique at the time, was nevertheless a case of seizing a recent development in the English game and applying the strategy more successfully than anyone else. In 1938, club secretary Walter Crickmer took over as temporary manager and established the Manchester United Junior Athletic Club from which players like Johnny Carey, Jack Rowley, Allenby Chilton and Stan Pearson emerged. All of those players would be important members of the United team that defeated Blackpool to win the FA Cup in 1948, our first trophy for 37 years, and yet they were merely the forerunners of a youth policy that would flourish to legendary levels under Busby in the fifties.

Patterns of footballing demographics since then have demonstrated just how far-sighted all of these developments were. Not only do we now live in an age of highly diversified patterns of support, but also one in which fewer and fewer fans across the top level of the game attach an importance to locality they once did, except in using it as a stick with which to attempt to beat United. The stark fact is that now match-going football supporters of clubs in the top division travel on average 40 miles to see their team and identify increasingly as their main 'rivals' teams from outside their immediate vicinity. [14] The little Englander mentality that embraces the calculated stupidity of the opinion that all United fans are Londoners similarly chooses to overlook that 95% of Arsenal fans don't live in the area of the ground [18] or that, in moving to Highbury from Woolwich in the first place, they failed to anticipate the growth of football as United did and made their eventual move away from their second ground inevitable, and could only carry this out by trampling all over the wishes of Islington businesses and residents [15] - and that's to use the example of London's – and indeed, except for United, the rest of English football's – historically most forward thinking club.

It's stretching credibility to claim that clubs in Britain's top tier envisaged a future of local clubs for local people when they were hiking up prices – against the recommendations of the Taylor report – on the back of all-seater stadia. Anyone with an ounce of business knowledge in the city-based clubs that make up by far the greatest proportion of the Premiership would understand that, in pricing out large numbers of inner city fans, they'd only make the numbers up by attracting them from an increasingly widening catchment area. United are unusual only in the sense that we've nurtured this growth in out of town support unashamedly and openly alongside the retention of a high level of local support, while others have sustained a myth of communality that they know to be a deliberately propagated falsehood. Though this doesn't reflect common prejudice, it is in full accordance with the facts that continue to show United as having a very high intensity of match-going local supporters. This achievement, along with the historical nurturing of the club's connections with non-local supporters, allows United to be successful nationally by exporting what remains a very Mancunian identity to the rest of football. That ship on the club's crest that represents the canal is a highly significant emblem, symbolizing not just the club's far-sighted and expansionist vision, but its intrinsically Mancunian character.

Rivalry between Liverpool and Manchester United has multiple roots, only some of which are revealed above. While the modern identities of the two clubs were forged in the images of Busby and Paisley (to credit Shankly is over-generous, as he got off the horse before it started seriously to complete in the race). That similarly intense levels of rivalry have never existed between Everton and city (or between United and Everton or Liverpool and city) shows that it's not only about geography. Footballing and other factors have been added to localised tensions already there since the ship canal and those political differences; recently emerging political radicalism among Liverpudlians does not have the deep roots of Mancunian socialism in the same way that Liverpool FC's football philosophy has always lacked the depth and historical resonance of United's, which is one of the reasons why hostility towards United from Liverpool was inevitable.

I pieced all of this together in a battlefield situation that, while not exactly like Wittgenstein composing his works in the First

World War trenches, was nevertheless pretty damn hostile, and growing moreso by the year. We, after all, only had the problem that we weren't accumulating trophies in anything like the numbers that they were, admittedly a source of not inconsiderable envy, but at least something we could rectify, given time, however far away that time seemed. ut having an identity that couldn't live up to your own dreams, having a history that was no less shallow, and having to accept that, whatever your own ideological leanings, your forefathers were the children and grandchildren of slave traders elicited more than envy and contained stains you knew you'd never be able to remove. This is why, it seems to me, Liverpool supporters have struggled to come to terms with their club's identity in a way that United fans never have, and why the conflict between us has been so liberally spiced in recent times with so many wishes, pretences, dreams and often plain lies, all arising from the psychological trauma that invariably comes from having to suppress and reinvent your own past.

[1] Robb, J. *The Stone Roses*, p3
[2] McKinistry, L. *Jack & Bobby*, p221
[3] White, J. *Daily Telegraph*, 6 February 2013
[4] http://www.chartists.net/General-Strike.htm
[5] Irving, S.
http://radicalmanchester.wordpress.com/2012/04/08/Elizabeth-wolstenholme-elmy-manchesters-free-love-advocate-and-secular-feminist. Interview relating to: Wright, M. (2011) *Elizabeth Wolstenholme-Elmy and the Victorian Feminist Movement*.
[6] http://alfiesantics.wordpress.com/4-alfies-architecture/founding-of-the-liverpool-free-state
[7] Bush, M. *The Casualties Of Peterloo*, p23
[8] Fielding, S. & Tanner, D. *The 'Rise of the Left' Revisited: Labour Party Culture in Post-War Manchester & Salford*, published in: Labour History Review, Vol. 71, No 3, December 2006, pp225-227
[9] Crosby, A. *The Lancashire Dictionary of Dialect, Tradition & Folklore*, pxiii
[10] Brown, Dr A. op cit p10

[11] ibid, p15
[12] Conn, D. *The Beautiful Game*, p66
[13] White, *Manchester United: The Biography* p54
[14] http://thechriswhitingshow.wordpress.com/2012/08/28/2012-football-rivalry-census-results
[15] Conn, D. op cit, p68

Chapter Five: A Different Kind of Tension

Portman Rd, 1 March 1980. Ipswich Town 6 Manchester United 0

You could have driven a bus through the middle of our defence the moment Alan Brazil received the ball to slot home the first goal with a decisiveness that had long deserted him by the time he later joined the hapless army of misguided signings United would make in the early eighties. Ipswich were three-up within half an hour, Paul Mariner's goal the result of something resembling a Hong Kong Phooey episode within the United goalmouth, only with no Spot the Cat figure to intervene and save the day. Gordon McQueen's pitiful double attempt at clearing the ball that led to a fifth goal had even more comic value. Apart from among United fans, of course. Ditto Coppell's woeful back-pass that let Mariner in for his hat-trick and Ipswich's sixth.

The unpredictable and a capacity to self-destruct have always been ingredients of the rich banquet offered to the United supporter through the ages but, through all of the travails of supporting United during the seventies and eighties, this one stuck in the gut most, its impact punctuated by the fact that this was a team supposedly in hot pursuit of a title that would once again be won by Liverpool. Ultimately finishing second at the end of that season would be the high point of the late Dave Sexton's reign at Old Trafford.

Going through the excruciating process of watching highlights of this game again, the cheers when Gary Bailey makes his three – yes, three - penalty saves sound amazingly loud, illustrating just how many United fans, as ever, were in the ground, the intensity of our away following during that largely unsuccessful period in our history, even though the first penalty came with us already 0-3 down, as always undimmed by the catastrophic events unfolding on the pitch. This was one of eight league defeats in season 1980/81. We won only nine out of 21 games at home and, overall, scored a total of just 51 goals in 42 league matches.

Despite this rather sorry set of statistics, United remained easily the best supported team in England with an average home attendance of more than 45,000 and the undiminished ability to add thousands to the gate at any away ground.

It all comes down, as Camus understood, to the unpredictability of that ball. This is true to some extent of all ball sports, but in particular football where there is no contact with the hands allowed, nor an extension of the hand in the form of a bat or racket. If the spherical object is elusive to begin with, it becomes even more so when controlled only with legs or, occasionally, head. This is a vital source of the inimitable excitement of football, because always we feel in touching distance of defeat, whoever we support and however often we experience winning. It is also the area where my devotion to United, I realised, clashed most emphatically with that of those Liverpool supporters I knew. The two clubs, it seemed to me even then, had responded to the game's unpredictable nature in two very distinct ways. Liverpool had devised a scheme in order to tame it, to neutralise its inherent danger and potential for creating mayhem, reducing and managing risk and chance; whereas United embraced the game's true soul by playing a form of the game where the danger and risk and sense of the unpredictable were still very much important elements and therefore, even in the more successful times of late, we always seem – to me anyway – to be within touching distance of either disaster or breath-taking, exhilarating glory.

I struggled to articulate this, and to understand how it fitted in with other aspects of my life, until I read that magnificent storyteller Yann Martel's early book of stories, *The Facts Behind The Helsinki Roccamatios*. In it, there is a story that recounts the excitement experienced by Martel's narrator on encountering an orchestral recital led by a part-time musician with a discordant violin. The narrator's reaction is the closest anyone's ever got to articulating my fascination for United and the various other divergent influences that converged on me during my childhood years; he enjoys the performance not for its perfection, but for its proximity to danger and propensity for things to go wrong, equating it with the thrill of punk, Jackson Pollock or Jack Kerouac. Football, where even the best player can tread on the ball, balloon it into the stands or miss an open goal, is closer than any other sport to this spirit.[1]

Such a description might adequately describe my thrill of hearing the Sex Pistols for the first time or seeing Gordon Hill either surge magnificently down the wing to cross for Pearson to head home, or alternatively over-run it, lose possession and stand with his hands on his hips. Insipid flawlessness was for Cliff Richard and Liverpool FC. Elsewhere was where true humanity lurked, in the hands of a guitarist who barely knew three chords but could create such unimaginable wonders with them or the unpredictable winger whose approach might lead to glorious success or ignominious failure but nothing in between. That's why, when I woke up on the morning of 2 March 1980 with the usual relief that it was a Sunday and therefore I didn't need to get up, there was a new feeling - or rather a realisation, a 'moment' as Virginia Woolf might have it; an epiphany. I felt incredibly lucky to be a Manchester United supporter.

I would experience it again, for example, on the morning of 27 April 1992, on missing out on the league to Leeds United and doing so, of all places, at Anfield; on 15 May 1995 after surrendering the league title to Blackburn Rovers who won it despite losing at, of all places, Anfield; I felt it particularly strongly on the morning of 14 May 2012 when city scored those two injury time goals to pip us to the league title on goal difference. I'm not claiming that I enjoy failure more than success; rather, that to grasp and enjoy the astonishing phenomenon of Manchester United requires us to do so when things are going badly as well as when they're going well: it's to understand the game's true nature and Manchester United's unique place in it. Because of the rather erratic period for United I grew up in, it's something I understood early in life, and I equally realised it was something the Liverpool fans around me could never, and would never, be able to comprehend.

Following 13 May 2012, surely the most devastating loss any English team has ever had to endure, the United forum Red Cafe was a hotbed of declarations of pride and love for Manchester United, easily as many as there are on the days when, thankfully more plentiful nowadays, we'd won something. Similarly, following the humiliation above – a 0-6 against Ipswich that could, had it not been for Gary Bailey, quite easily have been 0-8 - United's fans continued to turn up at Old Trafford in numbers that dwarfed other attendances in the top division. On the Saturday prior to the Ipswich defeat, we'd had 43,329 in the ground to witness the demolition of Bristol City. Every other attendance for the rest of that season would exceed this significantly, despite the fact that the Ipswich massacre brought the understanding that, though still riding high in the table, we wouldn't seriously be challenging Liverpool for the league that season, or any time soon. Even so, four of the six remaining home fixtures would draw attendances of well over 50,000. Don't misunderstand me: the feeling of euphoria after winning is something I wouldn't swap for anything, especially after having waited for such long periods to experience it on a regular basis. But to be United in defeat is something very special in its own way.

The great Dutch side of the seventies had only distant resonance by now. Everyone talked about Brazil, and would continue to do so, and we saw another great Brazilian team in the 1982 World Cup, one that clearly stood head and shoulders above everyone else in that competition even though they went out before the semi-finals. Further evidence that true greatness was something not intrinsically linked only to success. That to be truly great in a sporting sense was to have something more than just trophies. Recently a Liverpool supporter told me contemptuously, admittedly after I'd rebuked her playfully for soiling my desk at work by leaving a Liverpool FC official diary on it, 'United fans are just people who like football but don't know who to support, so they pick United'. It engages a stereotype of United fans that, I suspect, Liverpool fans have to comfort themselves with, but there's actually something in there that has unintended relevance.

Like those who saw Cruyff in 1974 and were transformed by the experience into loving football forever, United perform this role for even more nascent supporters, possessing a style and ethos that can turn somebody from casual observer into a confirmed lover of the game. It's not that such people like football and then think 'I'll support United'. Rather, they see United and decide that, if football can be like that, it's for me.

Comparable figures across other sporting fields are rare but their cases offer instructive parallels. These are individuals (teams are much rarer) who raise their sport to another level: Severiano Ballesteros in golf, for example; Muhammad Ali in Boxing; Alex Higgins in snooker; more recently Usain Bolt in sprinting. Larry Holmes easily surpassed Ali in terms of successful defences of the world title, but never achieved anything like the celebrated status Ali achieved, the latter lifting the whole sport with him so that, when I was a kid, heavyweight boxers were the most famous sporting personalities on the planet. Higgins was only snooker world champion twice, but his influence on the game's appeal vastly exceeded the honours accrued. Comparing Higgins with Steve Davis was probably sport's nearest parallel to United v Liverpool in the eighties, the latter walking off with every prize in the game while the former recorded only the occasional victory, but nonetheless possessing a panache, a certain something that rendered even a failure somehow glorious and spectacular and made a game that involves literally no more than potting little balls into pockets, for the period he was at the table, compulsive drama. Since then snooker has constantly willed a Jimmy White or Ronnie O'Sullivan to deliver the goods, in the hope that when they did the game would regain some of the unpredictable lustre that left it when Higgins drifted away ignominiously from it and the TV screens. Football has never needed to harbour such desperate hopes, because football still has Manchester United, and always will. Steve Davis did more than anyone to raise the performance level of professional snooker, but its legacy has been that the game is now played by perfect robots in bow ties that hardly ever make a mistake. Liverpool's legacy was the same, a game based on cold strategy, without character, attaining a kind of perfection that drained the game of football of its blood, leaving not a beautiful corpse, but a grey, rigid and unappealing cadaver. Thankfully, United would not die along with it and it would eventually be revived.

United, Ballesteros, Ali, Higgins and Bolt all have something else in common: the capacity to generate worldwide acclaim that goes well beyond immediate boundaries. A young golfing fan I knew, although professing to be highly patriotic, told me he couldn't bear to watch Nick Faldo and that all English golfers paled in comparison with the great Ballesteros, on whose example European golf was able to revive itself and compete with the all-dominant Americans. Ali and Higgins may have represented extreme, if very different, political ideologies, and yet they drew acolytes from an enormously wide demographic who were neither put off by Ali's forthright Islamic beliefs or anti-Vietnam stance nor Higgins' Thatcherism and Belfast Loyalist politics. The universal appeal of Bolt was such that, in the midst of the fervour around British successes in the 2012 Olympics, Bolt's 100m performance was still, for many, the highlight of the games, with thousands interrupting their viewing of other events in the Olympic Park to pour out to watch him run on the big screens. It's impossible to say with any precision what makes up the charisma of a Bolt or an Ali, but millions recognise it and respond to it, and their sport and the human race generally feels better for it. It is this spirit that United, uniquely in English football, represent.

Making such views known to the Liverpool FC dominated peer groups that made up the vast majority of the rest of my immediate world, it didn't take long to dawn on me just how much United pissed off other supporters, the inevitable other side of the coin. Our pride at supporting United was something I began to realise I could seriously wind other people up with, especially and increasingly Liverpool fans. A fan of Darlington, say, can declare, 'I support Darlington, the best club in the world,' and the spectrum of responses will only range from applause for his commitment to his team to a mild titter. Such a statement regarding United meets with wild, frothing-at-the-mouth outrage and finger-stabbing accusations of arrogance, then just as much as now. As the eighties kicked in and our trophy cabinet remained depressingly empty, simmering resentment of United among Liverpool supporters was nonetheless beginning to approach boiling point. From an almost dismissive attitude in the mid-seventies that only reached something of a peak during the Macari episode, they began to react to us with an indignant ferocity that at times threatened to be damaging to their health. I knew enough of them to become tiresomely familiar with the phenomenon. You'd see the blood rising in their faces, a strange grasping gesture affecting the hands as though attempting to strangle a small animal that wasn't there, and an increasing stammering incoherence as they struggled to enunciate some kind of sensible, rational and organised viewpoint, utterly failing and falling back on tried and tested banal and vacuous whingeing. I can't put a date on it, but I'd say that around 1982, with the arrival of Ron Atkinson as manager, such apoplexy reached a peak from which it has never subsided.

For me, the regular Liverpool trophy-hoovering during my primary school years had been bad enough, but since then Liverpool had won the league in 1976, 1977, 1979 and now in 1980 and would go on to repeat these successes in 1982, 1983 and 1984. They'd won the European Cup in 1977 and 1978 and would be champions again in 1981 and 1984. They would win the League Cup for the next four years (1981-84), a competition they'd professed not even to care about. And yet throughout that period of unprecedented success for any English club, my Liverpool-supporting friends had to choke down the knowledge that in every one of those seasons the under-achieving United side to whom I declared allegiance continued to draw in bigger crowds not just than them, but than anybody else in English football, and that people like me walked around with a, to them, inexplicable satisfaction as generously proportioned as Emlyn Hughes' arse. No matter how much they won, United still continued to inspire devotion at what seemed to them to be impossibly high levels. Indeed some of my mates claimed baldly that our attendance figures were just made up. My Liverpool-supporting mate Greeny argued feebly that it was only because we had a ground bigger than theirs. But they had a ground they weren't filling anyway, so the idea that a more substantial one would have resulted in higher attendance figures was to employ to say the least a somewhat underdeveloped logic, the sophistication of which was to set a standard upheld by Liverpool FC down the years.

Anyway, after Liverpool had won the league in 1981 I went back into school only in order to sit my O Level exams, and failed all but one. I'd pretty much got fed up of the place by the fourth year of senior school anyway and my lasting achievement was the number of times I wagged it during that year (the scouse kids called it 'sagging') without ever being caught. By the school, I mean. My mum and dad caught me when, on one misguided occasion, I'd decided to spend the afternoon at home only for them to return early and I hid behind the door in my bedroom, the Manchester United team poster I was breathing heavily into for once offering no solace — indeed, it seemed Martin Buchan was chiding me as I looked into his face and I wished someone with less of an impeccable moral code was staring back at me - as they marched up the stairs and confronted me. I'd made the idiotic mistake of turning the landing light on as I went past, so they knew exactly which area of the house to look in. Anyway, my mum pulled the door open to reveal me quivering behind it and it took all of my underdeveloped powers of persuasion and promises not to do it again to persuade them not to march me back into school. Promises I never kept.

In my parents' case, I regret those broken promises because they deserved better. School didn't though, with its petty rules and vindictive officialdom, not to mention Liverpool FC-supporting teachers and lads with LFC scrawled into their rucksacks in pen underneath 'AC/DC', quickly becoming the motif of choice as only the most loyal and hardy of us stayed true to our punk roots and the myriad musical variations that branched out from it while others became seduced by the New Wave Of British Heavy Metal, donned fishtail parkas on the back of their older brothers going to see Quadrophenia or preened themselves as the peacocks of New Romanticism. My rebellion, such as it was, was restrained and subtle. In addition to just not going into school, or leaving immediately after the register had been taken, jumping the fence and then sitting reading comics on the developed land that ten years earlier had been a disused railway line – the first signs of Widnes moving away from its industrial past, though it was years before it developed any idea of where it wanted to go – I started self-publishing a pen-written rag known as the Daily Insult which, presumably because of my plethora of gangster-like friends, managed to take the piss out of anyone I fancied, let others have a laugh at it and yet not see me end up as one of the Blundell Road casualties, the frequent fixture of a prone body lying on the ground amidst blood and homework which others walked round or, in some cases, over on the way home from school.

Apart from those O Level exams, the last time I went into school was the day they spontaneously adopted an unannounced 'zero tolerance' policy to lateness. I was barely yards from the school doors when I saw them being locked and a teacher emerging to direct all of us still outside over to the music block where something not unlike a reasonably upmarket refugee camp was holding around a quarter of the school (this being the newest building in the school. The rest of it just looked like a standard refugee camp). There we were scolded for our lateness and told that this kind of response to such tardiness would be happening on an ongoing basis now as we were all little bastards who ideally needed a spell in the army but, in the absence of that, would now face the icy blast of school discipline with periodical outbursts of corporal punishment should we continue to offend. Something like that anyway. I was enraged at this, because as far as my watch was concerned I was a good two minutes early when the doors were locked on us. I didn't have it in me to embark on the kind of rebellion favoured by my mate Paul who just swore profusely at them, following which he was taken into a room by a geography teacher who beat the crap beat out of him. I was waiting outside, receiving a milder rebuke as his grinning accomplice, so I heard it and saw the state of him when he came out. Teachers could get away with things like that in those days, and still stand up later perfectly comfortable with their status as Buchan-like exemplars of moral rectitude. Instead, I took my outrage to the head of year who told me there was nothing doing and I was late, end of story, and should go and get a new watch or learn to tell the time. So I walked out of the school grounds and didn't return, again a gesture rendered rather less valiant by the fact that I did go back for those exams – a proper rebel would have jibbed them all off with as little hesitation as Paul McGrath entering a boozer the night before a match.

After leaving school I decided just to stay at home for a bit and indulge my passion for doing sod all. The fact that there were no jobs anyway gave me the ideal excuse. I had a place at college but didn't take it. To say I had a chip on my shoulder was like saying Norman Whiteside was a tad zealous in the tackle. My political awakening was emerging at a time when the socio-economic landscape looked especially bleak, the odious dawn of Thatcherism followed by the election of Reagan emerging for me in a household and wider family that remained working class Tory, and the conviction so strong in the broader nation that the left was responsible for all of our economic woes that most stood by and allowed Thatcher to do pretty much whatever she liked. I started reading the New Statesman as well as the Guardian every day in the hope that I'd find some kind of genuine opposition emerging, but it seemed that the political left were either devoid of ideas or, when they had them, they were being crushed either by the political machine – as with the removal of the GLC and the metropolitan counties and the rate-capping of Labour councils across the country – or else were demonised, marginalised and effectively shut up by the Tory-dominated press. I felt completely detached from everything around me and, with the political left bereft of meaningful ideas and tearing itself apart, it's not putting it too strongly that Manchester United were, at that stage, quite literally the only thing I believed in.

Many Liverpool fans I knew clearly felt the same way, apart from the bit about belief in United of course. You might think it would give us some common ground but it didn't work like that. If any such mutual honour among northern desperadoes existed, it was very well hidden. My take on it is that the success of their club allowed many Liverpool fans to feel that they, after all, did have something significant to celebrate even as their city was ground under the Thatcher boot. The fact that United fans showed a level of commitment to our cause that they simply couldn't match in terms of bodies or anything else was taken as a kind of pissing on their parade, as if Liverpool fans had to believe that there was something unique, something about supporting Liverpool that was more than about being just another football fan to survive the woes of Thatcherism but, when looking up the East Lancs Rd, they saw a club who, without winning very much, possessed an appeal and aura they couldn't match, which demeaned their comforts and meant they directed ire at others that ought to have been reserved for Thatcher.

As far as the conventions of English football were concerned, the values represented by Manchester United in the fifties and sixties had similarly dropped out of popular consciousness as we were forced to accept a choice between the Charles Hughes up and under school and a very narrow definition of cultural refinement as represented by Liverpool FC. My own world was no different. I looked across the front room and saw Liverpool fans. I turned on the radio at night and, amongst some great music, I heard John Peel talking about being a Liverpool fan. And having stayed pretty much in my own room for about eight months from summer 1981 onwards, it was Liverpool fans who I should probably give some reluctant credit to for re-introducing me to the outside world. This was not as straightforward as it sounded, because human beings take time to adapt to any kind of change and, after several months of lazing around the house and doing little else other than listen to a lot of music and recover from eleven years of inadequate schooling, with some trepidation I decided to go out.

In addition to my immediate family – whose patience, understanding and support were unbelievable against the background holler of 'get a job' and 'you lazy bastard' from various uncles and aunties – I should give credit that's never yet been given to a couple of Liverpool supporters: Greeny and Dave. Greeny was, and probably still is, a Liverpool season ticket holder who would have died rather than miss a game and who for some reason took it upon himself to continue to knock on my front door and get me to go out after I'd long since decided the outside world was too irritating a place to inhabit; we'd go to The Music Shop – one of those independent record shops that would ultimately be wiped out in the bright new corporate world the Thatcherites created - to spend what little money I had on records, while Greeny moaned about life and very rarely spent anything at all. Dave was the kind of kid who was seriously bad news at school, whose eyes – scanning the near vicinity with that darting, Johnny Rotten-like sense of distrust and danger - would pick a fight with you as soon as look at you and to whom the mere words 'Manchester United' on your school bag were a red rag to a testosterone-fuelled bull, whose physique he resembled. Dave wasn't a match-going Liverpool fan at all, and was instead an active supporter of Widnes RLFC who grew to tolerate the round ball game partly because it allowed him to join the hordes travelling down to Lime Street when Liverpool were at home in pursuit of a ruck.

Dave wasn't so much hard as crazed, unpredictable and perpetually up for a fight, delighting in the nickname of 'Evil Dave' with a shrug ('Suppose I am a bit evil, really' he once told me, the way someone else might say 'Suppose I could have another cup of tea'), his only pretension to a welcoming gesture inspired by 'Shake Hands' in the last episode of *Boys From The Blackstuff*, where he'd make you the offer and squeeze until you either screamed in pain or allowed your bones to be crushed. 'You gotta fight dirty,' he once told me. 'Go for the face and the l'ks. Don't bother with anything else. Get 'em to bend over then, first chance you get, get 'em on the floor. Tread on the bastards. Stamp on their 'eads. They'll do it to you, so you gotta do it to them. Get in first.'

Fortunately, this Dave was gradually giving over to a new model, one who'd discovered weed down the stairwell of our local college when we attended one of several courses for the young unemployed, and embraced it with the eager fervour of a Remi Moses tackle. It calmed him down, made him at least capable of reasoned conversation without the potential for one-sided unarmed combat resulting, and made him into something resembling a civilised human being. Dave it was who first introduced me to the delights of the public house: The Gamebird, as it was then, run by ex-Everton defender Roger Kenyon in Widnes town centre. We had two pints and I was so unfamiliar with the stuff that I was pretty much off my head. I suspect Dave had taken something else in addition to the beer as he led me on a walk home through the foliage on a large roundabout, up the central reservation of a dual carriageway and finally onto and across a golf course, the notices at the entrance to which warned of dire consequences for trespassers and which would later be closed down because, having been built on a chemical waste dump, traces of arsenic were discovered within its bounds. Another example of the very slow march away from Widnes's industrial heritage, its 'Danger' sign still there now, the arsenic's reign of terror long outlasting that of Liverpool FC.

Once I'd got the taste for it, beer soon came to form the last of the three great pillars of my life, alongside football and music. It's also, along with football, one thing I like doing as a community activity and which I'd really prefer not to experience alone. Thus pubs joined football grounds as the two areas in which I actively enjoyed the company of other humans. The only problem was, unlike Old Trafford, it was difficult to get any kind of commonality among those I was drinking with, which meant I spent too large a proportion of those early drinking years in the company of complete dickheads, Liverpool supporters and usually both. The saving grace was that I've always treated friends a bit like they were part of some great transfer market of life, though obviously without money changing hands, and came to practise a rotation system akin to that of Claudio Ranieri in his heyday. Even as little as two years later, while United would sadly still be well behind Liverpool in footballing terms, my circle of friends and drinking buddies had changed considerably, and thankfully evolved to contain rather fewer of those whose conversation was limited to laughing at their own jokes, boasting about exaggerated and largely fictional romantic conquests and dull verbal treatises on the greatness of Dalglish.

The level of attachment to the game among this drinking fraternity ranged from long-standing season ticket holders to a guy who claimed to support Liverpool but went everywhere in an Ipswich Town shirt, while Greeny was one of those footballing fans for whom every silver lining has a great big cloud hanging off it. However much his beloved Liverpool won in those days, he had an irritating tendency to follow the latest championship or European Cup to enter the Anfield trophy room not with an enormous celebratory piss-up but with an observation along the lines of 'we'll win bugger all next year though'. Indeed, enormous piss-ups were pretty much off the Greeny radar anyway. He was the only dole-ite I knew who could keep a thriving savings account going, one into which he deposited a portion of his giro every two weeks. And when we went to the pub, it always seemed that the bell for last orders rang just before it was time for his round, a masterful piece of timing that I couldn't help thinking probably conspired against him actually enjoying himself. So it was with Liverpool FC. At some stage of every season he'd get his season ticket out of his wallet, offer it to me and say, with dour finality, 'You might as well have this. We'll win sod all this year,'. To which I'd respond, 'OK. But I'm off to the toilet and you probably won't want it back off me after I've come back out with it.' After which he always put it back in his wallet.

On 27 March 1983 Liverpool defeated a patched-up United side 2-1 in the League Cup Final with a last minute goal from Ronnie Whelan. As if to highlight the less than obsessive nature of his interest in the game, and the fact that it was taking place too far away for him to get down to for a spot of GBH, Dave knocked on my door on his way from somewhere to somewhere else after it had finished to ask me the score. I told him United had won 3-0. 'Fuck,' he said. I don't know when he found out the truth or even if he ever did. They sent Bob Paisley up the Wembley steps that day to collect the trophy, in recognition of his remarkable eight years at the club which had seen him become the most successful manager in the history of the English game. And on 28 March 1983, having just passed my eighteenth birthday and still without regular employment, I woke up regretting, yes, how much room Frank Stapleton had given Whelan as he did his best to fill in as a central defender, but nonetheless also still proud, very proud, loving Manchester United and understanding the nature of that love just a little bit more.

[1] Martel, Y. *The Facts Behind the Helsinki Roccamatios,* pp128-129

Chapter Six: Lucifer over Lancashire

Paul Rooney's epic 'Lucy over Lancashire' stands as one of the most remarkable musical achievements of the current century (if one that's overlooked to an appalling degree). Adapting its title from The Fall's similarly magnificent 'Lucifer over Lancashire', Rooney uses as the backdrop for his narrative the theme of a satanic presence in the area, drawing in examples as diverse as the Pendle Witch Trials, the ubiquitous Fall and our Red Devils. All of this is channelled through the voice of a sprite with a heavy Lancastrian accent who relates her story over mesmerising dub patterns until ultimately spinning off into eternal nothingness and perpetual damnation. Despite the track's creator being a native of Liverpool, the artistic palate with which he works takes in subject matter of an almost exclusively east Lancastrian hue. The supernatural shenanigans and witchy goings on all take place in Manchester or around the east Lancastrian mill towns

Although Rooney fills the song's sixteen minutes with enough to fascinate you for a good sixteen hours, it only really scratches the surface when it comes to legends of satanic influences afoot in the north-west of England. Lancashire is as much a home to Satanism as it is to cotton mills, cloth caps and Eccles Cakes. The famous 1612 witch trials unearthed a whole catalogue of local witchcraft allegations in addition to the renowned events in Pendle. The area now known as St Helens was an area allegedly teeming with satanic misdeeds and two of its female inhabitants had been tried as witches in Lancaster ten years earlier. A further twenty Lancashire 'witches' were tried there in 1634. To this day, the bus route between Burnley and Pendle is known popularly as 'the witch way'. Court records in Lancashire show well in excess of a hundred cases of witchcraft accusations in the county during the period and Kirsty MacPherson Bardell comments on how popular assumptions even under-estimate the powerful culture of magic in the area of the time; she identifies recorded cases of witchcraft across the county, in towns as widespread as Upholland, Windle, Aspull, Croft, Oldham, Bolton, Rochdale and Broughton.[2]

Looking further into these cases, what the bulk of them have in common is the presence of a strong anti-Catholic motive in bringing about the charges, the alleged 'magic' bearing a strong resemblance to then outlawed Roman Catholic rituals in most instances. Many of them are therefore more a result of contemporary protestant paranoia rather than responses to Satanism per se. [2] Indeed, when the trial of the three Samlebury witches – accused among other things of child murder and cannibalism – fell apart, the main witness for the prosecution was condemned for operating under Roman Catholic influences. The 'godly', or 'Puritan', element within the Church of England saw much of Lancashire as a haven for both chronic superstition and popist conspiracy. [3] Although only one of many areas in Britain – and indeed Europe - to play host to witch trials during the era, Lancashire was renowned as the most lawless and anarchic district of seventeenth century England, where popism and witchcraft were considered to be running rampant and therefore rumours of all manner of anti-protestant malarkey were as popular among seventeenth century gossips as were tales about who Charles II was knocking off. [4]

United's own associations with diabolism run deep, at least metaphorically, and I don't just mean in the form of over-hyped moments of alleged villainy like Cantona's kung fu kick or scars and bruises left by the studs of a Frank Barson or Roy Keane. Our Red Devils nickname is now so familiar that we can easily overlook how curious it is as a moniker and what rare associations it connotes. The name sits alongside Lincoln City's 'Imps' as a rare instance of an explicit footballing connection with the devil. The nickname was derived/pinched from the local Salford Rugby League Club, who used it throughout the decades before all rugby league clubs were harshly stripped of their historic identities in their own unholy pact with Sky Sports, in their case to be sanitised and re-named Salford City Reds. Others point to the club's original nickname of 'the Heathens' when playing as Newton Heath and see Red Devils as simply a modernised version of this. The connection of this nickname to the Red Devils comes only via coincidence and associated meaning and the Salford RLFC explanation is far more compelling, although it's worth also mentioning James Beckett's claim that the club first adopted the appellation on tour in France in the 1960s and that Matt Busby liked it so much he decided to co-opt it into the club's badge and give it official status as United's nickname. [5] Following the adoption of the nickname, the image of the red devil then entered the club's crest in the early seventies.

While the nickname itself is a second-hand one, it resonates with associations from United's unique early years. Much of football in northern England and elsewhere grew from church-based origins. Liverpool and Everton both emerged from the St Domingo's club, their president John Houlding a prominent protestant and freemason, while Bolton Wanderers were founded by the Reverend Thomas Ogden as Christ Church FC and were originally run from the church site. Both Sheffield United and Sheffield Wednesday have their origins in Methodism and the temperance movement via the influential Clegg family, while city began life as St Mark's, their name bequeathed by the CofE church of the same name in West Gorton, established by a couple of the church wardens under the guidance of Rector Arthur Connell. Aston Villa, Wolves, Blackpool and Barnsley are among many clubs in the north and midlands whose origins are also church-based. [6] Such origins are legacies of the church's active promotion of the game in this period as a means of encouraging self-discipline, based on values very much akin to those of Baden-Powell in his development of the scouting movement - basically to take young men's minds off the twin evils of sex and booze. That much of football soon after was liberally sprinkled with the latter, and football's history certainly contains no shortage of the former, suggests their aims of creating chaste and temperate young men were not wholly realised.

Although United weren't founded, as far as we know, by a group of Satanists, their unofficial 'Heathens' nickname when still in their Newton Heath days, saw them standing apart from the rest from the off. Although we aren't the only English club to begin among groups of workers, neither are these the conventional origins many suppose, and indeed those clubs in the north who weren't founded by God-botherers were more usually generated from within already existing sports (often cricket) clubs. While it would be going too far to suggest that United stood out from the pack as a completely solitary example of a club with labouring origins, we certainly are unusual in being a *surviving* and prospering club with these origins – most fell by the wayside either sooner or not much later - and we can surmise that early games featuring a contest between one of the many church-based sides in the region hell-bent on temperance and chastity and a bunch of hairy-arsed railwaymen more likely to be found in the alehouse or brothel would have possessed a certain frisson of cultural enmity. That United's identity was later rendered official via the Red Devil is emblematic of the way we developed our full character in the Busby era, the embryonic outsider status emerging fully realised from its nascent origins. That Busby preferred the Red Devils as a nickname to 'The Babes', a name he detested, illustrates just how much he was in touch with this essence. The name, usually taken so lightly, is actually loaded with meaning for the club and rightly encapsulates the origins of United and our inherent anti-establishment status, demonstrated so frequently by events on and off the pitch throughout the years.

The nickname has caused some controversy in recent times, with a fear that the global march of the United 'brand' may be interrupted by concerns arising from some Islamic countries about both the devil on the club's badge and our nickname. It was suggested that simply 'the reds' or 'Red Army' may be more appropriate, suggestions rightly greeted with hostility by Manchester United fans who understandably, given developments of more recent times, see this as yet another dangerous attempt to sever the club from its roots. The outsider association that comes with the satanic logo ties in strongly with our history of going it alone and defying convention. If it also, for rival fans, accords with their own identification of the club with evil, then so be it. The potential to draw acrimony from United's enemies goes to the heart of the club too and as such is, as far as I'm concerned, entirely welcome and part of the rich experience we buy into as United fans. In my lifetime, that United, began to attract the kind of attention among Liverpool fans that Bin Laden later attracted from the US military is entirely in keeping with what we are. It emanates from a rich identification with a kind of Miltonic, Prometheus-like Satan figure that Leeds, simply by descending into footballing hell, could never hope to attain.

As we've seen, this ties the club to the rich heritage of demonic forces in wider Lancastrian folklore. While the associations with devilry are relevant enough in themselves, the association and sometimes wilful confusion of the threats contained within witchcraft and Roman Catholic ritual during the period of the persecution of both in seventeenth century Lancashire are equally pertinent. Although the prevailing ethos that had driven the industrial expansion of Manchester was a predominantly protestant and non-conformist one, Newton Heath's non-church origins and early recruitment of Irish Catholic players placed United firmly outside the mainstream culture from day one. While the club's global support (using 'support' in a very broad sense) is inevitably pan-cultural and diverse in terms of religious origins, it's notable that surveys on the subject invariably reveal that United, among English clubs, have an unusually large proportion of Celtic 'supporters', indicative of continuing strong Roman Catholic roots or at least empathy among United fans. While the club's origins have no connections with institutionalised religion of any shade, it's fitting that a religious denomination that for many years underwent active persecution at the hands of the English establishment, and whose practitioners were barred from public office for centuries, should find common cause with this most single-minded, ostracized and rebellious of all footballing institutions.

This affiliation inevitably is viewed differently in certain other quarters. A Manchester Evening News report by Stuart Brennan in 2003 considered the strong levels of animosity towards United among Rangers fans. Entitled, bluntly, 'Why Rangers "hate" the Reds', the report looked at the context of and background to the violence at the United/Rangers match in 1974, spectacular even by seventies standards. What so irked the Glasgow loyalists, a bastion of blind bigotry through the ages, were United's strong ties with Ireland that had seen Newton Heath become the first English club to sign an Irish professional player (John Penden) and the newly named Manchester United even toy for a while with the idea of calling themselves Manchester Celtic. In the fifties, such associations became even more entrenched through the Irish-Scottish background of Matt Busby and the Welsh-Irish lineage of Jimmy Murphy. [7]

Despite the prominence of figures like Ulster's George Best and the Scottish protestant Alex Ferguson in United's history, the Roman Catholic associations have remained very real within the club and its hardcore support, and indeed both Best and Ferguson found themselves pilloried and, in Best's case, threatened by extreme elements of the loyalist communities in their homelands because of their outright rejection of sectarian prejudice, thus endowing them with an outsider status that was entirely in keeping with their new spiritual homes. An estimated 35% of Manchester's population is Roman Catholic in origin, much larger than the English average. Associations with it are another factor that places Manchester United outside the English establishment and another element that ensures that, however widespread, successful and global the club's image becomes, it retains its 'outsider' identity. Indeed, Stephen Wagg identifies the Irish Catholic associations as a vital thread between the two: he notes that the huge spread of Catholic communities throughout the English-speaking world allowed United to generate massive worldwide support long before globalization and the pernicious spread of the 'brand'. [8] Wagg shows that United's widespread support is not a product of recent penetration of global markets – to use the vernacular of modern owners – but something that's been a part of the club's identity for decades. The original owners of the Old Trafford ground, the De Traffords, were of Catholic origin and, although Alan Bairner disputes the view that Mancunians of Irish descent are inevitably

United supporters (the Oasis Gallaghers offer a high profile exception), he doesn't dispute the essential truth of the deep connection between United and Ireland. [9] During the seventies, as the British media ensured the maligned image of Irish Catholics achieved even further prominence as the 'troubles' wore on, United fans regularly wore tartan scarves and jackets as fashion accessories and indulged in chants of 'Celtic', which were invariably answered with calls of 'Rangers' from opposition supporters. The prominence of players like Crerand, Macari and Keane in successive generations of United sides has ensured the continuation of this lineage on the pitch. [10]

Although I was born into a Church of England family, it wasn't just the United connection that led me to find the heritage and outsider status of the Roman Catholic Irish something with which I could empathise. Not that I have much truck with either denomination from the point of view of faith or belief, the former religion having been created so that Henry VIII could divorce his wife and hence legitimately climb into a sack with Ann Boleyn, the latter a belief system created by the Emperor Constantine in order to give him a decent stab at keeping the Roman Empire together. The word 'catholic' means 'wide-ranging' or 'having broad interests', and the church itself was so-called because, in this spirit, it brought together a whole load of separate beliefs, including the myth of the Goddess Isis, from where you get your holy mother idea: through such bastardised contrivances did Constantine attempt to unite Christians and pagans under one belief system. Of course, at such times, any purity of original belief is completely lost. Hence the origins of the Roman Catholic Church resemble nothing much more than the ignominious origins of Dagenham & Redbridge FC, while the CofE is more in the spirit of Wimbledon FC being shifted to Milton Keynes, under the auspices of a Tudor monarch with the absolute power to do what the bloody hell he wanted. But, call it another outburst of the tendency to unite with the cause of the cats rather than the dogs, in my world Catholics were clearly outsiders and, whatever my own origins, I threw my weight behind them with a ferocity that was often unwelcome given the lack of one ounce of Roman Catholic blood in my English/Ulster/Swedish family background.

Although, as I've pointed out, my dad is as fair-minded and non-bigoted an individual as you're ever likely to meet, his family background is uncompromisingly of Northern Irish protestant stock, filled with devout Ulster loyalists and even, in my late Uncle Ted, a died in the wool Orangeman. So it was that he and my Auntie Pat, with the kind of broadmindedness you'd associate with the creed, banned me from their house because I had the temerity to be born on St Patrick's Day. Seriously. They finally relented after a few years – eventually persuaded, it would seem, that I'd not done it on purpose - but I would discover that being in their company was far worse than any ostracism, especially as it became apparent that their religious fervour went hand in hand with pretty much every form of bigotry under the sun. While enjoying much of my time at All Saints CofE Primary School, it also gradually dawned on me that the schemes developed by the headmaster to ensure that we and St Basils didn't grow up chucking bombs at each other were somewhat undermined by remarks in school assembly such as 'Apart from us only Our Lady's (another local school) have won the local football cup on a number of occasions, and they don't count because they're catholics'. The familiar distrusted stench of fettering norms entered my nostrils and I decided that, despite their theology being just as unacceptable as that of the protestants, whenever the dispute raised its head in my vicinity, I'd go with the RCs or at least make provocatively casual interjections such as, 'Tell you what, anyone who let King Billy just turn up uninvited and start running the show is on the same level as Lord Haw-Haw or Quisling, I reckon,' and watch the sparks fly. And my support for the plight of Billy Sands and the hunger strikers went down about as well as Frank Rijkaard offering to shampoo Rudi Voller's hair.

While we've duly noted the Roman Catholic influence at the heart of United and in Manchester itself, it should of course be recognised that there remains a large Catholic population in Merseyside also. Indeed, one of the reasons why Liverpool, unlike other northern urban centres, had failed to generate a sizeable socialist influence on its internal politics until as late as the fifties was the presence in the city of a huge political struggle between Irish Catholics and Orangemen which led to political factions along these lines dominating local politics and thus the city becoming immersed in a political debate more along the lines of sectarian divisions than of social class. It wasn't a simple matter for Liverpool of a large Roman Catholic influence ensuring a large voice for the politics of the underdog, as was the case in Manchester; instead, the influence of a loyalist/Catholic power struggle akin to that played out on the football fields of Glasgow muddied the city's political waters significantly and, as with the skilled/unskilled worker divide, did much to ensure the lack of common cause among its working population.

Although you can find a Liverpool-Irish population dating back as far as the 14th Century [11], even by the mid eighteenth century, Catholics were still very much a minority [12] and the first major influx only happened after 1798. The immigrants either (a) serviced the cheap labour needs of a growing industrial city or (b) used Liverpool as a stopping off point on a longer journey to America. The latter was the primary reason for the second wave of immigrants following the potato famine of the 1840s.

The Irish who arrived in Liverpool didn't exactly find the English population rolling out the red carpet or cheering them into port. Even well into the eighteenth century, George I had been imposing heavy taxes on Roman Catholics with little more justification that to secure recompense for the inconvenient disputes over the throne that had dominated British politics in the seventeenth century and the usual fear of a Jacobite uprising. Roman Catholics were not permitted to be landowners, nor therefore to vote, and standing for public office remained prohibited for many years into the future. Responses to this were roughly threefold. Some Catholics flipflopped Torres-like over their allegiance and simply recanted, becoming Protestants as a means of both protecting what money they had and giving themselves some small chance of future prosperity. Others stuck diligently to their faith, thus showing admirable loyalty, fortitude and tenacity in the face of immense political pressure. And others with a conveniently influential protestant friend got him to vouch for them that they weren't really catholics at all, saved themselves a lot of money and a lot of bother, and went off to confession. [13]

While much is made of the deep rooted Irish heritage of the Liverpudlian population, it's a bit disingenuous to claim, as scouse revisionists seem inclined to do, that the immigrants were neatly absorbed into the local population. In 1848, the historian Thomas Burke notes that 3,000 special police officers were sworn in on St Patrick's Day that year, so paranoid were Liverpudlians about the imminence of an 'imaginary' Irish uprising. [14] In 1931, the Liverpool Review argued that the Irish population, many of whom had fought as British soldiers in a world war and would shortly do so again, were to blame for bringing harm to the prosperity of the city, in a time when of course a lack of prosperity was generally being felt by everyone, and while other northern urban centres were rightly turning instead against the ruling classes for getting them into the mess. [15] The Liverpool-Irish population themselves, as we've seen, were far more preoccupied with turning on each other in the sectarian political forums of the time.

In footballing terms, various arguments have been put forward as to whether a firmer tie exists between Roman Catholicism and Liverpool or Everton FC, but in fact there are no solid roots linking either club to Catholicism or Ireland. That hasn't stopped people from inventing them, however. In October 2004, Geoffrey Wheatcroft stated baldly in *The Guardian* that Liverpool were Catholics and Everton protestants, while offering no supporting evidence whatsoever.[16] In fact, as we've seen, the origins of both clubs lie in a Protestant church and John Houlding, who broke away from Everton FC to form Liverpool in 1892, was a leading freemason. [17]

In Everton's case, the fact that a prominent figure from the catholic community called Dr Baxter joined the board shortly after the split with Liverpool is a plausible starting point for the putative association with Roman Catholicism that gradually evolved during the club's existence – he was, by all accounts, a very active individual in promoting the football club among impoverished locals of Irish descent, following the model of Celtic in Glasgow, and almost certainly ensuring a fair proportion of Roman Catholics were among the crowd of what was, for the first ten decade of professional football's existence, the club with the biggest support in the English league. Later, while nuns went around Goodison Park with collection tins, it was the protestant Salvation Army who did this at Anfield. Finally, a large number of Irish players joined the club in the fifties, leading many of those with Irish ancestry to find allegiance with Everton. For Liverpool, the only real connection with Roman Catholic support would be the stealing of 'The Fields of Avonrie' from Celtic, a rich source of plundering for the club following their annexing of 'You'll Never Walk Alone'. It's fairest to say, however, that neither club has the firm associations with Catholicism that United enjoy.

That the Irish landed up in Liverpool in such large numbers was more than anything else to do with Liverpool's proximity and its status as the main port, which was of course founded on its pivotal importance to the slave trade. Those Irish immigrants who were bound for America were really taking the same route as those who had been savagely wrenched out of West Africa. In effect, the misery of both fuelled the prosperity of Liverpool. As we've seen, political radicalism has only very recently set down roots in a city that, for much of its history, has been very much a seat of the prosperous classes, growing fat on the backs of the suffering and turning a blind eye to the hordes of Africans passing through the port to have their freedom taken from them, something for which the city finally apologised in 1999. Manchester, conversely, supported the north in the American civil war, fighting for the rights for the same oppressed African-American slaves on which Liverpool's prosperity was built. A statue of Abraham Lincoln was erected in Manchester as the John Laird shipyard in Liverpool was applying its own efforts to the building of ships for the south. In 1830, Manchester played host to its first black minstrel troupe to perform in Britain while Liverpool was still grooving to barber shop quartets. [18]

Such political radicalism, whether with deep roots or shallow, seemed a million miles from the experience of life in the grim eighties, either on the wider political stage or in my dull personal life. There was little of the enlightened outsider culture in evidence among anyone I knew. Greeny had started to follow that ludicrous and thankfully short-lived fashion of the half-and-half scally hat, whereby Liverpool football fans donned a red and green bobble hat to indicate support for Celtic, while Rangers fans sported a red/blue design. Everton fans did likewise. Although not unique to scousers, the fashion was particularly pronounced among their numbers and opposition fans would often stand bemused by the sight of supporters of the same club chanting 'Celtic' and 'Rangers' at each other, especially so as it was clear many of them were actually chanting the names of both clubs. I don't think Greeny actually supported either Glasgow side, but because he was CofE 'by birth' he went along with Rangers and pretended there was some substance to his involvement. It wouldn't be the last time during the eighties that Liverpool fans sought an association with success via somebody else's hard work.

Because my family, even in its extended form, consisted of no Roman Catholics whatsoever, even by marriage, in such surroundings the claim 'I'm a Satanist' would have been a less controversial one than 'I think the pope's OK' although the statement 'I'm a Manchester United supporter' was rapidly coming up on the blind side to usurp them both as the popular equivalent of farting in church. I discovered that the outsider elements in United's history went well beyond a half-hearted Catholic heritage and geographical associations with Lancastrian witchcraft and could be linked to far richer examples in the form of the club's management going it alone against the FA (most famously Busby's stance in taking United into Europe in defiance of the football league's protests in the fifties), but also, as we've seen, with making advances in football well ahead of anyone else and at times where the immediate result was more likely to invite derision rather than applause from the rest of the game. When United players Charlie Roberts, Sandy Turnbull and Billy Meredith instigated the idea of a players' union, they were relocating the socialist and rebel traditions of Manchester into the environs of the football club and, like the mid-nineteenth century strikers, doggedly stuck to those principles and held out far longer than anyone else. While it would be erroneous to identify the maverick Meredith with a specifically left-wing cause (his impetus came from the strict honesty and sense of fairness of the Welsh Methodist), others within the group certainly understood and embraced the class conflict and anti-authority stance deliberately and knowingly. Meredith, however, does represent perhaps more than any player in the club's history before Cantona that individualist streak that twice saw him refuse to be bought and sold for a transfer fee (both city and later United were forced to let him go on a free long before Bosman was even a twinkle in a Belgian milkman's eye) and his insistence on playing with a toothpick sticking out of his mouth, which didn't stop him destroying opposition full-backs with a panache not seen again until Best.

It's because of our deep-felt connection with outsider status that United fans, in contrast to Liverpool's, have never had a problem with applying a hefty dose of realism when making judgements on the character of their players or their club. There's never been any need or any attempt to sanitise, for instance, the off-pitch activities of George Best any more than those of, say, the later sexual exploits of Dwight Yorke, Ryan Giggs, Wayne Rooney or others. We accept that such players are far from being angels and take whatever putative flaws there might be in their make-up as part of the package. There's no need to deny or attempt to turn a blind eye to them. Similarly, in the more distant past, the almost unbelievable disciplinary record of Frank Barson, sent off nine times in the 1920s, during a time when you practically had to kill the ref to get dismissed from a football field, is no more denied or glossed over by reds than was the comparable legacy of Roy Keane or his oft-criticised but, like it or not, entirely honest revelation of the desire for vengeance that was the motive for his infamous tackle on Alf-Inge Haaland (to this day, wrongly identified in most quarters as the challenge that ended Haaland's career. Given that it was an injury to Haaland's other leg that was the cause of this, it's hard to see why this view has attained any credibility at all, other than that, of course, it makes a good narrative and allows the British press to wallow in its favoured state of horrified outrage, especially when it involves a United player).

Compare this with the default defensive stance adopted by Liverpool fans during the Suarez affair of 2011/12. Here, the mental gymnastics involved in refusing to accept that their player could do any wrong led to the logically and ethically embarrassing position of simultaneously arguing (a) that there was nothing wrong with the allegedly racist language used by Suarez and (b) that Evra had lied about the claims. Credibility was strained even further when, despite all television pictures of the event making it clear what had happened, many Liverpool supporters even refused to accept that Suarez had refused to shake Evra's hand in the next meeting between the two sides. Astonishingly convoluted arguments were devised to attempt to argue that Suarez had done no such thing, including the view that the BBC and Sky Sports had both chosen camera angles deliberately designed to show Suarez in a bad light. Manager Dalgiish even argued in a televised interview straight after the match that he *had* shaken hands with him (a statement which he apologised for the next day when it became apparent, to the club if not to many Liverpool fans, that there was only so far you could go with this without losing all credibility). In an earlier instance, when ex-Liverpool goalkeeper Bruce Grobbelaar had been filmed by Sun journalists accepting a bribe to throw a game, the supporters had been up in arms again, claiming this was an inevitable case of framing and that clearly the video evidence had been fabricated. Remarkably, this continued even though Grobbelaar's legal team didn't use this defence in the case (aware that such things are actually easy to confirm or refute and that there was clearly no way the film could have been a fake), instead opting for the defence that Grobbelaar was only playing along in order to generate evidence for the police. It's hard to see why, in both the Suarez and Grobbelaar cases it was so difficult simply for the club's fans to accept the possibility that a player who'd worn the Liverpool shirt might have done something wrong.

Football supporters are, generally speaking, disposed to adopt a variation on what psychologists call the halo effect. This term explains the phenomenon whereby our overall early impression of someone governs our subsequent views of him or her. Given the ferocity of the attachment between fan and football club, it's not surprising that this variant on the phenomenon has an even greater hold when it comes to governing subsequent views of what that club does. The halo effect as usually understood, allows for some loosening of the bond when we find that the person we've initially respected is actually a complete tit. The particular strength of loyalty to a football club for a real fan just doesn't allow for this. We can accept that some complete morons play for our club (although some have difficulty admitting even this) but the loyalty bond with the club itself is so strong that we maintain the attachment no matter what. Liverpool fans, it seems to me, have become so attached to the halo effect that they've mistaken a mere symptom of a football supporter's make-up for the real thing.

In the case of Leeds United, it seems, the halo effect is there but operates in a completely contrary manner. While Liverpool fans seem to need to believe that their club and players are absolute paragons of virtue, whatever evidence exists to the contrary, Leeds fans understand very well that their identity is that of a bunch of vile thugs and happily embrace it. Success on the pitch during the Revie years has influenced the Leeds supporter's view of his or her side for years to come, so that a team that is successful through gamesmanship and clogging the opposition will exert a pull that, it would appear, is just as strong to the individual supporters as it would be if the club were purveyors of the most stunning football imaginable. It's got nothing to do with logic or choice and everything to do with that mysteriously strong bond that prevails between fan and club. So the 20,000 or so fans who managed to remain with Leeds once the gravy train became a trickle retain an attachment to the ethos of the Revie years; it's like a coyote in a desert eating the maggot-ridden corpse of a skunk:

revolting as it might seem to the rest of us, it's the best he's ever seen, and the memory of the feast will be sustaining him throughout the years of famine.

It's not too esoteric to claim that all football clubs have a certain essence that underpins their identity and that governs fans' expectations. For United supporters, it scarcely needs to be said, the idea of not playing attacking football is anathema. Not all fans feel this way. Recall the success of Dave Bassett's Wimbledon, playing the ugliest form of football imaginable. Wimbledon fans actually liked it. You'd hear shouts from the Plough Lane terraces like 'put some snow on the ball' and calls for more kick and rush, not less. Not only did the 'Crazy Gang' image and long-ball game serve Wimbledon well, it also established an identity for the club that its supporters were more than happy to accept and even love. Ditto Jack Charlton's Middlesbrough side of the mid-seventies, who achieved a degree of comparative success with another particularly ugly and aggressive brand of football not entirely unrelated to what he'd learned at Leeds. Fans of these clubs happily accepted these traits and absorbed them into the identity of and love for their club.

Consider what happened when Charlton attempted to take these tactics to Sheffield Wednesday and Newcastle United. Supporters made it clear from the off that they weren't willing to accept their club playing in such way and repeatedly made their feelings known from the terraces. It was more than an issue of style rather than success: a question of the identity of the team and how to abandon that identity, regardless of results, is literally like someone you love changing beyond all recognition from the person you fell in love with: like finding a stranger next to you in bed, no less. These clubs, whatever else you might say about them, are founded on very different expectations about how the game should be played than Leeds or Wimbledon do and they weren't having any of it.

Although Wimbledon had a good go at it and Millwall fans have always sought to portray themselves in such a way, Leeds United under Revie were the archetypical team whom only their own supporters could love. Unquestionably their successes picked up supporters during that period but it either dwindled away once the trophies stopped coming or remained, with the same jaundiced expectation that it was not just OK to watch players going around the pitch kicking the opposition but that this was the way you went about accruing success: this became the expectation of what Leeds United were all about, literally the reason why their fans loved them.

Animosity between Leeds and United has a much longer and deeper history that than between United and Liverpool. This is perhaps not surprising because the rivalry emanates from a completely different source. While we can identify the geographical and historical element of Lancashire/Yorkshire emnity running just as deep, and having an even longer history, than that of the Manchester/Liverpool hostility, this has only taken shape between United and Leeds and not, say, city and Leeds because of what the two clubs represent: a diametrically opposed view to how the game ought to be played and, I'd argue, the fact that a sense of devilry pervades the identity of both clubs which both sets of supporters are happy to accept as part of their make-up.

Tension between the two arises from the very different natures of the devils within. The simple theological depiction of Satan as a wrongdoer cast out of Heaven by God we find very much mirrored in the Leeds identity: the legacy of Revie's approach to the game that bent and broke the rules and that saw them demonized within the game while attaining, among their own fans fans, a heroic outsider status. United's outsider status is somewhat different, representing a Satan myth that is more closely related to Prometheus, a creative demiurge, heroic not just for its his opposition to authority but as an artist, a rebel creative force very much in the image of the Satan depicted by Milton in *Paradise Lost*. The crucial difference between us is that hatred among others in the wider game towards Leeds is due to their devil's craven lack of style, whereas with us it's because our devil possesses so much of it.

Everbody wants to be like our devil; nobody wants to be theirs. What's really irked Leeds fans down the years is that players moving from Elland Road to Old Trafford have readily confirmed this view of things. While the most notable example is that of Cantona, there are many others who've hastily made a quick exit west down the M62 as soon as the reds came calling, high profile examples including Joe Jordan, Rio Ferdinand and Alan Smith. But my favourite quote on the matter, and the one that irked Leeds fans the most, was from Gordon McQueen who, on his move in 1978, shoved it nicely up the Leeds support by claiming that any player who said he didn't aspire to play for United was a liar. [7] After this, Leeds fans adopted the 'Gordon is a moron' line from Jilted John's eponymous single whenever we faced them. It further illustrates the nature of the rivalries being contested on multiple fronts by United fans that Liverpool supporters treated McQueen's remark as a slap in the face to them as well.

While very different in nature, what we might call a demonic variation on the halo effect influences subcultural norms within both Leeds and United fans with equal tenacity. My attachment to a stylish club with a culture of creativity and imagination is, perhaps, no greater than the Wimbledon's love of the long ball and roguery, no more strong than the Leeds fans' acceptance of gamesmanship and kicking people and certainly no stronger than the Liverpool supporter's commitment to the dry scientific principle or desire to be loved. Once committed, we can – if we are genuine fans – no longer alter our commitment to our club than a cat can turn itself into a dog; or into another cat, for that matter. United and Liverpool were destined to be rivals, because what our clubs represent have diametrically opposed foundations. With United and Leeds, mutual enmity comes from a sense of roguery lurking somewhere within both of our characters. Both sets of fans accept this as part of our identity, whereas the Liverpool fan becomes incandescent with rage should anyone dare to suggest that there is anything less than saintly about his club's character.. Leeds and United both accept they have a touch of the devil about them, but that's where the similarity ends, because they are very different devils.

United fans are also healthily aware of the faults within Manchester United as an organisation while those who follow Liverpool FC have generally seemed to me to be bewilderingly unable to accept that their club is anything other than a bastion of moral superiority. The position lays at the heart of the issues in the previous paragraph and goes back to the 'salt of the earth' comments about Liverpool fans made by my old maths teacher earlier in this book. I was on holiday at Butlins, Pwllheli on the night of the Heysel disaster, crowded into the television room as some bloke antagonised two disgruntled old women by turning off the soaps and putting the footie on. As the indignant blue rinsers left the room, we watched the appalling events unfolding. The place was, and is, a bit of a scouse playground so inevitably 90% of those watching were Liverpool fans. To be fair, not all of them were apologists or peddlers of excuses for the carnage and many of them sat watching, absolutely gobsmacked at what had been committed in the name of their club. A Wigan-based Liverpool fan sitting with me told me of his embarrassment at being associated with the club and said that he'd never feel the same way about Liverpool again. Whether he went through with this I don't know, but I actually argued against him, saying the proper course would be to carry on supporting the club but just get away once and for all from this daft Winnie-The-Pooh conception of Liverpool FC, recognise you're as fallible as the rest of us, denounce the wrongdoers, accept the stain on your characters, and get on with your life. Even then, as the events proceeded to unfold, loud-mouthed Liverpool fans in the audience began to invent scenarios that involved fictitious provocation or even infiltration from Juventus fans, every attempt possible being made to shift the blame away from Liverpool, a tide that continued to grow as the evening went on.

By the time I got back home, classic Liverpool FC doublethink was in full flow. The campaign to blame Chelsea fans, who allegedly had illicitly joined the Liverpool supporters on their trip into Europe with the sole intention of stirring up bother, was well underway. When a range of suspects identified from TV pictures was eventually shown to contain a large number with Liverpool postcodes (as well as some Londoners, admittedly, but then Liverpool, like United, have had south-east based supporters for donkey's years), such facts were permitted to have no impact at all on the headlong charge towards ensuring the club's name remained free of any taint of wrongdoing. All that changed was an incorporation of the claim that, as you couldn't tell from hundreds of rampaging Liverpool fans which ones had caused the deaths, you couldn't possibly prosecute anyone for it. The result of this beyond the myopic world of Liverpool FC was of course simply to compound the damage caused to the club's reputation among the rest of the population, which in turn only made the infantile arguments of Liverpool fans to secure a squeaky clean reputation for the club even more hysterical.

Liverpool's problem here was, as it remains, an apparent need to proclaim their club and its fans as morally pure. It's an impossible thing to unhold and one that no other club's supporters appears impelled to do with anything like this tenacity. For most clubs, the negative elements of a club's reputation are simply part of the package, and this is even more the case with United. I don't know any serious United fans who would seek to contest our club's reputation for hooliganism in the seventies and it's extremely well-documented in United fanzine articles and books relating to the era. Nor would we want it any other way. It's part of the history of our club and I think we accept that as such. I suspect it would make it much easier for Liverpool fans to take a similarly accepting attitude, but it simply isn't part of the make-up of the club or its fans to accept anything that might deflect from the implausibly angelic self-image they have. Instead, they smoulder with a chip on their shoulder the size of a docked ship full of African slaves. Had it actually transpired that, in fact, Chelsea fans *had* been to blame for the carnage, you can bet the campaign among Liverpool fans to clear the name of their club and ensure justice was meted out to the wrongdoers would have been pretty damn fervent.

For United, the outsider status and Miltonic Satanism that's accepted as part of our make-up sets us apart from other clubs in the game in a way that was always entirely welcoming to me and is clearly so to other United supporters. Part of this is the way in which we accept the potential for good and bad to be inevitably wrapped up in the same human package. The reason for this is, I suspect, a combination of solid Mancunian no-bullshit realism and deep affiliation with a club history so unique it doesn't require embellishment or sanitisation.

But then, unlike Liverpool, whose history began with a freemason sugardaddy with powerful local links and the cuckoo-like appropriation of someone else's ground, United's is a history very much founded in the harsh reality of the real world and the exposure to a whole barrage of difficulties and travails that make it surprising that Manchester United as a club ever survived this long. I mean this in an evolutionary sense, in the way that it's amazing how emperor penguins survive in the Antarctic or how that one wriggling sperm somehow manages to make its way to an egg. Other clubs in similar circumstances would have failed and died, and indeed have done so in far less perilous circumstances than these. United survived the collapse of our original Newton Heath forefathers and the astonishing levels of investment involved in building Old Trafford that burdened the club for years, before coming within a day of going out of business in 1930. The club then almost folded after the massive destruction to the ground during world war two, and then again following the Munich air crash. As with emperor penguins or sperm, if a hundred clubs were subjected to that kind of history, my bet is 99 would have bitten the dust. Other clubs can't buy this kind of history underpinning their identity so they either live with what they have or, like Liverpool FC, they create one and throw all of their energy behind maintaining the pretence.

While the pretentions towards angelic innocence and hysterical resistance to the identification of any kind of moral blemish are patently hallmarks of an unrealisable image anyway, much of the fingers-in-the-ears bullshit stems from the fact that, far from having anything similar to the survival-against-the-odds history of United, nor our long-standing socialist and outsider roots, Liverpool fans have to come to terms with the fact that they are a club born out of slave trade era prosperity, created by a freemason in a city that remained unconnected to grass roots socialism and the labour movement for at least the first sixty years of the club's existence. While Shankly took them some way towards creating a deep red socialist creed within the club, these origins were never built on in any convincing way and it's been the Paisley influence that more truly cemented the club's identity for the longer term anyway. Instead, Liverpool supporters, many of whom have undeniable left-wing credentials as individuals, espouse the kind of fraudulent bullshit that proclaims for Liverpool FC a utopian political purity as a response to not having the kind of solid left-wing background that United, from Charlie Roberts through Busby and of course Ferguson, have, and which remains an unshakeable part of what we are however much bogus corporate bullshit and disneyfication we're subjected to. Liverpool fans want their club to resemble their own beliefs and causes; United supporters don't have to do this because ours already does.

Ferguson's socialist and trade union roots are of course well understood. Long before he became United manager, it was heartening to see Ferguson giving support to the striking miners in the early eighties, at a time when the rest of the country was turning its back on social justice and shedding any sense of wider responsibility in the pursuit of an individualism that was defined only materially and about as far away from the creed espoused by Meredith as was the length of the average back pass to Ray Clemence. When Thatcher said she wanted to make socialism irrelevant, what she meant was she wanted to make democracy irrelevant, in the sense that a nation underpinned by free market principles with a population tied via the housing market to the yoke of interest rates coveting low rates of income tax would inevitably yield a political system where parties were bound by these same principles, and to hell with anyone else. Years before he became United manager, Ferguson's appeal as a rare figure in football who was prepared to take a fervent and vocal stand against this was firmly established, not to mention fully in tune with United's history. Although a protestant, Ferguson made himself a pariah among many of his fellow Rangers supporters, people who couldn't even bear to countenance the signing of a Roman Catholic player well into the 1980s. And although he had nothing to do with United yet, winning the European Cup Winners' Cup with Aberdeen in 1983 confirmed Ferguson already as a manager of considerable distinction and recorded a timely socialist-inspired triumph in that wholly unpleasant watershed year that would provide the Tories with a landslide and mark the true beginning of the Thatcher years in all their privatising, union-trampling, welfare state dismantling, industry base-destroying shame.

I'm not going to pretend I looked at all this and had the foresight to predict that Ferguson would one day become United manager. In retrospect, though, he had all the credentials not just to do the job successfully but to represent all of those strands of United's culture and history that were even more important. As a shop steward in the Clyde shipyards, he had the solid working-class left-wing background that linked back through Busby to the pre-first world war outcasts and the club's rail workers' beginnings that stood in stark contrast to the middle class sports clubs or church establishment beginnings to which so many English clubs owed their existence. Whether it's true or not that Ferguson's failure to make the grade at Rangers was down to sectarian animosity, it's certain he'd have felt the wrath of many at the Scottish club over his marriage to a Catholic; the now famous fire in Ferguson's belly came very much from his sense of being an outsider and forced to fight against establishment prejudice and stand up for himself in a position of severe isolation. It was clear he'd also used this experience when taking charge at Aberdeen, an unfashionable club on Scotland's east coast with what would have appeared to many the impossible task before them of breaking up the duopoly of the Glasgow old firm; to Ferguson it was just the kind of challenge he relished. And once there, having taken Aberdeen to the pinnacle of the Scottish game, he clung to it with backs against the wall temerity, picking fights regularly with the Glasgow giants and everyone else who stood in the way of Aberdonian supremacy.

Aristotle states that, in order to achieve the cherished state of fulfilment known as *eudaemonia* (a state of living at and experiencing the highest possible human condition) man must understand himself and sometimes seek, though when and only when the situation warrants it, to aim for characteristics that are opposite to his natural inclinations. [19] United's board were perhaps struggling with a bad translation of this when they replaced the gregarious and outgoing Docherty with the cautious and well-mannered Dave Sexton, then removed Sexton in favour of the flamboyant Atkinson. All these appointments served to do, though, was exchange one set of extreme characteristics for another, which is why it was never quite right and why the sought-after golden mean wasn't reached. Later we would understand why: the truly *eudaemon* football manager existed; he had achieved something close to that almost god-like state of footballing satisfaction already; but for now he was in Aberdeen.

[1] MacPherson Bardell, K. 'Beyond Pendle: the 'lost' Lancashire Witches' in Poole, R. *The Lancaster Witches: Histories and Stories* Manchester University Press pp106-107
[2] MacPherson Bardell, K. ibid, pp110-115
[3] Mullet, M., 'The Reformation in the Parish of Whalley', ibid p88
[4] Pumfrey, S. 'Potts, plots and politics: James I's Daemonologie and The Wonderfull Discoverie of Witches', ibid pp22-41
[5] Beckett, J. http://epltalk.com, 15 Nov 2010
[6] Conn, D. *The Football Business*, p131
[7] Brennan, S. *Manchester Evening News*, 22 October 2003
[8] Wagg, S. 'The Team That Wouldn't Die: on the mystique of Matt Busby and Manchester United' in Andrews, D.L., *Manchester United: A Thematic Study*, 1998, pp17-18
[9] Bairner, A. ibid, p141
[10] Worrall, F. pp201-221
[11] Muir, R. *History of Liverpool* Williams & Northgate 1907, p304

[12] Burke, T. (1910) *Catholic History of Liverpool,* http://archive.org/stream/catholichistoryo00burkuoft/catholichisto ryo00burkuoft_djvu.txt, p10

[13] *ibid,* p6

[14] *ibid,* p97

[15] http://www.merseyreporter.com/history/historic/irish-immigration.shtml

[16] Wheatcroft, G. *The Guardian*, Oct, 2004

[17] Johnstone, S. http://www.toffeeweb.com/fans/beingblue/religion.asp

[18] Robb, J. *The North Will Rise Again,* p7

[19] Aristotle, *Ethics,* pp94-97

Chapter Seven: Disorder

Wembley, 12 May 1979. Arsenal 3 Manchester United 2

Famously, United didn't turn up until four minutes from the end. I was watching from an armchair in my front room and my dad kept telling me to stop twitching and moaning as United wriggled and fumbled towards what looked like defeat from the moment Brian Talbot opened the scoring and inevitably so by the time Frank Stapleton had secured a 2-0 lead for the Gunners at half-time. No one called them 'The Gooners' in those days, incidentally; I suspect that variation on their nickname has arisen in the modern age rather as an attempt to lighten the image of Arsenal Football Club and lift it from its previously dour, establishment origins. But in those days they were indeed dour, though often lifted to a level above that via the footwork of a midfield magician called Liam Brady who, while he didn't dominate the game in the no-nonsense, take no prisoners way that Graeme Souness was beginning to do with Liverpool, had a more refreshing penchant for taking both Arsenal and the English game beyond its conventional low expectations and it was he who had provided all of the admittedly small number of splendid moments in this final thus far. And, unlike future United sides, this one definitely wasn't renowned for pulling back two goal leads against any opposition, let alone this late in the game against a mean-spirited team like Arsenal.

All of which contrived to make those last four minutes among the most memorable to me in my lifetime as a United supporter and, despite the fairly uninspiring fare on offer for the first 86 minutes, transform this into one of the most extraordinary of all FA Cup finals. Even when Gordon McQueen pulled a goal back it didn't strike me that there was much chance of a lifeline, but then Sammy McIlroy went past two players and steered the ball towards the Arsenal goal. It appeared to take about five minutes even to get there but, when it crawled inside the Arsenal post, it seemed there couldn't be any time left for Arsenal to re-establish their lead. And their players looked absolutely demoralised and out for the count, so it seemed inevitable that we'd cruise through the game in extra time and I'd see us grab our second FA Cup in three years. Unfortunately what happened next is inscribed just as clearly in my brain as is McIlroy's equaliser. Brady had the ball in midfield and released Graham Rix on the left wing. Rix floated in a cross that Gary Bailey flapped at, and which was always going to be out of reach. Wishful thinking later that day had the ball coming in lower, Bailey grabbing it comfortably and the game following a more pleasing course. In truth, he might have been better staying on his line. But what really happened was he missed it by miles and the (at the time) fashionable if entirely ludicrous footballer's perm of Alan Sunderland appeared at the far post and the Arsenal striker stabbed it home. I can still see Sunderland now, closed eyes and open mouth screaming up at the skies with clenched fists as he pulled his side back from an unlikely defeat to achieve victory in the most famous four minutes in FA Cup history.

As months go, May 1979 stands among the worst ever. On the 3rd Thatcher was elected as prime minister and began eighteen years of Tory government underpinned by an economic policy that shredded all sense of responsibility and decency with regard to working people and their communities and inevitably changed Britain for the worst. Not so close to home, The Soviet Union stepped up nuclear testing in Eastern Kazakh as the cold war gathered pace and my adolescent mind toyed with the increasing likelihood of imminent nuclear apocalypse. Even the overthrow of the odious Shah in Iran wasn't the cause for celebration we might have wished it to be given the hard line Islamist regime of Khomeini that followed it. And it got even worse. The first use of the words 'New Wave of British Heavy Metal' appeared in *Sounds*. *The Very Best of Leo Sayer* was number one in the album charts. And my geography teacher told us that punk was dead so those of us who were clinging to its mouldering corpse could carry on dying our hair and sticking things in our ears if we wanted to, but the future was glitterballs, flamboyant outfits and frizzy perms all soundtracked by the resurgent Bee Gees and he was inclined to dance a merry jig on its grave. And then the FA Cup Final happened. Admittedly, Greenland had secured independence at the beginning of the month so it was great for them and it crossed my mind when Thatcher was elected that I might emigrate there as soon as I was old enough. After the fourth Tory election victory in 1992, I did question whether it had been a missed opportunity. But then I suspected neither the footie nor the music scene in Greenland was up to much, so there was probably a downside to the move. Fortunately, among the many clouds of May 1979 one silver lining appeared. Malcolm Allison quit his job as Crystal Palace boss, soon to be unveiled in his second stint as manager at city.

I haven't said much about city yet, largely because for most of their history there's been little of any interest to comment on, and clearly in my case Liverpool were rather more of immediate concern as rivals went on a national, local and indeed domestic front. But suddenly, in 1979, they began to dominate the back pages of the north-west editions of newspapers, engendering a sense of optimism among their fans that would prove utterly unfounded and give United fans something to smile about during the dark Sexton era. The events of the next few years would, far from the new dawn initially promised, ensure city were financially crippled for the next couple of decades.

Those who see city's currently moneyed status as something new have either forgotten or didn't live through the beginning of the eighties, when, under the management of Allison for a second spell, they indulged in what must be one of the most careless, idiotic and ill-judged spending sprees in the history of the game. During a short period during 1979 and 1980, Allison squandered an English transfer record breaking fee to bring Steve Daley from Wolves, a footballer with no international pedigree either then or subsequently and the kind of English midfielder who wouldn't even get a game in today's Premiership, while similarly spectacular amounts of cash were splashed out on Kevin Reeves from Norwich and Michael Robinson from QPR in addition to a record fee for a teenager when Steve McKenzie arrived from West

Brom, for whom he'd never played a senior game. At the same time, young talented players at the club like Peter Barnes and Gary Owen were allowed to leave on the cheap.

The immediate results were disastrous, or hilarious, depending on your point of view: a narrow escape from relegation for the most expensively assembled club in the country, who finished 17th in the league. Following a terrible start to the following season, Allison was sacked and replaced with John Bond, the much televised and highly opinionated Norwich City manager who made regular appearances on the box to air his half-arsed views long before it became required practice for managers to do so. Bond took Allison's misguided signings and at least did enough with them to transform a relegation struggle into a mid-table position. However, ultimately the only thing city had to show for the Allison/Bond years was an appearance in an FA Cup final, their last for another 29 years. When McKenzie scored for city in the replay, which Spurs won, a London-based (yes, London-based) city-supporting friend told me the tears were streaming down his face. A familiar experience for city fans in the years to come. Following Bond's eventual resignation, in 1983 city continued what had seemed from the earliest days of Allison's tenure an inevitable slide towards relegation, memorably going down on the last day of the season.

During this circus, United were being managed by Dave Sexton. The Docherty years ended abruptly following revelations of his affair with physio Lawrie Brown's wife that emerged in the wake of the momentous victory over Liverpool in the 1977 Cup Final. No one can say how things might have gone had Docherty stayed, but what was certain was that his replacement (recruited, it was assumed, because of his low potential for any controversy with or without physios' wives, alongside his admitted pedigree as a coach) was not a popular choice among the small and indeed dwindling number of United fans at Bankfield High (as the steady drip of defections to European champions Liverpool continued) nor with the wider constituency of United's support.

A particularly contentious issue was the acquisition of Joe Jordan from Leeds, both because he appeared to possess a particularly Elland Road take on what was permissible within the rules of the game – totally alien to the Docherty years, where a booking for a United player, let alone a sending off, was about as common as a player lighting his own fart on the pitch - and his identity as a big, rough target man of a kind that United had eschewed in recent years, and indeed had never had much truck with before that. Many understandably saw the signing of Jordan as a regressive step towards a less stylish mode of play. When the highly popular and free-scoring Gordon Hill began to be left out of the side, this heightened misgivings towards the manager from within United's support, which grew to a peak when Hill was allowed to move to Derby County. Sexton soon acquired a reputation for conservatism in terms of tactics and team selections and for diluting the attractive style with which fans had grown familiar – and which was very much aligned with the great traditions of United - in the Docherty years. Indeed, to hear some seasoned reds speak of the period, you'd think that Sexton's model of play was a forerunner for the Charles Hughes/Wimbledon and Watford long-ball school of the eighties. When Sexton captured Garry Birtles from Nottingham Forest for a large fee in 1980, and the highly promising young forward then failed to score in twenty-five matches for United, this was widely viewed as the final folly of Sexton's reign and he lost his job in 1981, having failed to land a trophy in his four year tenure.

That's one version of events, but there is another, one much fairer to Sexton and perhaps more accurate. For a start, it wasn't as if Sexton could help not being Tommy Docherty, and indeed, many felt that one of the things that prevented the Doc's sides from becoming a consistently powerful force in the game was the lack of a truly physical presence in the side, both up front and at the back. In this light, the signing not only of Jordan, but also the big central defender Gordon McQueen, from Leeds, can be seen as a serious attempt to address these weaknesses and, rather than undo the Doc's good work, build on and fortify it. Regarding Gordon Hill, he could hardly be said to have gone on to achieve great things after United and his release could be interpreted as a shrewd managerial move given that the player's worth, though indisputable over the short-term, was quickly diminishing. Hill would make just 24 appearances for Derby before being sold to QPR, for whom he played only 14 times before heading off to North America. By 1984 he was playing indoor football in the States.

Jordan, on the other hand, strengthened his already fearsome reputation with United. Although never a prolific goal scorer, he improved on his goals per game ratio from his Leeds days and eventually secured a high enough profile in the game to be poached by AC Milan. The only regrettable thing about Jordan's association with United was that we failed to accrue a decent transfer fee for him on his departure, due to the way international transfers were regulated in those days. And while criticisms can be levelled at Sexton's transfer policy, it should be noted that, while Birtles was an unquestioned disappointment, then the acquisition of Peter Davenport from the same place by Ron Atkinson didn't exactly prove to be a shrewd move either. Indeed, over a period of time it became a characteristic of outgoing players from Brian Clough's Nottingham Forest that they rarely succeeded elsewhere. Possibly the only real issue here was that Sexton wasn't the man-manager Clough was, but then that accusation could have been levelled against anyone in the English game at that time. It should be noted also that Sexton brought the cultured Ray Wilkins – another player whose growing reputation saw him eventually leave for Italy - from Chelsea, so the idea that he invested only in hard men and failures is undeserved.

Sexton managed United on the day we lost that 1979 FA Cup Final to Arsenal in dramatic circumstances. The following year United finished second to Liverpool in the league and at the end of the next season Sexton was sacked directly after a winning run of seven games. While it's true United didn't win any trophies during his time in charge, it's worth remembering that Alex Ferguson took a similar period of time before winning his first honour.

It's usually claimed that the reason for Sexton's departure was that United's attendances had begun to dip. Despite that win of seven games, which included a 1-0 away win at Liverpool, it was speculated that the one thing United's board weren't prepared to accept was falling gates as these provided incontrovertible evidence that United fans simply didn't want to see the kind of football Sexton's team was playing. It's true that attendances dropped in the season he took over from Docherty, and, while they recovered approximately to their previous level in the 1979/80 season, this wasn't sustained the following year; it's also true that United fans, if they're turned off at all, are far more likely to be turned off by the team's approach to the game not being right than a losing streak which, as we've seen with the evidence of the relegation season, if anything often sees a rallying of support for the club. Yet Ferguson presided over a more significant decline in home attendances during his early years in charge; attendances under Sexton still remained above those of the all-conquering Anfield side and, contrary to received opinion, were actually beginning to recover at the end of the 1980-81 season prior to the manager's removal. It's true there had been some poor individual attendances during that season, home gates even falling below the 40,000 mark for games against Aston Villa, Wolves, Stoke, Birmingham, Forest and Crystal Palace; however, the last two home games of the campaign – despite being against relatively unfashionable opposition in the form of West Brom and Norwich – were back above 40,000.

I believe the real reason why Sexton had to go, and it seems more and more plausible as the various facts are considered, was because of city. While we've seen the disasters that Allison and Bond presided over during their brief reigns, there was a real fear among United fans at the time that their spending power was reaching a point where they were rivalling and indeed overhauling us in the transfer market. That this money was being spent with the profligacy of Stan Bowles in Ladbrokes, making Sexton's acquisition of Birtles appear a minor financial indiscretion in comparison, wasn't widely acknowledged at the time. City suddenly had financial muscle, and they were flexing it. Even more importantly, they were appointing high profile, media-friendly managers, something that Sexton was not and would never be.

During these years there were signs that English football was stirring restlessly from its torpor and beginning to wake up to changing times. The decision to allow non-British players into the game had been finally made in 1978 after years of stern and narrow-minded resistance, and the likes of Osvaldo Ardiles, Frans Thijssen and Arnold Muhren had made an instant impact. Similarly, after years of claims that televising football beyond the annual England-Scotland game and the FA Cup final would administer a fatal blow to attendance figures, regular live televised football was now looking an inevitable prospect and, though many remained unconvinced by the move, there was a momentum already gathering that would lead to live screening of the first televised league first division game in 1983. Given the ensuing surge in media coverage this would bring, it may well have been felt that Sexton, particularly when compared with his talkative Maine Road hot-seat rivals, would struggle to hold down even a quick word with a reporter let alone regular post-match interviews and certainly didn't have had what it took to continue to preside over Manchester United the high profile new era. If this sounds unconvincing, consider that the main boardroom battle surrounding Alex Ferguson's later appointment concerned an oppositional faction favouring Terry Venables, one of their central arguments being that Venables had the media savvy to deal with these very challenges. [1] It should be noted that Leo McKinstry offers a different version of events, claiming that the entire United board was unanimously behind the offer to Atkinson. [2] If this is true, it was probably only due to the fact that by that stage they'd already admitted that prising Venables away from Barcelona would have been beyond them, and indeed board member Mike Edelson pretty much confirmed this. [3] Otherwise, Venables it might well have been, an appointment that would have very much in line with the view that United at this time needed someone who was going to secure an enhanced media profile for the club. Though many names were on the list for replacing him at the end of the season, the one thing that would have been agreed was that Sexton was exactly the wrong person to spearhead this charge into football's television revolution.

If this is true, then the sacking of Sexton, if questionable on performance grounds, can be seen as mildly visionary given that football's profile would follow this small scale uplift with a very large scale one not too far down the line. Another, slightly more cynical way of reading it is that we'd fallen so far behind Liverpool that we weren't even looking at overhauling them in footballing terms and that the reduced objective of staying ahead of city was driving events at Old Trafford at the time. Certainly, despite what would happen in the early Ferguson years, any concern that we might be in danger of falling behind Liverpool in terms of attendances seems unlikely, given that they'd drawn in a paltry crowd of just over 31,000 when we'd beaten them late in the season, a figure well below any league crowd at Old Trafford that year.

But there is something else here that we can only understand by taking the Docherty and Sexton years not in isolation but together, and which may be just as relevant when considering the unease about Sexton both on the terraces and at board level. There is something about the period of their dual tenures that makes the Dochery/Sexton era stand out from Manchester United eras before or since, which is this: at no point in the period between 1974 and 1981 did the team have a figure who oozed the individual class and charisma that, either at the time or in retrospect, can genuinely be said to be fully synonymous with the spirit and character of United. The period stands out in United history, whatever the teams' collective abilities, because of the lack of a Duncan Edwards, Eddie Coleman, Denis Law or George Best , an Eric Cantona or Roy Keane figure. While there were some extremely good players, none of them – not the quietly inspirational Martin Buchan, nor the terrace favourites Gordon Hill or Pancho Pearson – stamped his character onto Manchester United, absorbing something of that club's charisma in the process so that he became almost synonymous with United, and the lack of such a figure marks these periods as somehow incomplete, as if they were merely stepping stones on the way to re-establishing the identity of Manchester United and none of us, whether supporter, board member or player, could be absolutely sure whether we were heading in the right direction or not. Perhaps we enjoyed the ride more under Docherty than Sexton, but these were transition periods for the club and one of the big problems for United at the time was that we were probably unaware of exactly what the transition was to or what the future even looked like. On this analysis, Sexton was perhaps simply unfortunate that his period in charge came second, by which point the gap at the heart of United's playing style had become too significant to ignore.

The game and its potential future now looked very different from that of the fifties and sixties, where United had created a template within the English game and positioned itself unequivocally at its forefront. While we remained easily the best supported side in English football, the direction of the game was being determined by other forces. English sides were winning European Cups by adopting a model of football chiefly influenced not by us but by an all-conquering Liverpool side. The successful incorporation of the best overseas players was being led, not by United, but by Spurs and Ipswich. And to top it all off city had appeared suddenly with great wodges of cash and a manager prepared both to spend it and talk endlessly in the media about doing so.

It's folly to assume that, when a manager is ousted, the board always have a clear idea of what has gone wrong and what to do next and the circumstances described above only muddied the waters even more. And in Sexton's case it's much more difficult than is popularly admitted to identify exactly what *was* wrong – other than that there was something about the team that wasn't quite what you expected of a United side. In Docherty's case, it's impossible to say what would have happened had he continued at the helm: would he eventually have found such a figure? The portents weren't good: despite his positive stewardship of the team he'd presided over the retirement of Bobby Charlton and departure of George Best, improving the team in the process but without pulling a similarly influential figure out of the hat or showing the inclination even to look for one, and his falling out with and decision to get rid of Willy Morgan, who appeared the player most likely to assume the mantle, suggests the Doc's priorities lay more in the creation of a side in his own image rather than someone else's as well as a realism regarding Morgan's limitations and his inability to fit this particular bill whatever he (or his mum) thought about that. Given what Docherty inherited, this seems a reasonable and pragmatic approach. But when have Manchester United ever been known, or wanted to be known, for their pragmatism? Somewhere in the Docherty-Sexton axis, although superficially we might understand them by their differences, was something that didn't seem right. And if the word 'pragmatic' doesn't sit easy with you as a description of the Docherty period, I'd contend that, had the truth of Docherty been in line with the public image he acquired, he'd never have been able to bring the club forward in the way that he did, skilfully negotiating a boardroom minefield that had already seen two very recent casualties, surviving relegation and eventually getting results with perhaps the most outrageously attack-minded system ever seen in English football. Only a very skilled and adept planner, and shrewd politician, could have achieved all of that.

Richard Kirk, that most iconoclastic of all Manchester United scribes, rightly celebrates the spirit of individualism at the heart of the club as well as the thrilling fluctuations it can provoke: that's all part of being a Manchester United supporter. And whatever else was right within the club, by the end of the Sexton era, United fans were pretty much in agreement that this special characteristic of United sides wasn't there,[4] though Kurt's conclusion that this is the reason why United have a global support that Liverpool lack [5] is a tad misconceived given that the size of Liverpool's international support is undeniably large. More accurate to say, I think, that the international appeal of both clubs rests on very different premises: Liverpool's on that highly ingenuous but nevertheless fervently believed in 'You'll Never Walk Alone' themed sense of spurious community, and United's on a sense of pioneering individualism that is characteristic of both our supporters and our teams, as well as of Manchester itself. Sexton's downfall, I believe, arose from his failure to engage with this ideal both in terms of his managerial style and playing personnel rather than by anything tangible like falling attendances or uninspiring tactics. He would be replaced by a manager with whom the personality contrast could not be greater and who has often not had his role in fully returning United's heartbeat to its rightful place adequately recognised.

[1] Charlton, B. op cit p312
[2] McKinstry, L. op cit p351
[3] ibid, p352
[4] Kirk, R., *United We Stood*, p62
[5] ibid, p6

Chapter Eight: New Dawn Fades

Old Trafford, 21 March 1984. Manchester United 3 Barcelona 0

It's a revealing reflection on United fan culture that, among all the trophy-winning occasions down the years, and despite the rich memories attached to Barcelona in 1999 and Moscow in 2008, not to mention the holy grail-like regaining of the English champions' mantle in 1993 and so many other great occasions that fans of other clubs would kill to experience just one of, the defeat of Barcelona in a 1984 Cup Winners' Cup Quarter-Final still ranks above any other event as the most memorable of all among so many hardcore reds.

It's not like it led to anything much, at least in terms of any immediate success. We were knocked out by Juventus in the following round and it would be another six years before we saw off Barcelona in the final of the same competition to give a firm hint that the glory years were really underway. But the manner of this victory was about something more important, confirming that, after more than a decade, the true character of a Manchester United team had been re-established, and how long it would take for that to transform itself into trophies was, even though we might not have understood this at the time, not as important to United fans as others might think.

It's curious that Jimmy Burns, in both of his otherwise excellent books *Barca* and *Maradona – The Hand of God* remembers it so differently. I can accept that a Barcelona fan would inevitably have different feelings on the game and about the result, but Burns writes that this was the first leg of the tie, and talks instead of the ill-fated attempt to pull the score back at the Nou camp coming to nothing in the wake of an injury to Maradona. [1] [2] Not the way any of us remember it, and certainly not true. The first game took place at Barcelona in front of 70,000 on 7 March and this game, two weeks later, was the second leg. Even though it followed a fine 4-0 win for United against Arsenal the previous

Saturday, no one gave us a prayer of pulling back a two-goal deficit against a Barcelona side featuring both Maradona and Schuster.

In the event, we played them off the park, the on-field action surrounded by an almost permanent Old Trafford roar a million miles from the meek, civilised appreciation you get even on European nights in these post-corporate days, a fumble from their keeper that led to a Norman Whiteside effort looping just the wrong side of the bar early on a rich portent of things to come, followed by Robson exploiting much the same uncertainty to nod in from close range and give an already rampant United the lead midway through the first half. Robson added the second in the second half, but his close range finish only applied the finishing touch to the brilliant build-up play that led to it, our legendary opponents penned back to the edge of their own penalty area by the pressing of Robson and Wilkins until a nervous back pass almost put Whiteside in, the goalkeeper's last-ditch interception falling to Robson to finish it off. As the players celebrated in front of the Stretford End fences, there now seemed little doubt we'd go on to win it and, indeed, only moments later, as United poured forward, Albiston found himself some spare grass on the left and, released by Robson's cross-field pass, crossed for Whiteside to nod down to Stapleton, who finished emphatically, a firm full-stop to close the most powerful statement of what it meant to be United in a generation. Despite those fences, hundreds of United fans poured onto the pitch, a large group of them holding Robson aloft. It was he who most symbolised United's spirit on the night and around whom a side in the true image of United was being created.

Two years later, Liverpool fans I knew would scoff at Bobby Robson's assertion that, had he had his world class namesake available to him in the quarter-final of the World Cup to match the threat of Maradona then the result might have been different. But we knew what he meant. And the fact that Bryan Robson would be so universally vilified by Liverpool supporters as the decade wore on wasn't, I believe, unconnected with the fact that, for the first time, we'd seen at United something, and indeed someone, who other supporters at other clubs didn't, couldn't understand, but which represented something important to us, even if it was hard to put into words exactly what that was.

Ron Atkinson's arrival as United boss has him cast as the anti-Sexton, in some senses a throwback to Docherty in that we returned a larger than life character to the club's hot seat but one who, ultimately, can be criticized for pulling us too far in the other direction, creating a debilitating media frenzy around his reign and blowing our best chance in years of winning the title, not even in the manner of some glorious failure but with an embarrassingly weak petering out that saw us, in 1986, as the Liverpool fans who surrounded me gleefully proclaimed, finish fourth in a two-horse raise. To our enemies, Atkinson represented the glamour without substance they asserted was all United had, his jewellery and sun tan synonymous with a façade beneath which beat nothing of any true value – like United themselves, they sneered. History has fingered him for instilling a lack of discipline at United at a level well beyond any other boss in our history (despite his egregious countenance and flamboyant media image, Docherty didn't have a champagne lifestyle and certainly had enough fall-outs with players to suggest he wasn't as avuncular and tolerant as he sometimes appeared in public). Under Atkinson, a debilitating drinking culture was allowed to flourish, festering away at the prospect of any serious attempts at prolonged success.

But the danger is that, in accepting the criticism of Atkinson for crassly misappropriating the club's image, as with Sexton we over-simplify it with even greater crassness. In his four years at the club we ended a run of only one trophy in fifteen years by winning the FA Cup twice and, while league and European success eluded us, we did at least get some consistency. So unfamiliar were we with such a thing that a top four finish for five years running for the first time since 1964-68 seemed almost a novelty to those of us who were too young to remember the great years – and an enticing doorway to great European nights for the first time since the late sixties for those who could recall them. More importantly, Atkinson made a significant step forward from the Docherty-Sexton years by giving us the first true great United individual for the first time in years when he brought Bryan Robson with him from West Brom for a then record fee, a catalyst for the club's future in more ways than is often understood, even by some of the United fans who rightly identified him as the club's saviour.

Liverpool fans to a man detested him, which only served to make him more popular in our eyes. He gave the club a direction that had been missing for a decade and that determined the way forward for the United legends who followed him during our eventual glory years. He was, we felt, uniquely ours. Understandably, that meant that the United haters and Liverpool fans in particular would see him rather differently.

Like every other footballing phenomenon associated with the club, Robson was somebody who only we could truly understand and appreciate fully. We only got Cantona so cheaply because neither Howard Wilkinson nor anyone else in the country could understand his true value and almost unbelievable potential as a player. I recall Tommy Smith scoffing before our victory over that appalling designer-suited and over-coiffed 'spice boys' Liverpool side in the 1995 cup final, modelling contracts stuffed down their shorts, about newspaper reports linking Ryan Giggs with a huge transfer fee move to someone or other with: 'if he's worth that what's Robbie Fowler worth?' Much less, obviously, but he didn't get it, and never would. There were many who would write off the majestic Roy Keane as a clogger and Cristiano Ronaldo as a luxury player who you'd rather play against than alongside. In the end, they just don't have beating in their hearts the same appreciation of these figures that we have, and couldn't possibly get close to understanding what they represented. These are United men, definitively. Bryan Robson was the first example of such a figure we'd seen in years and United fans understandably clasped him to our collective bosom.

Even better, it didn't just stop with Robson. Another well-documented myth, and this propagated by many United supporters as much as anyone else, is that the youth system before Alex Ferguson got hold of it was crap. While I'm not about to underplay the success of Ferguson in this area, it's another over-simplification to suggest that United had no decent young players coming through under Sexton and Atkinson, though true that before them Docherty's young side were mainly the product of clever deals for young players in the lower leagues and there was a lack of attention to our internal development system, perhaps understandably given the speed with which he needed to address the decline of previous years.

Bobby Charlton has expressed his dissatisfaction at watching United's reserves during the Atkinson period, shaking his head as none of the lads on view clearly had what it took to make it at the top level, a key factor in his desire to get shut of Big Ron. [3] But to get a bit of perspective on this, I've often watched the reserves under Ferguson and thought exactly the same thing. While his management has undoubtedly brought our youth system up to scratch in many respects, it's still the case that some crops of young players are inevitably better than others and only a minority of players who come through it will ever be United regulars, let alone legends. That's just the way a youth policy works. The famed Youth Cup winning team of 1992 was an unusually rich seam of talent that has never been replicated since, and the more common pattern has been for the occasional talent to break through (a Wes Brown, Darren Fletcher or John O'Shea, all of whom have been good servants to the club, but hardly matching in quality or number the class of '92) while some years have seen as little on the horizon as the pre-Ferguson prospect as denounced by Charlton.

It should be remembered that United reached the Youth Cup Final in 1982 for the first time since 1964 and that the period saw the breakthrough of some fine players, two of which – Norman Whiteside and Mark Hughes – realised very quickly their clear potential to join Robson among a breed of Old Trafford players that surpassed anything we'd seen for years. If Atkinson was guilty of anything in this period, it was in letting go prospects like David Platt and allowing Peter Beardsley to slip through our fingers, but this in itself is further testimony to how many excellent players the youth system and scouting network were bringing through at that time and Atkinson's explanation for letting them both go is, understandably, that there was so much talent emerging and he couldn't have hung onto it all. [4] Again, you can point to the Ferguson era and the loss of the likes of Ryan Shawcross, Giuseppe Rossi and Paul Pogba, while Gerard Pique remains the finest defensive player I've seen to come through the ranks at United, as he unfortunately went on to prove in Spain (I know his case was rather different, but if a lad with his potential's homesick, you'd like to think that the club might anticipate this and do something about it. After all, George Best suffered from homesickness too, although I accept the pull of playing for, say, Linfield might not compare with Barcelona). Ultimately, there are only so many places in the side and you can't hang onto them all.

In the end it was Atkinson's failure to win the league, given the enormously talented squad he'd brought together, that made his downfall inevitable. Consider the potential of a squad that contained, during a relatively short period of time, not just Whiteside, Hughes and Robson, but Steve Coppell, and Ray Wilkins at their peak, along with Frank Stapleton, Gordon Strachan, Kevin Moran – a man who probably, literally, shed more blood for United's cause than anyone in history – and the emerging Paul McGrath, and you begin to see the shape of a United side that, for all its success in two FA Cups in three years, flattered to deceive. There ought to be recognition for Atkinson, however, in helping us catch up with the likes of Spurs and Ipswich – clubs who should never have been allowed to get ahead of us in the first place - and finally engage with some top talent from overseas. While Sexton had already made United's first continental purchase with Nikolai Jovanovic, he hadn't exactly set the world on fire in the way that Spurs' Argentinians or Ipswich's Italians had - something that was emblematic of so much of Sexton's time at the club – and the signing again represented a creed of gentle, barely noticeable evolution rather than the richter-scale registering leaps forward that United should really be about. Atkinson's purchase of Jesper Olsen turned out not to be the world-changing event we'd hoped for either, but did show the first sign of promise that United could compete with big European clubs for the best talent and, although Olsen proved to be a bit lightweight for the English game of the time, the acquisition of the phenomenally talented and proven Arnold Muhren from Ipswich was one of the best and shrewdest United signings for many years. It's easy – and correct – to criticise Atkinson for spending good money to bring the likes of Peter Davenport, Terry Gibson and Alan Brazil to the club even if statistical cases have been made for at least two of the trio to have been better than their maligned reputation suggests, but for me the overall judgement has to be that, despite under-achieving, Atkinson began to make United look a lot more like United again. And not only in terms of flair and style: a quick glance at the team sheet for that famous game against Barcelona and you'd have to conclude that any side featuring Robson, Moses, Moran and Whiteside would have its fair share of steel and resilience too.

But it was the introduction of Robson, Whiteside and Hughes to United that, for me, raises the tenure of Atkinson above the level of his predecessors in terms of his role in restoring the identity of United to what it once was. These three were the first United players in a generation to look the real deal in terms of genuinely embodying the club's true identity and heritage. Robson was like Stiles, Crerand and Charlton rolled into one, equally at home winning the ball on the edge of his own box, making devastating runs to set up attacks and getting decisively on the end of the ball in the opposition area. Inevitably compared with Best because of his Northern Ireland background and the fact he arrived in the first team at such a young age, Whiteside was actually the least convincing of all of the supposed 'new George Bests' we'd seen coming and going at the club and therefore perhaps more immune to the burdens the comparison brought with it than the rest. He became United's youngest debutant since Duncan Edwards when, as a sixteen year old, he appeared in the first team towards the end of the 1981/82 season before going on to represent Northern Ireland at that summer's World Cup, breaking Pele's record as the youngest ever player to appear in the competition. Initially a forward who converted to a highly combative midfielder,

Whiteside even at times surpassed Robson as public enemy number one in the United side during a period in which detestation by Liverpool supporters reached new heights, not only for the robust style of his play but also because of his frequent match winners against the Anfield club in a period in which opportunities for me to put the record straight among Liverpool fans in the pub became gratifyingly regular. 'A merry Christmas to everyone, with the usual exception of Norman Whiteside,' said John Peel at the start of his Boxing Day show in 1986, after big Norm had grabbed the winner at Anfield. The third of the triumvirate, Mark Hughes, emerged from the ranks in 1983/84, and quickly established himself as United's first genuinely prolific goalscorer since Denis Law, with 25 goals in the 84/85 season and a further 20 in 85/86.

For the Liverpool fans I knew, Robson was the most high profile manifestation of their increasing common and absurd belief that United weren't actually capable of actually having good footballers. Because of this, however well Robson performed it seemed that no one with an affiliation with the Anfield outfit were willing to depart from the party line that it was simply impossible for United to have a good player. Prejudice is easy. You just stick to the default position and dismiss every piece of contradictory evidence by pointing to selected refereeing decisions, claims of a biased media, a crap England manager or a combination of all three. One Liverpool supporter said to me, completely seriously, that he'd never seen a United goal that was legitimate – that every time we put it in the net it was due to an overlooked foul or something the referee had let go further down the pitch. Seriously. Absolutely deadpan. When you're dealing with that kind of individual, logic goes flying out of the window. The reason United's eventual years of success hit them so hard was that they dismissed every possible sign of it in this way and therefore its eventual arrival was as tumultuous an event as the end of apartheid or the coming down of the Berlin Wall, while they sat there with their fingers in their ears and shouting 'la, la, la' with their half and half hats on and history crashing all around them.

Those years of success may have been still some way off, but if the history of United and Manchester teaches us anything it's that nothing comes about without long-term commitment and belief and that the individual who is, rightly, praised for bringing it about often has someone in the years before them who did a lot of the preparatory work. For Busby, read Gibson. For Ferguson, it's a more controversial claim but for me, read Atkinson. And for the most vivid sign of our future success look no further than that triumvirate of Robson, Hughes and Whiteside.

What was significant about the emergence of these three players, and the real reason – I believe -for the abnormal levels of vilification of each of them among Liverpool fans, was that they not only represented the true spirit of Manchester United, but all possessed attributes hitherto either unseen or very rare in the English game. Liverpool, with their emphasis on systems and functionality, found a team fired up by key individuals in a way that United had been back in the great days of the fifties and sixties completely alien and indeed threatening. And because fear and ignorance are always fertile breeding grounds for prejudice and intolerance, the level that the Munich taunts reached during that period became predictably deafening. On one occasion, walking home through Widnes town centre on a Saturday night, around twenty of them, faces red from booze and anger in roughly equal proportions, walked towards me singing the song they'd honed and perfected as their own; as they went past me, their severely pissed off gnarled faces looked very similar to those seen in National Front boot-boy scenes of the late seventies and early eighties. Not having any United regalia on my person at the time, I escaped unidentified as the enemy, but the memory has remained with me and I honestly believe that, had I been wearing my United scarf, if I were here now it might only be in a severely disfigured state. My immediate thought, as I saw the last of them walk past, was that, if four European Cups and six league titles in the last eight years had made them into this, either they were past saving or perhaps success just wasn't the right thing for them. The more they won, they more they seemed to become more unhappy about us, football and life in general.

While Robson's detractors saw him as no more than a caricature of the over-physical, energetic and ultimately one-dimensional English player, United fans saw beyond that and understood a player who combined a whole range of elements that would provide a model for the box to box midfielder for the English game of the future. Although they criticised him, Liverpool had their own pale shadow of Robson in Steve McMahon, a player who was to become more and more significant a player in their team as the decade wore on ('their leader' Vinnie Jones identified him as, before nobbling him). Robson was the forerunner of players likes Frank Lampard and Steve Gerrard, only much better.

The young Whiteside scored goals of a kind never seen from a United player or anyone else, exemplified by his semi-final winner over Arsenal in the 1983 FA Cup and the clincher against Everton in the 1985 final. On both occasions, Whiteside scored from positions that other players wouldn't try a shot from, and it was this contempt for the training manual as well as his 'Scourge of the Scousers' reputation that added Whiteside's name quickly to the pantheon of United greats. Rather pitifully, those self-proclaimed scouse wits on the Kop couldn't do any better than label Hughes 'elbows', allegedly because he only got where he was by fouling his marker. It's through such examples of legendary scouse humour that I begin to understand how the likes of Jimmy Tarbuck and Stan Boardman reached such dizzying heights in their profession.

Familiar with pigeonholing players in accordance with established and unchallenged models, it was understandably rare if not entirely beyond the experience of fans of other clubs to witness the emergence of players who would foreshadow genuine changes in the way the game was played. This is why a player like Duncan McKenzie, when he arrived in the seventies, was said to be ahead of his time. McKenzie wasn't ahead of his time at all – he was simply a less wayward version of what we already had: Frank Worthington, Tony Currie, Stan Bowles etc, whose style on the ball and hedonistic off-field activities were foreshadowed by the genuinely new model of George Best. McKenzie simply offered a more clean-living version of these players and, while undoubtedly possessing natural talent, was never a player who was going to change the way we understood the game. Robson, like Best, Charlton and Edwards, did this and that's why their influence remains stamped on the game to this day.

So, it may be asked, am I claiming here that only Manchester United could produce such players? No, but what I am saying is that United, via the model established by James Gibson and Matt Busby, were better placed to absorb such talents, understand their significance, nurture them, not be hindered by the question of where they might fit into pre-established systems, and thus move the English game and Manchester United Football Club forward via their influence. No other club had this heritage and therefore wouldn't notice it if it bit them in the arse, and for supporters of Liverpool FC, the acceptance of this was, perhaps understandably, an especially difficult pill to swallow. They'd been more successful than any other English club had got even close to, had four European Cups and were winning the league almost every season, but somehow, they were gradually understanding, they didn't have what we had. I saw it etched in the faces of Liverpool fans I'd known for years, whose dismissiveness towards United had turned into outright vilification and irrational hatred. Placed before them was a model of football that they couldn't understand., that operated by unfamiliar and therefore derided rules. We existed in different realms. Liverpool were science. United were art.

That venomous hatred concealed a deeper psychological torment similar to that which Jason might have experienced if, having defeated the nine-headed hydra, he found that the golden fleece was back in Greece after all, and had for years been resting with the Argonauts' biggest rivals who were all passing the cigars around and laughing at him. It was the spirit of vilification arising from this that led to the ugly scenes at Anfield in 1985, when United's players were tear-gassed. Given that Heysel was still fresh in everybody's mind, the response from Liverpool fans I knew who cared more about Atkinson's criticism of them in the press than the appalling scenes committed in their name was sadly as characteristic as it was indefensible; to their credit, it wasn't a view the Liverpool board took and from that point on they worked hard with United's directors to defuse what was becoming an out of hand situation, a move that soon led, thankfully, to the diminishing frequency, if not complete removal, of those Munich chants. Those responsible for the tear gas incident were the ape-like ancestors of the missing links who attacked Alan Smith's ambulance in 2006 as it left the ground and whose semi-involved descendants go to the lengths now of taking a shit, collecting it, putting it in their pockets, and dropping it onto the United fans below them in the Anfield Road end. The tear-gas incident also occurred at the height of a period when, further insult was being added to injury among Liverpool fans because, during Atkinson's period in charge, despite still being well behind in the trophy stakes, United didn't lose a game at Anfield.

So does this mean I'm taking the view, actually common in the press at the time, that Atkinson had been dealt a bit of a shitty hand when he was dismissed in 1986? After all, he oversaw Whiteside and Hughes emerging from the youth team (alongside others such as McGrath, Hogg and, er, Sunbed) which suggested there wasn't a lot wrong after all with United's ability to nurture and develop young talent in that period and we were certainly looking a lot more like United again. Was this an unfair end to Atkinson's tenure?

I'm sure Charlton at this juncture had a point regarding his appraisal of the reserve team and its potential to produce anything more lasting than a lot of perspiration and a few strained hamstrings, but then again Eric Harrison, the key developer of young talent for Ferguson, had been brought to the club by Atkinson in 1981. Dare I accuse Ferguson of using that time-honoured management tactic of making the claim that everything that he found at the club when taking up the reigns was in need of an overhaul when, in fact, some of it needed far less tweaking than he claimed? As a manager, assuming such a position can help to emphasise the scale of your own improvements in years to come.

Ditto the club's notorious drinking culture of the time. While it can scarcely be argued that Ferguson didn't approve of it and courageously and successfully rooted it out (willing to shed fans' favourites like Whiteside and McGrath and thus court animosity along the way), heavy drinking was an established part of the English game then and had been pretty much since its origins, where the rituals of the pre-game swig of whiskey and post-game beer were as much a part of the Saturday routine as the match itself. [5] One reason why Billy Meredith stood out so much in the game's early years was his lifestyle of obsessive fitness and abstinence – most other players were swilling down the good stuff like Oliver Reed in a lock-in.

If we want to talk about a drinking culture in the eighties, we should also apply some historical context and recognise that Jimmy Murphy instigated one very successfully among the Babes in the fifties [6] and we didn't do too badly out of it then. And we should note along the way that the only successful England side on the world stage ever contained more than its fair share of imbibers, with Ramsey not only frequently having to deal with Jimmy Greaves' excesses but also those of the (by reputation) ultimate professional Bobby Moore, his regular drinking buddy. [7] So the levels of drinking at United in the mid-eighties only appear shocking now that the idea of moderation in this area is more firmly accepted in the culture of the English game. Then, as Arnold Muhren found, it was being tee-total that was likely to make you stand out.[8]

Despite these caveats, it was the right time for Atkinson to go. A fair summary, I think, would be to say that he presided over some significant steps forward for the club but gave the impression of not knowing what needed to be done once he got there. Having won the first ten games in 1985-86, what should have been a serious assault on the title fizzled out until we had about as much chance of winning it as Teddy Sheringham had of receiving a post-match rub-down from Andy Cole. Having discovered the amazing talent of Mark Hughes, the club quickly agreed a sale to Barcelona and then, even worse, made it public half way through the season.

Atkinson then got involved in two notorious and ill-advised spats with Bobby Charlton, newly appointed as director and a huge critic of Big Ron, whose style was always going to find about as much favour with Bobby as would George Best necking a bottle of Scotch at half-time, the first his objection that Charlton's soccer school coaches were interfering with United's training of young players, and the second Charlton's refusal to allow Atkinson the funds to buy Terry Butcher.

I'd find it within me to have some sympathy with Atkinson on the first point, but less so on the second. A pattern appeared to be emerging in his transfer dealings. Peter Davenport, Terry Gibson, Terry Butcher and others seemed to have something in common, examples of players hailed by the English tabloid press, who by this point were plumbing ill-informed depths well beyond the world of football, as players who United ought to be interested in but who in truth had nothing of what it took to be a genuinely first class United player. Butcher, in particular, was an effective but very much old school English centre half, a blood and guts type that the English press tended to love but who lacked the sophistication of, for example, Liverpool's Hansen and Lawrenson, and thus a tried and tested national model rather than someone who was going to transform a football team. Was it possible that Atkinson's relationship with the media (and, as we've seen, that relationship appears to be a large part of the reason he was brought in) became a case of the cart leading the horse, and that Ron was in bed with the press to such an unhealthy extent that he was allowing it to, at least partly, whisper sweet nothings in his ear that dictated transfer policy? Richard Kurt, who begins his excellent *United We Stood* book on the early Ferguson years with a chapter on the last days of Atkinson is among many United fans who think so [9] and indeed he goes further by putting forward the view that, rather than possessing a manager fitting the image of the club, United were instead rapidly coming to take on the stereotyped image of their manager. [10]

Thus, we're left with a United that had begun to parody itself by spending big on whatever the current flavour of the month might be while being prepared to sell off a player like Hughes who, fortunately, returned to the club in the Ferguson years and confirmed his status as a colossus with a contribution that dwarfed those of any of the forwards paraded among the big Atkinson signings. The effects of United's pandering to the more negative elements of its public image were all too visible by that time, not only in the aforementioned big money failures and Hughes, but also in the case of Peter Beardsley, sent back by Atkinson after being given a single outing in a League Cup tie, and soon transforming Newcastle United and about to be a major player in arguably the greatest Liverpool side ever. Despite Atkinson's plausible protests that there were too many players coming through for him realistically to hold onto Beardsley, it's hard to believe that someone of his considerable talents couldn't have been fitted in somewhere.

It's understandable that most of the press following his departure felt he'd been treated unfairly. This was, after all, a press who'd feasted voraciously on the titbits thrown from the Atkinson table and were now salivating at the thought of the feeding frenzy on the carcass of a United side who, in 1986/87, now had the look of relegation contenders despite Atkinson's five years of top four finishes. All of this meant that, as a United fan, you could debate the symptoms and find some way of defending Ron's youth policy and taking a sideward glance on the issue of his players' penchant for boozing, but still conclude that somewhere things weren't right and it was going to need someone with a hell of a lot of character as well as a genuine feel for the heritage of Manchester United to put it right.

[1] Burns, J. *Maradona – The Hand Of God*, p117
[2] Burns, J. *Barca*, pp256-257
[3] Charlton, B. op cit, p310
[4] Mitten, A. *We're The Famous Man Utd*, pp250-251
[5] Burn, G. *Best & Edwards*, pp156-157
[6] Charlton, B. op cit, pp72-73
[7] McKinstry, L. op cit pp171-172

[8] Mitten, A. op cit, p227
[9] Kurt, R. *United We Stood*, p4
[10] ibid, p3

Chapter Nine: These Things Take Time

Anyone who attempts to draw genuine comparisons between music and football has to accept that the two worlds are really very different. Music regulates the emotions; with football, you are a slave to those emotions and a hostage to fortune. Every time I go back to Joy Division's *Unknown Pleasures*, I get the same indescribable buzz that was there the first time I encountered it. My reaction might potentially change over time, but that's because of me and not the records themselves. With football, whatever club you support, you never quite know what level of performance you're going to get. Admittedly, these variations were more pronounced in, say, the Sexton years or the early Ferguson years than they have been post-1992. However, even in a year like 1997, when we won the league comfortably, we suffered significant stuffings at the hands of Newcastle (5-0) and Southampton (6-3) on the way, and in the space of six days. Even in the year of the treble we managed to lose at home to Middlesbrough.

Whilst recognising the futility of making too much of comparisons between the two realms, the nearest comparable musical phenomenon to Manchester United is that of The Smiths. Not that the Smiths shared any of the features of a football team identified above (despite 'Shakespeare's Sister' representing a conspicuous loss of form in an otherwise triumphant unbeaten run) but because, with The Smiths, I got that same feeling that you were part of something that, as with United, other people just didn't get and that in many cases this sense of exclusion drove them to a frenzied and irrational hatred however much they tried to convince themselves they weren't missing out on anything. In fact the most frenzied and apoplectic responses came from those who denied it most vehemently. Never having felt that way about anything in their lives, they'd refuse to believe anyone could do so and therefore refused its right even to exist, or tried to ridicule it out of existence.

It's futile, because this is something that, like the canal, was too good an idea not to prevail. Over the years, appreciation for The Smiths has resonated through the words of music critics with, on the face of it, very different reasons for appreciating them. I recall one time in spring 1983 suddenly having them thrust at me by adoring acolytes as eminent as John Peel and David Jensen on Radio One and, the picky and notoriously hard to please Sounds journalist Dave McCullough. They were responsible for no less than restoring Nick Kent's faith in music. [1] John Robb regards their emergence as of equal significance to national and Mancunian musical history as the fabled Sex Pistols gig at the Less Free Trade Hall, [2] while for Dave Haslam they represented that peculiar form of Mancunian individualism that involved essentially doing what you liked throughout the hail of ridicule, defiantly knowing that at some point everyone else would have to catch up. [3] For me, The Smiths resonated through my life like an answered prayer, even though I hadn't prayed since they'd forced us to at primary school.

I can't speak for other United fans, but for me such reactions to The Smiths were bang on the money and replicated pretty much precisely the thrill of my discovery of United: no one else seemed to be much interested, those that were seemed almost universally disparaging and I found myself once again right out on my own. To me, Liverpool remained the Cliff Richards of football – undeniably successful in a materialistic sense, but bland, predictable and completely lacking in originality; faced with a phenomenon like United – or The Smiths – and the excitement stirred by it, those with this narrow mind set see a disturbing mirror held up to the object of their own devotion and they don't like it one bit.

The Smiths were the first Manchester band to celebrate that sense of Mancunian attitude identified by Haslam in a direct way as opposed to reflecting its spirit only tangentially. In pre-rock and roll years Salfordian Ewan McColl had evoked the spirit of the city brilliantly in some of his folk songs, but 'Dirty Old Town' had been composed back in 1949 and, though frequently covered, little of its influence was discernable in modern Manchester music. While Joy

Division perfectly depicted a sense of post-industrial alienation within which a Mancunian influence was easily discernable, they didn't actually sing *about* Manchester. The inhabitants of LA or New York were entirely familiar with hearing their city or bits of it celebrated in song, but in England only Liverpudlians had really absorbed their city's identity directly into their popular music canon. The artistic zeal for locality – such as it was – that gave us 'Ferry Cross The Mersey' even dodged the tearing up of the rule book that was punk, with a whole raft of post-seventies records such as The Mighty Wah!'s 'Come Back', Frankie Goes To Hollywood's *Liverpool* album and cover version of the aforementioned Gerry & The Pacemakers abomination, lost gems like 'Kardomah Café' by The Cherry Boys and The Icicle Works' 'Up Here In The North of England'. The general tendency of Manchester bands in the era was to use a wider, less geographically specific canvas for their musical masterpieces. The power of Joy Division, say, or Magazine was something that reached beyond the direct and immediate, while remaining, like United, still distinctively of the city itself.

We shouldn't assume that there was anything definitively Mancunian about this way of doing things. The work of the Old Trafford-born L.S. Lowry, much of which depicted scenes of industrial Salford and Pendlebury, is a prime example of localised art that still possesses the capacity to have meaning for those who've never been to these places, and yet retain a defiantly Mancunian/Salfordian spirit. Lowry's attachment to his industrial roots were such that he consistently resisted the pull of the bright lights and he remains, to this day, the only person in history to have turned down five invitations to be honoured by the establishment (an OBE, CBE two CHs and a knighthood) [4], although it says much about his affinity with his industrial north-west heritage that he did accept the freedom of the city of Salford and honorary degrees from Salford and Liverpool Universities. Lowry's hatred of the limelight, and desire simply to be left alone to do his own thing, is encapsulated in the story that he always kept a suitcase by the door so that he could claim to be on his way out if a visitor called. He was also, it's only fair to add, a city fan.

But then, so was Johnny Marr, which is one of the less significant parallels between Lowry and The Smiths; far more meaningful are those between Lowry and Morrissey. It's certainly possible to imagine the latter adopting the suitcase routine. Why there was such a time lag between Lowry's passing of the baton to the Smiths in terms of depicting artistically the bricks and mortar of Mancunian life is hard to say; perhaps it's because of that lack of a definable impetus or direction to modern Manchester music prior to the late seventies. Music of the area had been nurtured very much in the year zero spirit of punk; perhaps it took an eccentric figure like Morrissey to reach back over a far longer period of time and find connections with Lowry just as he was able to with, say, Oscar Wilde. Certainly, the Mancunian reference points are scattered throughout the musical legacy of the band from the very beginning. The first song Morrissey and Marr wrote together, 'Suffer Little Children', is a haunting and disturbing reflection on the Moors Murders and future works would continue the local thread both in the music and in the sleeve art, which featured images of, among others, local institutions such as Viv Nicholson, Pat Phoenix, Shelagh Delaney (the Salford dramatist who also inspired 'Sheila Take A Bow' and whose words are quoted, among other places, in 'Reel Around The Fountain') and Salford Lads' Club (where United's Eddie Colman was once a member). Musically, the terrors of Manchester schools are directly evoked in 'The Headmaster Ritual', the violence and raw appeal of the fairground in 'Rusholme Ruffians'; the local prison provides the title for *Strangeways Here We Come* and other local scenarios frequent songs like 'Vicar In A Tutu', 'This Night Has Opened My Eyes' (another song that evokes Delaney's *A Taste Of Honey*) and 'Still Ill'.

Delaney obviously crops up quite a bit there. Like Lowry, she was a ground-breaking and idiosyncratic artist who was one of the first playwrights to cover what still remained in the late fifties uncomfortable issues for audiences, such as homosexuality and teenage pregnancy. She is now recognised as a ground-breaking proto-feminist and an influence on many later radical female authors, but her palette was much broader, a key inspiration her desire to encompass a great sense of the dignity of northern working-class life. She objected to the theatrical convention of the gormless northern stereotype every much as she did to the plight of marginalised voices and sought to give much greater depth to the depiction of northern characters. [5] Her masterpiece *A Taste Of Honey* debuted on 27 May 1958, when Delaney was still only eighteen and just three weeks after a patched-up Manchester United side had gone down to Bolton Wanderers in the Cup Final in the wake of Munich. There are many similarities, too, between the way that young Manchester United side had breathed life into football, challenging accepted and stultifying norms and the tearing up of the rule book by northern writers like Delaney in the theatre and in other areas of literature. This uncompromising spirit reverberates through novels and films like Yorkshireman Stan Barstow's *A Kind Of Loving*, a novel set in Manchester and filmed on location throughout Lancashire, and the work of other 'kitchen sink' dramatists and authors, and Salford-born actors like Tom Courtenay and Albert Finney (another Smiths cover star). [6] *Coronation Street*, well established and uncontroversial though it is now, was a product of this same cultural movement, the Salford-set soap opera at the time seen as highly radical and indeed almost documentary-like in its depiction of the life of northern people with a rawness that's sadly diminished over time.

The colossal impact of Busby's young Manchester United's side in the fifties shouldn't be separated from the wider developments in northern culture during the period. As with *Coronation Street*, while we might now be tempted to accept the conventional view of the birth of the babes as something that was immediately welcomed by the British public, the reality is somewhat different. The early *Coronation Street* was widely criticised and dismissed for its vulgarity and, similarly, there were those whose feathers were distinctly ruffled by the appearance of the young, brash United side and the threat they posed to the established order of English football. The 'Teddy boys' gibe thrown at United by Burnley's Bob Lord [6] involved a telling choice of words, connecting United with the establishment-threatening media image of young rock and rollers. In Bolton, the appalling level of animosity towards United in the run-up to the 1958 Cup Final is often seen simply as a result of having their noses pushed out as a result of the Munich-oriented publicity, but documents of the time reveal a contempt among Bolton supporters for the whole emerging aura of Manchester United during the period that has been largely airbrushed out of popular history. [7] While many city fans try to justify their detestation for United as something that emerged only as a post-Munich phenomenon, and however much city-wide mourning there was in the wake of the disaster, there was certainly enough hostility already there for some city fans openly to testify breaking the general mood of city-wide mourning and go out and celebrate hearing news of the crash. [8]

Nor should we see the Football League's refusal to sanction United's involvement in the European Cup as purely borne of a desire to protect the eminence of the league as the game's primary competition: much of it stemmed from a concern on the part of the game's establishment about the impertinent rise of Busby and his new ways. It failed, but we shouldn't allow that failure to blind us to the truth. United's arrival in the fifties was seen by many as representative of the kind of impertinence that *Coronation Street*, Shelagh Delaney and the folk devils from musical subcultures would bring to staid, conservative British life. The Manchester post-punk explosion was a modernised manifestation of this threat and the later hedonistic acid house era would provide another. The arrival of The Smiths in the mid-eighties was simultaneously very new and vibrant and an extension of that much older Mancunian legacy of cultural provocation and challenge.

I admit I got it wrong myself at first; not with The Smiths themselves – whose music I obsessed about from that first Peel session in May 1983 – but of what they meant in terms of their wider context. Their appearance coincided with a time when I'd begun to explore other areas of football, where I found myself visiting non-league grounds around the north-west in the mistaken belief that 'indie music' (when the term still meant something, rather than later when it just became another industry label inhabited by sterile forces like Coldplay, Stereophonics and Travis) could have a direct equivalence with non-league football, which seemed, on the face of it, to possess many similarities, not the least of which were a lack of big celebrities, low budgets and a genuinely intimate approach to a game that, even then, was in danger of losing touch with its roots. While I frequently attended games at Altrincham, Northwich Victoria and Witton Albion, my most serious attentions were focused on Runcorn who, like Altrincham and Northwich, were in was what then the GM Vauxhall Conference, and on whose games I was writing match reports for the local paper as my first real stab at doing something worthwhile with my life.

Far from providing me with a Smiths-like buzz, it was my experience with Runcorn that helped to explode the myth of localism in football, so prevalent in the blunted armoury of the ABUs that would grow over the next decade. I've been told by a Chelsea fan ('born a fackin' stone's throw from the Bridge, my san'. OK, he didn't actually say 'my san') that, in choosing whom to support, Frank Skinner once proclaimed that the only legitimate method was 'you draw a line from where you were born, and the nearest club, that's who you support'. I have met many who have nodded, confident in their sagacity, at the wisdom enshrined in such a methodology, and indeed who have used it in order to castigate me, and many of my Manchester United brethren, in our choice of allegiance. It does, after all, involve a journey of 28 miles for me to get to Old Trafford, while the football grounds of Liverpool, Everton and Wigan Athletic would all involve a shorter trek.

In reality, this stance is completely bogus, not to say highly disingenuous There are, in fact, very few football supporters who abide by the rule and many occasions when an application of it would be preposterous, at its worst akin to a kind of dictat, arising from a Nazi ghettoizing mentality. Certainly careful consideration of Skinner's case itself shows he doesn't live in accordance with it. He was born not in West Bromwich, whose club he supports, but in nearby Oldbury, and so by his own logic he ought to support Oldbury United, his nearest football team. The club Frank Skinner chose to support was not the non-league outfit who were his real local club, but instead the nearest 'big' club, if indeed such an epithet can be applied to Albion. This is the case with many people who publicly trumpet their views on this matter. Even the venerable John Peel, who, in shows from the nineties onwards, was heard to bemoan the large number of Manchester United fans who didn't come from Manchester roughly at the same time when Liverpool fans in general decided they would choose to have a problem with this as they couldn't point to our lack of trophies anymore without looking even more foolish than they'd already begun to. This despite the fact that Peel was from Heswall, on the Wirral, and therefore his nearest league team, Tranmere Rovers, plus a plethora of non-league clubs, had been passed over in favour of supporting a team from across the Mersey who had a far better chance of winning things.

Were it my habit to attempt to seize the moral high ground, it would have been very easy, using the argument of geographical proximity (Anfield is a mere 11.6 miles from my home), to have followed the road to supporting the all-conquering Liverpool side, as peer pressure and even familial influence would have impelled me to do. Should some gun-toting officer from the ABU secret police force me into a situation where I had to accept allegiance to the Premiership team geographically closest to me or accept death, I would of course choose death because there is nothing in my soul that could even consider a situation, however remote, that would find me supporting Liverpool. And, given the geographical spread, there would be thousands of Liverpool supporters in that mass grave with me.

Recent Premier League surveys on this matter show that, on average, supporters of premiership teams travel about 40 miles to see their team play at home. Although this rises in the case of Liverpool and Manchester United (an average of around 70 miles), this is a revealing figure, showing that support for football teams, and not just for the biggest clubs, is now drawn from a very wide area. [9] The fact that United and Liverpool draw it from an even broader area presumably accounts for the higher average figure. All of which perhaps explains why, when away supporters at Old Trafford sing the banal and cringe-worthy 'we support our local team', they do so in such a variety of accents. Presumably, as they claim as the whole basis for not liking United is that our fans don't come from Manchester, city fans ought to turn upon themselves at the revelation, that even their average supporter travels in from as far away as east Yorkshire or Leicestershire.

I recall a conversation with an Everton fan who trotted out to me the claim, popular among supporters of his club, that they were the real Liverpool club, both because they were the first to lay down roots there – which is fair enough - and because Everton fans all come from Liverpool while Liverpool fans were turned on merely by the prospect of silverware and come from everywhere but. During the course of our conversation, he proceeded to tell me, without any trace of irony, of a very enjoyable evening he'd once had at the London branch of the Everton Supporters' Club's annual meeting.

In fact, the more you scrutinise the spurious logic of the claim attributed to Skinner, the more preposterous it gets. Even if we leave aside the fact that most fans will overlook a smaller team that interrupts the 'line of legitimate support', as I will call it, and restrict it to top level professional teams, it would mean, for instance, that those in the towns and villages in the very north of Cumbria should support Gretna in Scotland, as their ground would be nearer to them than that of Carlisle United. It would mean that someone from a West Yorkshire village like Cornholme or Lydgate should presumably support Yorkshire in cricket but Burnley in football, as the east Lancastrian club are the nearest league football team. On these grounds it would also be out of the question for anyone from my home town of Widnes to opt to support Everton, given that their ground is 0.8 miles further away than that of Liverpool. And, moving outside the football league to consider the case of Chester City, I'd love to be a fly on the wall if someone were to suggest to a fervent Wrexham fan from the Welsh town of

Buckley that they should support their hated English rivals, which, on grounds of proximity, would have to be the case.

In reality, the north of Wales is chock full of Liverpool fans anyway, just as there are swathes of Arsenal and Spurs supporters across the south of England, Aston Villa fans all over the Cotswolds and West Midlands, Leeds fans across Yorkshire and even, despite their conventional identity as a one-town team, loads of Newcastle fans throughout Cumbria and Northumberland. I've had, in fact, the pleasure of watching United playing away at Newcastle on the telly in a Lake District pub (my joy tempered by the fact that it ended in a 2-2 draw) and found myself completely alone among pseudo-Geordies with the exception of one very passionate Sunderland supporter who formed a temporarily alliance with me for the evening and a barman who, in his thick Penrith accent, declared himself a lifelong Liverpool fan and kept serving other punters before me.

My involvement with Runcorn exploded the myth still more convincingly. If I were to follow Skinner's line properly it led me to Runcorn's Canal Street ground, but despite my sincere affinity with the club for a time (and the fans seemed to find my reports on the games fair and balanced), there's no more affinity between Runcorn and my home town of Widnes that there is between two cats in the same bag. A deep cultural chasm lurks between the two towns. Pre-1974 Runcorn was in Cheshire and Widnes in Lancashire and bringing them both together at that point as the borough of Halton didn't do anything to encourage anything remotely resembling neighbourliness. Relations between Widnes and Runcorn remained no more harmonious than between a nun and a Satanist locked in the same room, and indeed got worse due to the enforced cohabitation. The new leisure centre that was built in Widnes in the eighties pissed off Runcorn residents, who alleged a bias for Widnes within Halton Borough Council and the final straw was the annual Halton Show, situated on Spike Island in Widnes but close enough to Runcorn for marauding old towners, fired up on special brew and god knows what else, to stream over the bridge and do battle with the legendarily handy West Bankers. To many on both sides, the Mersey might as well be the Atlantic Ocean. Ludicrous as it may seem to outsiders, entrenched Runcorners do not accept my labelling of the bridge as the Runcorn-Widnes Bridge. They refuse to use the word 'Widnes' in the title, labelling it purely as 'Runcorn Bridge' out of a denial, formed across generations, that the word 'Widnes' can have any connection with their town's identity.

Of course, being me, I didn't feel much of a connection with either place outside of happening to live there, so didn't believe the vitriol on both sides had anything to do with me. I was rudely awakened from my innocence on the coach back from watching a Runcorn away game Boston United. This meant travelling along the M62 and dipping down into Lincolnshire, and following the reverse route home. For me, this also meant that we'd be heading through Widnes on our return and down across the Runcorn-Widnes bridge, so I made the driver aware of this on the way back and he agreed to drop me off on the way.

What I hadn't reckoned on were the cold eyes fixed in shock upon me as I made my way from close to the back of the coach, to the doors and off. It was evidently bad enough that the coach had touched base in the foreign territory of Widnes (I think some on board even advocated ignoring traffic lights in order to avoid even temporarily dropping anchor in the town). A flabbergasted 'he's from Widnes – what the bloody hell's he doing on our bus?' hung like a silent fart in the air, misting up the windows with disbelief as the coach continued on its way without me, having discharged with relief its alien cargo. My next visit to a home game was met not so much with outward hostility (though I had no doubt it existed out of ear-shot) but an amused curiosity that was certainly accompanied by a tendency to stand a foot or so further away from me than had been habitual prior to my cultural origins being exposed. 'Don't get a lot of Widnes people round these parts. I think the last one was in the seventies,' said one older guy, his tone only a notch or so above an Arkansas badass giving forth in a redneck bar, spitting on the ground, his finger twitching at his gun. Others just gave me ostracized glares. From then, my match reports seemed to be scrutinised a little more critically. They were no longer the trusted words of an insider.

No football club, local or otherwise, could give their supporters what United have done for decades, and I'm not talking in terms of trophies. Despite the amount of money swilling around the game these days, and certainly swilling through United and out the other side, the essential spirit of the club remains far closer to that of the ostracized, the outsider and the individualist than any non-league club could get close to. I became to see more and more the truth behind Runcorn's 'local club for local people' image. At one FA Cup match – where there were bigger crowds than normal and therefore more of a police presence – I was stopped by one bobby at the turnstiles as I made to go in via the Runcorn end. 'Are you sure you're from round here?' he asked. 'I don't recognise you.' People might use the international breadth of United's support as a stick to beat us with, but it's a beating we can take and give back in equal measures: ultimately, I've never felt anything other than welcome at Old Trafford, in contrast to the reaction I experienced when turning up at a ground just a few miles down the road from where I live.

Runcorn folded in the nineties following a series of disasters that started when a wall fell down at an FA Cup game under the pressure of accommodating more Hull City fans than the ground could safely hold. Even here, the response of the local press (I didn't provide the report for that game, which was abandoned anyway) and many fans was to blame the Hull supporters for putting too much pressure on the wall, an unwillingness to accept that their small and therefore, in football terms, inevitably loveable club could possibly accept any responsibility for something that might easily have resulted in a more serious incident. Prior to their demise, a proposal had been made to move the club from Runcorn to Widnes, to ground-share with Widnes Rugby League Club, around half a mile from my house. The proposal was treated as if it were a request from Jimmy Saville to become chief tucker-in at a girls' boarding school. A petition went around Runcorn and quickly secured 6000 signatures, successfully putting a stop to the initiative.

The average attendance at Runcorn games was around 400 before the petition and remained around the same immediately after it. The club struggled on for a couple more years before closing.

Had a courageous decision been taken three years earlier – one that tore a leaf out of the John Davies book perhaps - rather than listening to the views of people who, while local, had no intention of ever going near a Runcorn match wherever they played, the future of the club may have been different. Runcorn's fate was sealed by a rigid application of Skinner's law. There is a reason why premiership clubs bring in support from an average of 40 miles away and that even the worst supported among them operate on an average of at least 20 miles. No club with any desire to survive can operate purely by considering only the opinions of those up the road because the idea that they will somehow automatically have a level of interest and attachment to sustain you on their own, purely because they're on your doorstep, is and always has been complete bullshit. Whatever the putative authority of Frank Skinner's line, the one that went from my house to Runcorn's Canal St ground was a seriously tenuous one. Just like the line separating Wrexham and Chester, the cultural complexities unique to an area are such that simply taking a tape measure and using this as a basis for legitimate allegiance doesn't cut it. As the coach rumbled on its way towards the bridge and I trudged homeward in the opposite direction, I reflected on the gulf separating this small club from the mighty United and its swarming cultural metropolis, within which James Gibson had seen no contradiction in dreaming of a fully Mancunian team and opening up the rail routes around Old Trafford to accommodate all-comers more easily, where the protestors of Peterloo opened their arms across Lancashire to those who shared their political plight, and across which and beyond the footballing 'outcasts' who established the players' union reached to encompass hands that withdrew themselves in fear and cowardice, leaving only the solid rump of proud United men to stand firm against the forces oppression. Herein lies much of the power of Manchester and of United: the ability to stay true to your own culture while not seeing like-minded outsiders as contaminators of its purity.

It had been a huge mistake on my part to equate non-league football with outsider music. The truth is that the world of semi-professional football is an inherently conservative one, filled with people with a genuine attachment to their club but also those who support them, not always out of some fierce loyalty that knows no bounds, but because they kind of like it the way it is, and to whom the prospect of new supporters arriving to join them is as much of a threat as an invading army turning up on the beach (not that any army would survive landing on what passes for a beach in Runcorn). There are exceptions to this – in the eighties, Barnet achieved a brilliant club identity, underpinned by real style on and off the pitch, and whose attendances rocketed as a consequence; recently the Chester phoenix club is one I've visited on many occasions and found to be of a different kind of small club all together, progressive, far-sighted and accommodating; Yeovil Town developed a highly meaningful niche for themselves over a long period and drew in support from a massive area of the south-west even when they were in a league below Runcorn, while Crewe Alexandra remain the paradigm example of how to run a football club - but unfortunately I came to realise that Runcorn weren't one of them.

I found that everyone I knew who watched non-league teams thought magazines like 'Team Talk' and Non-League Football' were great when actually they were crap, filled with platitudes and clichés like 'cosy' and 'nice little set-up' that many non-league fans I met liked to use themselves. In the end I stopped visiting such grounds not because of incidents like the trip home from Boston, but because there was something essential missing from the experience, something about the appeal of football that these clubs couldn't match and only pretended to understand. Being a small operation, I realised, doesn't by its nature make you an outsider or a rebel: in any scrap between the cats and the dogs, most supporters I rubbed shoulders with on the non-league terraces would have been firmly on the side of the dogs.

The Smiths, like United, were about being a part of something that people on the outside looked at it with a particular kind of envy as well as savage dislike, their ears pressed to a door within which were noises of a kind of enjoyment they didn't understand. And it wasn't like anyone was keeping them locked out – this was, again to paraphrase Timothy Leary wildly out of context, a self-selected elite and not being part of it simply emanated from your own failure to grasp its appeal. You couldn't just fake that taste or pretend to acquire it as a means to something else – you had to have it, to really know it, to gain entrance. And if you couldn't fathom out quite what it was or why other people seemed so obsessed with that particular taste, well then, that said rather more about you than it did about the thing in question.

In considering what these footballing and musical entities do have in common, one thing leaps to mind: Manchester itself, and the central figure of the maverick genius that is so bound up with the identity of Manchester and Manchester United from Billy Meredith onwards, inevitably becomes magnified across the decades because ultimately such figures will be celebrated in the future to an even greater extent than they were in the past. If you live in Widnes, St Helens, Leigh or somewhere like that – as I did - you face up to the reality on an everyday basis that no one's going to take much notice of what you do while you're there. So the only option is to move or comfort yourself with the notion that you're misunderstood too and that you're in pretty good company with it.

I've lived in the area long enough to have become aware that those who can't come to terms with their outsider status either live a life of self-delusion or become enraged, often violent human beings, the sort of people who start a fight in a pub because someone looked at them funny. Better to accept you aren't part of any kind of cult-like clan whose rigorous rules you're required to follow, and embrace what you are; and if you're going to join any sort of clan, make it one that doesn't insist on giving up your individuality as a condition of membership. The appeal of United, again, was that you could feel a part of it without sacrificing anything about what you are, while the embarrassing experience of watching kids trying to pronounce 'dickhead' in the right way at school showed me just how much of your dignity you had to give up in order to become accepted as a Liverpool supporter in that environment. Liverpool and United both have massive out of town support, but with the former the initiation has always seemed to involve some pretence to actually be part of the place, while with United a cultural connection with Manchester and an affinity with what it stands for are what are important.

Hence the power of a figure like Morrissey who, like United, inspired a devotion among followers that transcended any of his peers, irrational contempt among non-believers and a cult of allegiance among even those who identified and accepted any character flaws. As with United, these were just part of the overall package. But there was something else too. A defiance; a fortitude that enabled you to stand up for your beliefs, again something fully bound up with the identity of Manchester United ever since Charlie Roberts and his colleagues made their stand against the football authorities. Better for the game had the rest joined them in their defiance; better for United that they didn't. And through the ages – Davies's Old Trafford project, Busby's defiance of the football league, and pretty much everything Ferguson has done during his years at the helm – it's stuck to the club every bit as much as the legacies of Meredith, Best and Cantona.

In 1984, not only unemployed but living in a borough with the highest unemployment rates in the north-west of England, I went for a half-hearted interview with some company based in the West Bank area of Widnes. I walked out of the place knowing I hadn't got the job and looked up to see the giant iron presence of the Runcorn-Widnes bridge above my head. I thought of the ' iron bridge' line in 'Still Ill' by The Smiths, which I'd first heard in session on Peel the previous year, got back on my bike and rode over to the Music Shop in Widnes town centre to purchase a copy of their debut album, out that day. In truth, all the way through the interview I'd been thinking about it and couldn't wait to get away from the artificial ritual of discussing a job I didn't want and wasn't going to be offered anyway with a couple of nodding, serious-looking stuffed shirts and back to the real business of life.

Many people I know who despised The Smiths at the time admit now that there's more to them than they originally realised, that they were put off by the unflattering image woven around them and found themselves objecting to a crude stereotype which meant they didn't probe with any serious scrutiny what lay behind it. Their loss. This provocative juxtaposition of artifice and message was a big part of their attraction and very much central to the appeal of Mancunian music at least from Joy Division onwards, and probably back to Devoto's Buzzcocks, evoking a kind of exclusivity of culture you had to have something unique about you as an individual in order truly to feel a part of. The music press had been searching for a new Sex Pistols ever since the original impetus of punk fizzled out, looking for it in completely the wrong places, seeing in the notoriety of fakes like Sigue Sigue Sputnik a rebellious individualism that was only ever put on. The Smiths, a band led by a celibate vegetarian who preferred an evening in stroking the cat to a drink and drugs fuelled bender, were the first truly controversial band to appear in the eighties, purely because they challenged in a very unfamiliar way accepted norms of rock and roll rebellion. Aside from their obvious greatness, they appealed via the cultivation of deliberately uncool reference points like flowers, hearing aids and undisguised protestations of alienation and misery.

Because of my age during the punk era, pretty much all the bands I grew to love were ones I heard about from somewhere else first and who fitted to some extent a scene and identity I'd already determined to inhabit, but nothing prepared me for first hearing The Smiths on the Peel and David Jensen shows in 1983. And because of the animosity they generated among others, it was so easy to take The Smiths into my own private world in the same manner as I had United at primary school, like a re-engagement with the isolated spirit of those years, perversely masochistic and yet exhilarating and rewarding to a degree others couldn't comprehend. And I think it says something telling about United that, while we might draw parallels with the likes of Higgins and Ali, the comparisons that seem most appropriate are with artists, and primarily artists of Mancunian/Salfordian origin.

Inevitably, non-United fans won't understand this any more than those who didn't understand the Smiths. In the latter case, what they failed to understand was the creative context of the band and, without that, you won't get the music. Similarly, supporters of other clubs who denounce Manchester United do so out of a complete failure to appreciate that same context, simply because for the majority of football clubs it doesn't exist, not as a clearly defined condition anyway. So Barnsley being 'just like watching Brazil' is a temporary state comparable to an average singer songwriter coming up with the occasional better than average tune. Liverpool raised their game above the level of the merely temporary, admittedly, but in a different, mundane and uninventive direction: a raising of standards in football, but of a completely different nature to what we stood for. The logical positivist philosopher AJ Ayer understood the kind of distinction identified here more than most, and this was the reason why he believed that moral disagreements could only take place between those who actually agreed on the same fundamental principles – for example, a debate on the rights and wrongs of capital punishment as a response to murder can only take place between two people who agree that murder is wrong in the first place – while, in the case of Liverpool and Manchester United, our football clubs have developed according to quite different principles and therefore we don't even inhabit the same space that would allow a sensible debate between us to take place. We operate in, quite literally, different universes. I was going to say aesthetic universes, but to Liverpool fans it isn't even an aesthetic universe, which is precisely the point.

United will never be 'just like watching Brazil' – it's always about watching United. Brazil have their own special identity and it is entirely distinct from ours, which is why United fans would consider it demeaning even to make such a comparison. Similarly, The Smiths found themselves in that rare – and, in modern music, very Mancunian - position in music of making no sense if they were compared with accepted norms and values in the rest of rock and roll. I was asked once, by one of the many people who were so pissed off that I liked them so much (they really took it personally, like it was some immense judgement on their artistic sensibilities and values, which I suppose it was), 'How can anyone even dance to The Smiths?', a question so inane it clearly didn't deserve to be dignified by an answer. Again, we were two people who existed in two entirely distinct universes in terms of our positions, which rendered any attempted discussion, as Ayer would have said, quite literally meaningless.

Even more than Joy Division, The Smiths were the band whose distinctive appeal resonated across my area of Old South Lancashire. The raw violence in lyrics like 'Rusholme Ruffians', the institutionalised educational cruelty of 'The Headmaster Ritual' and the emotional wounds opened in tracks like 'I Don't Owe You Anything' and 'Pretty Girls Make Graves', all done with a kind of detached humour and observational panache that you had to understand or you missed the point, spoke to me via references to the aforementioned iron bridges and rivers the colour of lead, taking the backdrop of the post-industrial wasteland I'd inhabited since birth and pulling together strands of understanding about my situation that went well beyond music. Once again, Manchester had provided the source for both self-knowledge and a self-defining detachment both for me and the geographical area in which I continued to exist.

[1] Kent, N. *Apathy for the Devil*, p362
[2] Robb, J. *The North Will Rise Again*, p192
[3] ibid, p210
[4] http://www.bbc.co.uk/news/uk-16736495
[5] Conti, P. 'Shelagh Delaney' in Lichtenstein, C. & Shregenberger, T. *As Found: The Discovery of the Ordinary*, p266
[6] Burn, G. p139
[7] Mellor, G. 'We hate the Manchester Club like poison' in Andrews, D. op cit, p35
[8] ibid, p32

[9] *National Fan Survey – Summary Report 2007/08 Season*, p32

Chapter Ten: A Rush & A Push & The Land Is Ours

Anfield, 31 March 1985. Liverpool 0 Manchester United 1

There were certain events that could disturb even my dad's normally benign and accommodating demeanour, and this would prove to be one of them. I was sitting alongside him in a front room that, exactly two weeks earlier, had been the venue for my (my choice, somewhat low-key) eighteenth birthday celebrations, but this was much better: watching United nick a 1-0 win at Anfield and allowing Everton to widen the gap at the top of league, and finding ourselves in that latterly rare position of having as much chance of catching them as Liverpool did. Which, I suppose I'd better add, meant pretty much no chance at all.

There's a video posted on YouTube [1] that reproduces brilliantly the conditions in which football matches were watched in that era: thousands of United fans being herded through the back-to-back terraced streets around Anfield by police on horseback then lined up against fences while uniformed officers deliver finger-wagging instructions. One fan is shown being held at the ear by a scuffer on a horse and ushered in the other direction: it's unclear which side he's there to support. In the game itself, Liverpool enjoy more possession and have a couple of ridiculously optimistic calls for a penalty turned down before a cross from the United left finds Frank Stapleton, who's clear among unusually ragged and out of position Liverpool defenders, and scores with a firm header.

The scenes shown on YouTube of disgruntled Liverpool fans outside the ground were nothing compared to our house, where my dad, steaming at his side losing a match they'd dominated and in the process thrown away any chance of winning the league, turned – completely out of character – on me and my beloved United, claiming we hadn't even turned up to play football and telling me that if that was the kind of rubbish I supported then I didn't even understand the game. To which I responded, fairly childishly, by storming off upstairs and chucking a maiden full of clothes down after me.

Just seventeen days later, United would knock Liverpool out of the Cup, thankfully wrecking any chance of the nightmare prospect of an all-Merseyside final. I'd be watching it at my granddad's house, a place where my hatred of Liverpool would be welcomed, and indeed at times even exceeded. We would, of course, go one better and beat Everton in the final, to which my granddad would respond with scarcely less ire than that of my dad. 1984-85 would end, for the first time since 1968, with United winning a trophy in a season in which Liverpool for once drew a blank, though of course we would be robbed of a place in the Cup Winners' Cup, as Everton would be of a first tilt at the European Cup for fifteen years, by the events at Heysel.

Perhaps less momentous on a national scale, 31 March 1985 would be the last time I'd ever watch a United v Liverpool game with my dad.

That same month, The Smiths released 'Shakespeare's Sister', which would remain their only single release not to secure a place in John Peel's end of year Festive Fifty. It didn't matter. They'd already released more great records than most bands would manage in a lifetime and would never put a foot wrong after it. Like United, The Smiths joined a small band of individualistic forces, driving forward British culture whether it liked it or not and asking awkward questions along the way, destined by the very nature of what they did to be misunderstood and maligned by a large proportion of the population. They knowingly cultivated this and did it in a way that identified and offended the most deserving targets. As such they were a realisation of something that had been stirring in Manchester music for some years and in its culture and history for centuries.

It was something those meatheads I'd been drinking with on Saturday nights for far too long would never be able to understand, and were certainly offended by, and so much the better for it. It was an individualism that stood out in a time when the whole concept of individualism had been redefined, and politically desecrated, as something credible only in terms of financial value. Thatcher's materialistic sense of individualism was given hegemonic supremacy by a British press dominated by her orthodoxy; if you believed in something else, something other than the narrow Chicago school doctrine of market forces, you were decreed an enemy of Britain just as surely as were those victims of Peterloo or the 1841-42 strikers. If you didn't want to be an enemy of Britain, you had to join her repugnant crusade for a narrow, fundamentalist brand of economic individualism. The Smiths were standard bearers for a different form of individualism, one that prevailed entirely separately from this, that didn't view economic gain as the sole driving force of human endeavour; it continued to stand for an individualistic creed that saw personal freedom as something that involved going against the grain, being prepared to stand up for the unpopular and dispossessed and was nothing to do with making money or screwing someone else out of it (although I'll leave you to draw your own conclusions about the infamous financial recriminations the band allowed themselves to dissolve into after their split). There was no contradiction, in short, between this form of individualistic creativity and the belief in social responsibility and communal values, precisely as those nineteenth century Mancunian socialists and creators of the Co-operative Society in Rochdale had understood.

The greatest leaps forward in human understanding don't necessarily come from the introduction of new information or knowledge, but from a shift of angle, a new perspective – Darwinism, Platonism, Freudianism, Berkleyan idealism and thousands of other world-changing ideas all had at their root a different way of seeing reality rather than a different reality – and I don't think it's overstating things to say that The Smiths, during their brief period of existence, line up alongside The Beatles, Dylan, The Velvet Underground and very few others whose influence emanated not, of course, from being better musicians than anyone else, but in offering a different way of seeing and in presenting what they'd seen. It was something that had been stirring in

Mancunian music for several years and was now brought to full realisation as The Smiths joined up the dots to connect it with LS Lowry and Shelagh Delaney, the result being a Mancunian music culture that understood its identity with even greater clarity and boldness.

In the rise of northernness that had grown out of the kitchen sinks of the fifties, Liverpool and Manchester had both acquired sudden and significant centrality. In Liverpool, it was essentially music-led, from The Beatles and Merseybeat onwards, and Liverpool Football Club, taking on 'She Loves You' and 'You'll Never Walk Alone' as badges of identity and terrace anthems, followed that lead without contributing anything essentially new beyond it. For Manchester it was the reverse. Football came first, led by Busby's Babes and music didn't really follow at all, at least not for a time. While The Hollies knocked out some belting tunes (and let's give 'Listen To Me' and 'I Can't Let Go' some credit for having some of the greatest vocal harmonies ever put onto record), they were pretty much alone in this and there was nothing identifiably Mancunian about what they did, and even less so the embarrassments that masqueraded in the forms of Freddie & The Dreamers and Herman's Hermits. Great Manchester bands appeared in the late sixties and early seventies (Stackwaddy and Tractor, who featured on John Peel's Dandelion label and short-lived late sixties Peel favourites Sweet Marriage are examples) but these appear in retrospect disparate, sporadically emerging, if brilliant forerunners to the explosion of Mancunian innovators who would appear in the wake of Buzzcocks' 'Spiral Scratch' and continuously ever since, just as Billy Meredith foreshadowed the model of Manchester United which didn't truly become fully established until the fifties. This is not to say that there weren't important musical movements in Manchester in the fifties and sixties, but largely speaking these were club-based rather than live music-based phenomena that characteristically incurred the full wrath of parliament who'd identified the city as an unhealthy haven of pills and depravity and forced most of the city's bars to close down, taking any emerging music scene along with it. There were further dots here that Manchester music would succeed in joining up before the current decade was out. [2] For now, a defiantly individualistic Mancunian music had caught up with other spheres of the city's culture.

McCartney and Lennon met in 1956 and set out on their journey that would ensure that the most significant influence on change in the world of music would have its genesis in Liverpool. That year, the United babes were becoming champions for the first time and ensuring that the template devised in Manchester would be the one that would cast a radical influence over football. Liverpool FC were a good decade away from establishing even the first prototype of their own lasting template and, once formed, there would be nothing they could do to affect or compete with the glorious model that had already been cast in the east. The most important figure in cementing that model is often not given full credit for it, especially by United fans of later years. While we were robbed of seeing what Duncan Edwards, Eddie Colman and so many of the great Babes side might develop into, it was Bobby Charlton who matured to become the first nationally renowned footballing figure of a new kind of individual flair and character, and indeed at the time a figure of no little controversy, to a degree that's all too easily overlooked today.

Like *Coronation Street*, time has seen Charlton acquire a kind of safe and conservative gravitas, not to mention the aura of a national institution (something that always dilutes the appeal of a player among United fans), his abiding on-field images pile-driving shots at Wembley such as the goal that saw off Portugal in the semi-final of the World Cup and the unfortunate wafting piece of stray hair across a bald pate, with the result that the early controversies and disagreements concerning his merits and style of play have been largely forgotten. Unlike Best, Charlton didn't look individualistic or stylish and certainly didn't, in a footballing sense, live fast and die young. History, if it records it at all, has him cast more as an avuncular Bill Haley figure to Best's Presley. Yet arguably no English footballer before Charlton had so polarised opinion or challenged conservative notions on the field of play within the game of football in England. Had he not been such a crucial figure in England's World Cup victory or metamorphosed into Mr Diplomacy, it's very possible that Charlton would have continued to be viewed as the maverick figure he was once seen to be by so much of the English football world. Leo McKinstry recalls how, as a young player, his unique class and style drew time-honoured criticisms that his was a kind of flair that could never thrive in the physical environs of the English game: such a thing had been for wingers like Stanley Matthews, not players in the centre of the action as Charlton desired to be. [3] It was largely for this reason that Charlton, despite the loss of so many top players at Munich, was left out of the 1958 World Cup squad. That his replacement Derek Kevan had the nickname 'The Tank' says everything about the perpetual ethos governing selection policies of the national team and everything about the suspicion with which the talents of the young Charlton were greeted within the game. [4]

Best, whose youthful challenge to conventions – not to mention his drinking and sex marathons - tied in far more easily with his rather more effervescent personality traits, meant he, rather than Charlton, represents the creative ideal among so many United supporters and within the game itself. Both (though certainly not natural allies off the field) are, with the predictable addition of Law, collectively more responsible than any other players for affirming a cherished identity of individualists and convention breakers among United players, but we shouldn't let image or subsequent events allow us to forget that Charlton came first.

Despite my own experiences in that far flung playing field at the south-western edge of Old Lancashire, the identity enshrined in those three players remained vibrant and a central factor in the persistent influence of Mancunian culture across my part of the world, an identity of which Liverpool had no part. Wrapped up in this whole rich Lancastrian mythology and history, United's influence resonates powerfully across the rest of the country in a way that no other north-west football club or institution can achieve. It's another reason the figure of Charlton is so easily rejected by United fans: like David Beckham in another age, his early dynamism and unquestioned loyalty to the United cause were co-opted, brushed down and sanitised by a national media more interested in what he did for the England team. The Republic of Mancunia so often proclaimed in United flags and unofficial merchandise is the source of this resonance, an independent, value-generating, innovation-perpetuating state in its own right, which has no time or need for official recognition from elsewhere.

The music of the region has a similar drawing power. Experience of the Manchester music scene was what led the southerner Roger Eagle to discover a deep northern heart beating beneath his breast [5] and what led even an exiled scouser like Happy Mondays manager Nathan McGough to prefer Manchester's enticing combination of inclusiveness and individualism.

Not only did they carry this heritage around on their backs, The Smiths knew it damn well and consciously played with and manipulated the identity through a series of brilliantly chosen record sleeves as well as lyrics, and their eminence in this field can only be challenged by Prestwich resident Mark E Smith and The Fall. It can scarcely be questioned that city fan Smith's unique brand of obtuseness and refusal over a long career to be pigeon-holed or easily classified means he, even moreso than Morrissey, most fits the bill of Mancunian (or rather Salfordian) maverick and pioneer. City, for all their faults, do have a part in all of this. The fine footballing calypso from the fifties, Lord Kitchener and Fitzroy Coleman's 'The Manchester Football Double', offers an impartial celebration of the footballing ethos represented by both Manchester sides, while even the partisan Keith Dewhurst recognises the two clubs as essentially twin standard bearers of true footballing creativity [6] It might also be worth recalling that United fans in the Docherty era bated city fans with accusations of copying our style [7] something that of course may be understood rather differently through pale blue eyes.

I've never been entirely convinced by the portrayal of Morrissey as a committed Red (although Andy Rourke definitely is) so Johnny Marr's city affiliations always came across as the most prominent footballing influence within The Smiths. I've never sought to claim that you had to be a United fan to reflect this spirit; so why not city as well as United? Indeed, why not? They, even before United had won the league, were flying the football flag in Manchester with serious ferocity, and indeed were the first and last footballing home of the great Billy Meredith. A commitment to football played with style has always been a feature of city's identity. The problem with city is that, unlikely United, they've always had something about them similar to those small clubs discussed in the previous chapter, a determination simply to be just another club. They could have been what United are, but they aren't.

What city lack are two things. Well, *at least* two things. For one, both the club and its fans have sought to fix a parochial image for themselves via the myth that all of their supporters come from just down the road, only just stopping short of pencilling in whippets and cloth caps, while the true identity of Manchester is nothing if not outward-looking and expansive. They are, at heart, a small club in a big city who, by their own decree, have written themselves out of representing the spirit of the place from which they originate: the worst kind of betrayal. Secondly the creativity at the heart of United is of a different kind, one that ties in with that (Paul) Rooney-esque dark heart of Lancashire discussed earlier and one to which city, so determined to represent a cuddly side to their city it just doesn't have, can never get close.

Everyone can possess a dark side, but you have to be confident enough with your own identity to admit it's there and understand its nature. Like Liverpool, city have never possessed this secure self-image. Leeds United have, but in their case they've let the dark side get out of control and it's consumed them, Darth Vader-like. As the embodiment of the Miltonic concept of Satan, United are not only the creation of a political republican but of an artist who painted his devil a distinctive hue of political red; in 'Paradise Lost', Satan begins existence not as an evil presence at all, but as an outsider, a challenger to authority and a creative spirit and only becomes identified with evil due to his challenging of the *ultimate* authority. As we've seen, all of this has embedded itself within the identity of both the Red Devils themselves and in Mancunian/Lancastrian folklore and culture. It's something in which city have opted to take no part, indulging instead a small club-small mind narrowness and rejecting any essence of true Mancunian character in the process.

This heritage not only imbues Manchester with a self-belief that has historically enabled it to stand up for itself when the rest of failed to live up to its standards of progressiveness, whether technologically or politically, but also a prevailing healthy enlightenment when it comes to refusing to join in with fashionable bullying of those perceived to have a heretical outlook or to represent challenges to conservative values. Not only did this ethos permit the north-west's most prominent gay community in Manchester's Canal Street, it also made it the centre of the fight against Section 28 with Canal Street a veritable battleground for values in the face of Chief Constable James Anderton's concerted war against the community in the mid-eighties. It was alleged that Anderton directed his force actively to search on foot and in motorboats for homosexuals indulging in any form of intimate behaviour. [8] Of course, Anderton's values and the fact that he was prepared to spend so much public money pursuing them puts to bed any ludicrous claim that there's no homophobia in Manchester, any more than that there's no racism there either, but a general culture of openness to outsiders and a willingness to embrace notoriety makes Manchester a far easier place for the peripheral and marginalised to thrive in larger communities than elsewhere. It's exactly the same value that drove Shelagh Delaney to go against prevailing values in her representation of unmarried mothers, Lowry to keep turning down knighthoods and Morrissey to stand up for those wearing hearing aids or, er, bunches of flowers in their back pockets.

It's also inevitably true in terms of race. We've already spoken of Manchester's stance against the slave trade and both John Robb and C.P. Lee stress the multi-ethnic influences on the Mancunian music scenes of the fifties and sixties in comparison with the predominantly white Merseybeat scene, however much greater the immediate influence of the latter was nationally. [9] [10] This nurtured a musical culture that drew far more on the influence of black music than that of Merseyside and ultimately spawned the northern soul explosion based primarily in Wigan but with Mancunian involvement in the seventies and eventually the innovative, varied and far less homogenous Mancunian music scene that emerged in the late eighties.

It sometimes seems to me that lurking beneath those contrived accusations that United's support is non-Mancunian lies a brooding racism; certainly the multi-ethnic mix in United's matchday crowd is more apparent than is the case at many grounds, where crowds have taken years to grow away from a predominantly white male identity and in some cases still don't show many signs of doing so. Indeed, the tendency of clubs lower down the league structure to proclaim their identity as inherently 'local' should be considered alongside an acknowledged failure to bring about an increase in ethnic diversity among crowds at lower levels than has been the case at many larger clubs [11] In such a context, taunts about supporting our local team – given that the facts show they can't relate to living within the immediate vicinity of the ground – begin to take on a deeper, potentially more sinister, meaning. Even in 2012, it was still being noted that, among English clubs, only United and certain London clubs have anything like a genuinely ethnically mixed support.[12]

That's not to say there hasn't been movement at other clubs in this respect, just that, if it appears a little slow, maybe the conservatism of the 'local club for local people' mentality has something to do with it. It's well-established, however, that on Merseyside progress on this front has been slower than elsewhere. By the mid-eighties, Liverpool and Everton were the only clubs left in the old first division who didn't have a single non-white player in their first team squads. Players like Howard Gayle and Cliff Marshall had, it seemed, come and gone without ever being fully accepted. When Kenny Dalglish thankfully ended this shameful period by securing the signing of John Barnes, the player was greeted at both Anfield and Goodison by a hail of bananas, [13] with Everton's racist support achieving particular notoriety by chanting the word 'Niggerpool' at their local rivals. The loudness of the taunts revealed that, regrettably, the actions couldn't be attributed only to a small minority. Remarkably, many Merseysiders have sought to re-define this as simply another example of that irrepressible scouse humour, misguided if that, but only a bit of fun, with no malice intended towards John Barnes or the large black community in Liverpool. Indeed, Barnes happily fell in with this view this himself. [14]

Some three years prior to Barnes's signing, I found myself in the unusual and inadvisable position of standing in the queue for tickets at Goodison Park among a bunch of Liverpool fans. The reason I was in that position was that I'd been to Liverpool Royal Court to get tickets to Billy Bragg and the Sid Presley Experience (the line-up also featuring a young Phill Jupitus in his early guise as Porky the Poet) and Greeny and a Liverpool-supporting friend of his who were on the same train told me they had a problem: they were on their way to Goodison to get tickets for the derby and it was one person one ticket. However, they had a friend who couldn't make it. If they passed the money to me, could I travel down to the ground with them after I'd been to the Royal Court and get a third ticket on his behalf? Foolishly I agreed, and was now regretting it as in the queue outside the ground they joined up with an individual called Ste who turned out to be one of the most revolting individuals I'd ever encountered. Prior to his arrival, they'd been referring to him as 'Fatman'. The epithet turned out to be in no way ironic, I noted, as his hefty deportment waddled down the street towards us.

Perhaps ill-advisedly, I wasn't prepared to shield my allegiances – footballing or otherwise - from anyone, which led to the loud-mouthed Fatman constantly addressing me in a loud voice as 'Manc'. Many of the hundreds of Liverpool fans in our immediate vicinity responded with mirth, seeing it as a wind-up and finding it unbelievable that a United fan would have the temerity to stand alone in such surroundings. Thus, I survived. However, in far more sinister a fashion, Fatman began talking about something called 'the party' and espousing such racist bullshit, including some appalling comments about Martin Luther King, that I had to challenge him over it. 'He thinks they're all right,' said Greeny, warming to his unpleasant colleague and clearly no longer feeling bound to disguise his attitudes now that the arseholes held the balance of power. We'd go for a pint at Ma Egerton's near Lime Street station later on but for me and Greeny that was pretty much the end.

You can get away with being a Manc here,' Fatman told, 'just about. But come out here and share yer views about n*****s, and you'll get yer fugghhing 'aaarse kicked by everyone.'

I'm not suggesting for a moment that Fatman is as representative of every Liverpool supporter as he appeared to believe. None of the Liverpool fans I know now would have any truck with such an individual or his pronouncements. However, Fatman's complacent belief that his mission would find support with all of those around him had a credibility that was reflected in the hate-twisted faces of many of them, none of whom joined me in challenging his racist tirade. I'm not saying that such attitudes were nurtured deliberately, but the stance of the two Liverpool clubs in the eighties allowed his type to flourish in a way that was already thankfully on the way out at other grounds. You'd certainly hear racist chanting at other grounds, including Old Trafford, but the trend was already discernably in a more positive direction. Barnes was hardly a militant campaigner for change, but the quality of his appearances in a red shirt undoubtedly made it easier for those silent dissenters to be heard at Anfield above the loud voices of obnoxious types like Fatman. It shouldn't take a talented black player to achieve this, but his impact was such that it made the petitioning of pricks like Fatman and his odious 'party' so much more difficult to gain a foothold on the gullible individuals that sadly form a fair proportion of so many football crowds.

Whatever the nature of this ridiculous party, Fatman managed to combine his racism with the sporting of a badge that read 'I Support Liverpool Militant Council', which on the one hand said much about his confused ideology but also reflected the failure of the radical left who'd vociferously taken the fight to Thatcher in the city to get to grips with what, for their city, was a highly pertinent issue. While left-wing councils, including the one in Manchester, were finding in equal rights issues a far more productive platform for the fight against the political right, the agenda can charitably be said to have been underdeveloped in Liverpool. Militant had as its primary focus the politics of the white working class and supported policies on race and gender, where they existed at all, that certainly had little to contribute to the campaigns being waged by councils across the nation run by the non-Militant left. The Liverpool Black Caucus was damning in its appraisal of the effects on black people of Militant rule in the city, which it claimed had allowed race relations to deteriorate significantly, citing, among other examples, the abolition of Liverpool's race relations liaison committee, under-recruitment of black council workers (less than one per cent in a city with a large black population) and the cancellation of the River Avon Street housing project to serve the ethnic minority despite central government providing a grant towards the plan. [15] Julia Sudbury notes that, during the period of Militant control, other groups promoting black and feminist collective action in the city were, marginalised,. pejoratively labelled and increasingly found themselves on the wrong end of grant aid cuts from the council, whose tactics in this area can in some respects appear worryingly similar to those of the Thatcher government itself [16].

It's scarcely surprising that, with such scant support for the voice of ethnic minorities in the city, racist attitudes that existed among the likes of Fatman could be enunciated with a much louder, and largely unchallenged, voice than elsewhere. I don't believe there's anything as sinister as intentional racism at the heart of the city of Liverpool or of Liverpool FC, but I do believe in the dictum that all it takes for evil to flourish is for good men to do nothing. What allowed it to flourish in Liverpool in the eighties was a general head-in-the-sand attitude towards the issue which unfortunately, for all the changes wrought in the post-Barnes years, doesn't appear to have completely gone away. Unless you come out against racism uncompromisingly and incontrovertibly, there'll always be some arsehole who takes it as a green light to practice his or her malignant creed to the fullest possible extent.

That such vigilance was still being inadequately practised well into the 21st century, and that loud racist voices continued to find it very easy to make themselves heard in the city, became all too apparent during the damaging Suarez affair of 2011/12. Following the allegations (later upheld) that Suarez had racially abused Patrice Evra on the pitch, it shouldn't have been beyond the club to extract themselves from the controversy at an early stage with no real stain to their reputation. Although the issues involved were clearly very different, it would have been entirely possible and appropriate for Liverpool to behave as United did in the wake of the Cantona kung fu kick incident: admit it was unacceptable, talk to the player behind closed doors and reassure the authorities that they viewed the matter seriously by imposing some kind of suspension. While you could argue that Suarez was clearly Liverpool's prize asset at the time – easily their best player – and therefore, however deplorable, their support for the player was understandable on a pragmatic level, United found themselves in precisely that situation with the Cantona episode and managed to find a way of taking action while allowing the player to feel supported. The only difference, I would claim, is one of scale: Suarez's actions were, in the wider scheme of things, far more serious. Instead, they chose to hide behind the defence of racist apologists through the ages by claiming that directing the word 'negro' at a black player on the pitch was no more than the non-controversial use of descriptive language and a case of oversensitivity (or worse, dishonesty) from the target of the abuse.

I don't think that the issue is necessarily one of a racist culture prevailing at Liverpool FC. It's more about a victim culture that prevails, and has for years, within the club. The tendency of Liverpool football club to see itself in the victim's quarters when any mud is flying are what brought about consequences that were hugely damaging to the game, the reputation of the club and the city of Liverpool. When the entire team donned t-shirts in support of Suarez they did so with complete disregard for any potential consequences that might result from it. Dalglish's reaction to the storm over the issue was to voice his determination that the firm bonds of allegiance to each other within his club would not be broken up by outside forces. [17] The rest of us were somehow viewed as a mass group whose only mission was to destroy the work of Liverpool FC, and any higher level obligations – ie the supposedly agreed policy of 'kicking racism out of football' – were completely dismissed, to the club's considerable detriment. The night the official complaint was being covered in the media, I was in the Millfield in Widnes watching the footie when a Liverpool supporter walked in. Seeing the match on telly, he began shouting his drunken head off about 'fucking n*****s destroying the game'. To be fair to everyone else present, he was widely reprimanded and the bar staff removed him from the pub, but it's an example of what is unleashed when a club fails to send out a firm and unequivocal message on such an issue.

There ensued a surge in racially-motivated incidents in the club's locality as a result of the affair. An Oldham Athletic footballer alleged that he'd been racially abused by a Liverpool supporter during the FA Cup tie between the two sides shortly afterwards, an event which was quickly followed by pro-Suarez chants from fans around him. A Facebook page set up by a Liverpool supporter, entitled 'Evra=Scum' quickly received over 1000 likes. The Facebook page for Love Football Hate Racism UK was on the receiving end of violent abuse from Liverpool supporters. Gloria Hyatt in The Guardian reported a number of outbreaks of racism in the city which included the ritual labelling of black people as 'Evras', incidents of that hardy standby for what poses as scouse racist wit – the banana – being thrown repeatedly into the gardens of black residents and local youths marauding black neighbourhoods with Suarez masks on.

Hyatt reported that her company Teach Consultancy had written to Dalglish about these issues, and the letter remained ignored. Following this she wrote again on behalf of eighteen anti-racism organisations to Liverpool FC, again raising concerns and offering advice on a potential way forward, receiving only a response stating that Suarez had already apologised (though not specifying to whom) and leaving the matter there. [18] Many Liverpool fans on the internet seemed unable to take a line that admitted any wrongdoing on behalf of their player. A typical response criticised over-sensitivity and PC-gone-mad mania for accusations of racism among the UK population, regretting only that this had been allowed to sully the undisputedly good name of the club. [19]

It's this kind of institutionalised defensiveness, rather than any malicious intent, that has ensured that Liverpool Football Club remain, at base, an extremely conservative and inward-looking institution. It's characterised by a refusal to admit that there are any problems there in the first place, to which the inevitable logical progression is to ask 'so why look?' and to which the response to any problems that do exist is to blame the rest of the world for them. It's for this reason, and not because of racism as such, that the club didn't see the need, as other clubs did, to move away from its conventional view of the world in the eighties. It's what conservatism, with a small 'c', means: the world has always been this way, so why change? In the eighties, the club was perfectly happy with an all-white playing staff and white-dominated support, and it certainly wasn't having any discernable detrimental effect on their performance on the field. It was exactly the same attitude to its refusal to adapt the club's playing style or the restrictive dressing room culture that bequeathed it. If Dalglish deserved congratulation for disrupting this complacent attitude – both to race and to stylistic variation – partly through the signing of Barnes, it's a shame he didn't recognise years later the dangers inherent in such public support for Suarez.

Such a history, combined with their default defensive tendency when faced with any criticism, imbues Liverpool with an internal identity clash that ultimately, I believe, has proved very destructive for the club in recent times. Its city so wants to be seen as a champion of the downtrodden and the common man and yet it is hog-tied to its history and position in the slave trade, something that wasn't been helped by its refusal for years make any earnest efforts to distance itself from that past. Dave Hill goes further than this in his critique of the endemic racism he sees at the heart of Liverpool's civic identity, drawing attention to the city's ghettoization of its large black community to the point where it had almost been, prior to the Toxteth riots going off, erased from the Liverpool map. [20] While Dave Haslam has correctly shown that, despite a greater racial tolerance prevailing historically in Manchester, the social and economic forces that created Toxteth are not noticeably different from those that went into the shaping of Moss Side.[21]. Cultural developments in Manchester throughout the eighties - including the increasing importance of hip-hop culture, dance and the emerging eminence of the DJ and exemplified by Barry Adamson's remarkable *Moss Side Story* album – have quickly and significantly broken down any emerging chasms between black and white culture in the city. The poverty that afflicts areas like Moss Side and Hulme hasn't been erased – far from it – but these areas had become, culturally, vital sources of creative energy in the city [22] , something which. has never truly been the case with Toxteth, and that relations between white and black communities in Liverpool have serious ruptures not far below the surface was demonstrated only too well by those outbreaks in the incidents and viewpoints that emerged in the wake of the Suarez affair.

This is not just about racism. It's not even just about social liberalism and the forces that create or prevent it. It's about a civic history based on distrust of 'the other' in Liverpool that's manifested itself over centuries, in the Ship Canal protests, in the workers who refused to band together in a common interest because they worked in different industries and had different interests, in the sectarian politics in the pre-war years which also helped to thwart any developing socialism due to citizens of different religious backgrounds refusing to accept the other lot's difference as anything other than irreconcilable. It shouts out loud at you from almost every page of Dave Hill's *Out of His Skin*, written by a Liverpool supporter who suffered prolonged abuse from his fellow fans for daring to step out from the group and attempt an honest depiction of how things looked and, perhaps, attempt therefore to steer a more positive course for the future. It's also why United are, for Liverpool Football Club, the enemy because we represent, more than any other entity, the spirit of otherness, values and sensibilities that they find so difficult to trust.   If Liverpudlians sometimes appear to try too hard to achieve for themselves a sense of solid community identity, it's probably because they know that such an identity is, at best, an extremely fragile one.

I don't take any pleasure from this.   Over the next few years circumstances would mean I would spend rather a lot of time in Liverpool, time which I very much enjoyed. Were Liverpool to rouse itself from the torpor of conservatism and inertia represented so baldly by its main football club, I'd applaud. If anyone were to offer me the prospect of Manchester and Liverpool taking simultaneous cultural leaps forward, as the latter did once via the Beatles and as the former has been doing in much of the time before and since, I'd grab with both hands the mouth-watering prospect that these two north-west heavyweights might both seize the initiative and embark on a creative rivalry that would drag not just England but the world forward by the scruff of its neck.

Sadly, despite the enjoyment I experienced in the pubs and clubs of Liverpool in the late eighties and early nineties, any such parity of influence seemed centuries away as, in the ensuing years, Manchester continued to take these huge strides while Liverpool was standing still, affected by the same cultural paralysis that had rendered it unable to stand up to the confederate bullies of the slave trade or embrace a political radicalism that could serve the interests of its working people even during the recession years of the thirties.

Liverpool's failure to match Manchester as a cultural power, certainly from the late eighties onwards, had an awful lot to do with this. Liverpool had never given its citizens the unifying, common purpose that a great city needed and this was illustrated most distinctly by the stark and visible absence of racial harmony in the city which, if it existed, was well-hidden. Everywhere I went in Liverpool at that time, it was impossible to assume anything other than that you were in a white-dominated city. You might expect this in places like Knowsley or my home town of Widnes where there just wasn't a racially mixed population,; but Liverpool *did* have a large ethnic population and it was alarming to see it so concealed from sight within the city and impossible to stave off the impression that, within streets still carrying the names of slave traders, the large and long-established black population of Liverpool was still being hidden away in its ghettos, much of the rest of the city's population able to indulge themselves in the myth so loudly voiced by supporters of its two football clubs at the time, not just occasionally but consistently, that Liverpool was white.

Culturally, Liverpool in 1987 couldn't have been any more different from Manchester than it was from Antarctica, and its once celebrated music scene was becoming about as productive as the latter. That year The Icicle Works' third album clearly marked the end of their creative journey, the two albums that followed it lacking any of their early energy and spark. Echo & the Bunnymen's artistic legacy came to an end even more abruptly, their fifth self-titled album beset by a huge vacuum of ideas that betrayed the majesty of the four near-masterpieces they'd put out previously. The Las's, whose debut single 'Way Out' came out that year, emerged as the city's bright new hopes, but only boasted an identikit rehashing of the city's musical heritage, in stark contrast to a whole range of Mancunian bands and DJs who were eagerly searching for a new in a city that was moving so fast you had to get off the pop escalator and use your own feet in order to keep up. Some Liverpool bands, like The Farm, did this and began taking their musical lead from Manchester because that was where such inspiration resided, now more than ever.

Liverpool's own divided city, deaf ears still turned to demands to apologise for the slave trade, calls that would take another decade to be heeded, with its ghettoized black areas and stunted, one-dimensional politics, was in no position to contribute to a world in which multicultural and cosmopolitan energies had arrived so suddenly at the fore, fuelling a classless hedonistic spirit that hit the country in a massive explosion of vitality, Manchester's gift to us all a gigantic party to celebrate the final chapter of the Thatcher years. If, when the party started, much of Liverpool gave the impression of standing around at the side clutching a glass and staring malevolently at the fiesta before them, then such was the unfortunate legacy of their historical contempt for 'the other'. They had as much contempt for Thatcher as anyone but, as with the Militant debacle, had little to offer on the way forward beyond tired gestures and slogans.

The late eighties culture rush in Manchester grabbed anything (black or white, middle or working class, native or settler) the city's ragged mix of styles could throw up, in a seismic lurch forward that dragged the whole nation out of all of its comfort zones all at once. It wasn't just that the ground was fertile enough to raise Ruthless Rap Assassins, 808 State, A Guy Called Gerald, Krispy 3 and MC Tunes alongside a whole load of fresh white indie bands, but that cross-fertilization took place among the participants to a degree that just hadn't happened before, anywhere. That would be the legacy of the late eighties Mancunian music scene – and it would have implications far beyond music. While the footballing ideal of Manchester United was, putting it mildly, still struggling to find its fullest expression in the eighties, Manchester music found its creative zenith and then, incredibly, improved on it. Manchester being Manchester, the zenith wasn't enough. In June 1986, The Smiths released their masterpiece *The Queen Is Dead*; within a year the central source of musical creativity would be somewhere else entirely, yet still in Manchester.

During 1986 and 1987 I sensed my own firm foundations rumbling beneath my feet. Even as I marvelled at the magnificence of *The Queen Is Dead*, I could sense the changes in the air crowding the LP's grooves. I heard a documentary about the house music coming out of Chicago on the radio and, although I admit I didn't get it at first, the ideas and formulas being deployed seemed so far removed from my accepted canon of 'good music' that it was impossible not to take notice. During spring and summer of 1987, a series of milestone events occurred: Phuture released 'Acid Tracks' and the birth of acid house was announced to the world; in Britain Manchester was there before anyone else: The Hacienda opened their seminal 'Nude' nights.; the first Happy Mondays album came out and Stone Roses' 'Sally Cinnamon' saw them ditching their somewhat unconvincing beginnings and moving decisively into a sub-psychedelic sound that would provide a vital stepping stone towards the truly spectacular. Even the release of New Order's *Substance* compilation seemed to denote the closing of one era and the beginning of another. The Smiths, sadly but as usual with impeccable timing, announced their split.

You sensed a real wave of change, and Manchester was right at the epicentre of the quake. It shook the foundations of the world within which I'd grown so comfortable. The time for bedroom radicals like me was coming quickly to an end; I quite literally had to move on or simply give up, suffering a living death in the cocoon I'd wound round myself, as indeed you'd expect it to as that was what Manchester had always been about: it was as if the same wave of change that rippled so emphatically through Lancashire and the world during the industrial revolution had gathered themselves for another, equally decisive cultural push. Liverpool could talk about that ley-line that allegedly ran down Mathew Street, reflecting as it did some kind of inner complacency that required no human effort or intervention to make it work. Manchester had its roots in blood and sweat as well as ideas and innovation; those ripples were man-made and, again, looked outward to shake ground that would never be the same again following its tremors.

The pulsing squelches of Acid House disrupted my inner peace and pointed the way towards a future that demanded moving feet and bodies as well as minds. Acid House didn't instantly provide great new sounds that I could absorb into my world, because frankly at the time I didn't understand it, but it showed me that the future very clearly lay somewhere else and that I couldn't be part of it unless I re-examined myself and my life. More significantly, it offered up a similar challenge to everybody.

I realised that for long enough I'd been a receiver of the world rather than an active participant in it, like I was waiting for something to happen – like United winning the league or some desperate publisher appreciating one of my half-arsed attempts at writing the great British novel – that would make everything all right. Manchester sent me a message in characteristically blunt, no-bullshit tones and I responded

The next morning I got up and went to the local college. I paused at the gate, walked back in the other direction and went and bought the NME, then stood around reading it for a bit, stalling. There was no Greeny, no Dave, no pub full of arseholes. No mum or dad, nor siblings nor other family members. I was completely on my own. Memory tells me it was the edition where they looked at this brave new world of music, where the sounds coming out of Chicago and Detroit were arising to challenge the decades-long supremacy of the guitar in youth culture, and winning convincingly. But I may well be imbuing the moment with a coherence it didn't really have.

I returned to the college gates, walked past them and circled the building. Then I circled it again. After reaching the gates a fourth time, I went in. I was enrolled by some lecturer who smelt as if he'd just farted and he told me to write some details down on the cover of my NME about where to come on Monday at the start of term. I'm not one of those who believes education solves everything, but I can say with complete certainly that, had I not done that, a large portion of my life since would have been completely different and I'm certain nothing like as enjoyable. What I didn't know then was that the impending appointment of Ferguson would, in time, bring about a similar change to another vital portion of it.

[1] http://www.youtube.com/watch?v=KKgSivBlf-U
[2] Robb, J. *The North Will Rise Again*, p1
[3] McKinstry, L. op cit p138

[4] ibid pp105-106

[5] Robb, J. op cit p9

[6] Doherty, K. op cit p241

[7] Egan, S. op cit p296-297

[8] Campbell, B. *The Guardian*, 7 August 2004

[9] Robb, J. *ibid*, p3

[10] ibid, p7

[11] http://www.guardian.co.uk/football/blog/2010/sep/24/british-asians-premier-league-football

[12] Skidmarx, http://shirazsocialist.wordpress.com/2012/03/19/muamba-turns-from-sponging-black-immigrant-to-footballing-hero

[13] Hornby, N. *Fever Pitch,* 188-191

[14] Hill, D. pp177-178

[15] *Liverpool Echo*, 17 January 1986

[16] Sudbury, J. *Other Kinds of Dreams: black women's organisations and the politics of transformation*, p188

[17] Hayward, P. *Daily Telegraph*, 23 December 2011

[18] Hyatt, G. *The Guardian*, 24 February 2012

[19] http://thekop.liverpoolfc.tv/_Racism-Abuse-and-Equality/blog/5700650/173471.html

[20] Hill, D. op cit p122

[21] Haslam, D. *Manchester, England,* p225

[22] ibid, p258

[23] Hill, D. op cit pp27-28

Chapter Eleven: Transmission

Anfield, 4 April 1988. Liverpool 3 Manchester United 3

At the time it appeared a bit of a curate's egg, but with hindsight it's in contention for a place among the top ten defining moments of Liverpool's slide and United's rise under Ferguson. Liverpool were nailed-on certainties to win the league title, having entered April with only two defeats all season, and this wasn't going to change that. They were by some distance still the best team in the country. Indeed, arguably this was the finest of all Liverpool sides, adding, fleetingly, a degree of artistry to their play lacking in all previous Anfield teams. Only two years later, however, they'd win their last league title for two decades, and counting.

Looking back at a YouTube clip of the highlights, what you notice first are two things. Firstly, again, the crowd. United's away support is light years ahead of our home support in intensity now, but then it was something else altogether, the roar when Robson knocks in the opener absolutely deafening. The other thing is the BBC commentary, which begins by talking of Liverpool suffering past injustices and remains heavily weighted towards the Anfield side's point of view throughout the game. This was at a time when Liverpool's paranoia at 'the meejah' being allegedly pro-United was at its height, and such bald and blatant fawning at the altar of Anfield by the BBC was just ignored by those who always prefer to enjoy the moral superiority afforded by the victim complex, even when they're winning everything in sight.

Although United had a great record in one-off games with Liverpool during those years, this one was a bit different. When Liverpool go 2-1 up after Gillespie nods in Barnes' lay off, Motson starts purring about 'vintage Liverpool', and I wonder how many takers I'd get if I laid a bet that every commentary on the side that season would feature that phrase at least two or three times? 3-1 down after 47 minutes to go after McMahon's long-range strike ('one of the best goals of the season, even by Liverpool's standards'

– Motson), recovery looked hopeless when Colin Gibson picked up a second yellow ('a position Liverpool are ready-made to exploit' – Motson). However, Robson's deflected shot brought a 'desperate' United who were 'in danger of losing their discipline' (commentary again) back within range before Strachan took advantage of some comedy Liverpool defending to equalise. The commentary inevitably finishes with the comment that, despite the result, there was 'no doubt who the better team was'.

In that game, you can see what a powerful presence Steve Bruce is already becoming in the United defence. A Liverpool fan I knew had been praising him to the skies when he'd played at Anfield with Norwich, but now of course he was 'crap' , a typical English carthorse centre half, light years from the cultured industry of Liverpool's defenders. In this game it was easy to see how much Liverpool benefited from the creativity and guile of Beardsley and Barnes, giving them that unfamiliar individual craft that had been so recently added to their make-up, allied to the midfield power of McMahon, the dynamism of Hodgson and the versatility of the excellent Steve Nicol, but cracks were beginning to show. In Gillespie and Ablett you had two defenders who wouldn't have got a sniff of the Liverpool first team in the late seventies, and the confusion in the back line that allows Strachan to slip in for the equaliser was starting to become a more frequent feature of their game. A couple of years down the line, such defensive frailties would be the key crumbling blocks upon which an empire would fall.

However, for the TV coverage, there is only the moment, and how that fits into the conventional narrative of the all-conquering Liverpool side. They had no idea that we were so close to the dynasty's end and, frankly, neither was I. The bafflement in Motson's reaction to United coming back into the game is perhaps understandable given how assured Liverpool's position of dominance seemed at the time, as good a marker of the strange twists and turns that were about to come as you'll find.

The roots of Manchester United's ascendancy in the nineties lie in Liverpool's hatred of us in the eighties. As the successful team the English game had ever seen at that point, the delight they might have taken in their own success failed to flourish fully as a result of their feelings towards us and, without intending to do so, they helped secure for us again an eminent position among the footballing elite. I'm absolutely clear on this: had Liverpool fan simply soaked up the envy of others, accepted it went with the territory of being at the top and simply *behaved* as if they were a big club, they wouldn't have allowed us the centre stage we took from them. They established a trend among clubs across the spectrum of England's top division for teams to define themselves in comparison (or more often contrast) with United which flourished well before we began piling up the trophies. Back then, Liverpool had the field largely to themselves in terms of hating us at that kind of intense, silly and ultimately self-defeating level, but because of their much greater desire to procure the status of victim they opened it up to others and, although we might have taken a while to realise what was happening ourselves, Ferguson was leading us right through that wide open door.

A bloke I knew from Rainhill (near St Helens) told me around this time that he was beginning to despair of his son, a Liverpool season ticket holder, because he seemed no longer to derive any pleasure from his club's dominance of the English game. 'He comes home from the match,' said his flummoxed dad, 'and I try to talk to him about it. All he wants to talk about is Manchester United. "They only drew at home today," he'll say. "Why doesn't anyone want to talk about that?"' Even his dad – a highly amiable chap with only a passing interest in the game – was seen by this paranoid Liverpool fan as a source of the malaise that Liverpool fans saw as tainting their own success. 'Let's shift the focus to how crap Manchester United are,' they'd want to say. 'That's what we want to talk about'. So the attitude of the English press, who inevitably gave generous coverage to the triumphs of the Liverpool team whatever is claimed by the club's supporters, was roundly condemned because they (a) refused to talk at length at how crap

United were and (b) they had the temerity to give some coverage to United also, and any such coverage was viewed, from that jaundiced angle, to be some kind of slap in the face to Liverpool.

Inevitably, having now meandered into further education and on the verge – at the age of 22 – of actually doing something with my life, I continued to encounter the persecution complex at first hand, as well as discovering some rather more unexpected and welcome things along the way. I suddenly found that the previous half dozen years I'd spent largely idling, reading and writing the time away hadn't really amounted to doing bugger all, as was popularly supposed. Instead they'd given me what I now realised to be a rich body of knowledge about the world and the well-honed ability to put it down on paper. As a result, having scraped just two O Levels in my misspent school years, I managed to get straight As in my three A Levels. More importantly, I came into contact with a whole crowd of mavericks, cynics and subcultural desperadoes that altered my social world for the better.

This wasn't a traditional sixth form college I'd walked into. It was a second/last-chance FE college filled with social outcasts and dropouts and they had an axe to grind with the world every bit as sharp as mine and in some cases even sharper. The long-term young unemployed held sway behind barricades Thatcherism was destined never to break down and from which, though I didn't realise it then, she was already beating a retreat, though with a damaging scorched earth policy laying waste to the no man's land that was Britain's industrial base. Reformed heroin addicts rubbed shoulders with nerds blinking as they came out into the sunlight, alongside unreformed heroin addicts and other members of the young unemployable. Older acid casualties lined up alongside flaming gays hell-bent on standing up against Section 28 and holding a firmly proffered two fingers to the purveyors of back to basics values and pseudo-Victorian morality. Girls with long hair who couldn't face the day until they'd had at least three spliffs happily shared learning space with losers raddled with lice and incontinence who weren't afraid to tell you about it.

Among them I found one young bloke whose teeth would have given Shane McGowan's dentist nightmares and whose hair had mostly fallen out in clumps by his early twenties. The son of well to do parents who'd tragically died in a car crash, he represented the downwardly mobile underbelly of Thatcher's Britain, having lived a feral lifestyle on smack and beer in the company of biker gangs who'd helped him to spend his not inconsiderable inheritance and then ridden off when the pickings got less plentiful. He'd started college because it meant he could save on heating bills during the winter. Then one day I encountered Graham, arrogantly blowing smoke rings on a chair in the staff room, where bohemian leftie teachers allowed us to sit and play things like *The Basement Tapes* and *Axis: Bold As Love*, hitherto unexplored gems to me thanks to my punk-dominated youth.

'You wear a paisley shirt and you can't even recognise a Jimi Hendrix record?' said Graham to me dismissively in his Canadian accent, nurtured via a childhood spent there, although the rest of his family all spoke with thick Widnesian dialects. I was thus instantly looked down upon and only found favour with Graham – who refused to accept anybody who he didn't regard as his intellectual peer and politically sound on every issue – during a college assignment at the local Pentecostal church when I'd interviewed a born again Christian and bullied him intellectually to the point of him admitting he couldn't be sure of God's existence. Because of my unintended obnoxiousness as much as my display of intelligence, Graham was happy to accept me. He was the only person I'd met, and would ever meet, whose extreme disregard for anyone who he didn't agree with put my own anti-social tendencies into a very deep shade, to a point at which I realised I actually wasn't that anti-social at all. In class, you put forward a half-thought out or too-conventional viewpoint in Graham's hearing at your own risk.

'I do think that, for a soap opera, Eastenders at least covers serious issues.'

'It's a fucking car*toon*!' yelled Graham.

'At least we've got good public service broadcasting in this country.'

'I don't share the conventional view that the BBC is worth two shits,' was Graham's reply.

'Can you stop smoking in the classroom?

'I don't listen to anti-smoking types. No, I'll rephrase that: I don't listen to anti-smoking FASCISTS.'

Causes that Graham fought on behalf of, either within the classroom or in the pub afterwards ranged from the right for all sportspersons to take whatever performance-enhancing drugs they liked, the return of Julie Burchill to her rightful place in the literary and journalistic canon and the bombing of large areas of our home town, on the grounds that a sufficiently large proportion of reactionary dickheads resided therein,

These were far more interesting circles to move in, filled with bohemian attitudes and contempt for convention to an almost self-defeating degree, populated by young people with an axe to grind and tutors who, certainly in my case, helped to give my stunted rebellious attitudes shape and yield the realisation that the radicalism I'd assumed I alone felt was shared and ran deep into history, that the version of the British nation's heritage fed to us by Thatcher's propagandists was bollocks and that, after all, I wasn't quite as marginalised in my left-wing view of the world as the Tory press and most of the people I'd known till then would have liked me to believe.

I didn't, however, find much to mirror my view of the footballing world. My teachers included Brian, a kind of non-native born again scouser and Liverpool season ticket holder; an exile from the south-west now living in Liverpool and another convert to the LFC dream, who littered lessons with interjections and reflections on the wonder of John Barnes; a former Spurs football hooligan who hated United with relish and one of those Evertons fans who happily bought into the all-scousers-together-anti-United bollocks that was fashionable at that time.

Most of the students were Liverpool fans as well, although Graham felt that football support was just another form of mindless tribalism and inherently capitalist and berated me for taking it seriously. A few years later he and his girlfriend would have the temerity to turn up at my flat during the penalty shootout between United and Spartak Moscow; while I died a million deaths in front of the telly they sat there laughing me as if I were some form of novelty animal in the zoo. My complete deflation at the end when United went out brought the loudest laugh of all.

Graham was the first close friend I'd ever had who wasn't a Liverpool fan. There were enough around to make up for it, however. When Hillsborough happened, towards the end of my second year as an A Level student, I felt more surrounded than ever before although at the same time, for a short while, I was conscious of a certain spirit of amnesty descending. Even the rabidly anti-United Brian was heard to utter sentiments about football being put into perspective and musing that, after all, we didn't really hate each other as much as we liked to make out, did we? He talked of finding himself in a pub in Salford not long after the disaster and being bowled over by the warmth of the United fans he met there, feeling a post-disaster camaraderie he'd never before experienced.

It wouldn't last. We were soon back to Monday morning lessons filled with gloating and goading on a large scale among Brian and his Liverpool-supporting students and which always kicked off with an astonishingly puerile assessment of whatever was on the sports pages that weekend. Inevitably, whatever it was, the Liverpool fans, determined to find misery amongst the joy of victory and equally determined to find more evidence that the world was against them, would root it out like famished pigs grubbing around for truffles and ensure they discovered something to object to, however much shit they inhaled in the process.

Liverpool FC at the time took an attitude to media coverage that would make Alex Ferguson, in his refusal to pander to the whims of the fourth estate, look as media-friendly as Alan Partridge. In his heyday, Bob Paisley would deign to honour the BBC with one appearance all season – right at the end, and only if they'd won it, which they usually did. Joe Fagan was slightly more amenable and invariably convivial on camera, though still granted about as many interviews per season as did the average member of the royal family. At the time they stood in stark contrast to those rent-a-gob first division managers, always good for a quote and the occasional controversial interjection of the sort that was apt to generate further copy for the media. Brian Clough was the undisputed king in this respect, but in those days managers weren't contractually obliged to be media personalities and so most chose not to be.

Kenny Dalglish was not so much awkward in front of the cameras as belligerent and difficult, refusing to engage with the press at all if he could help it, suspicious and irritable with them when he did, treating even the most innocent of questions as intrusive and provocative, and in turn fanning the flames of his own fans' insularity by making an interested journalist's questions appear the height of impertinence. Nothing wrong with that, as far as it goes; managers are paid to do their best for their clubs, not for the media. As soon as you get a boss (and Atkinson was often accused of this, even by United fans) who puts responsibilities to the media above his own club, you're in trouble. Liverpool kept things behind closed doors as much as possible, and they were right to do so. Alex Ferguson himself noted how far the Anfield secrecy ring extended when in temporary charge of the Scottish national team in the lead up to the World Cup in 1986: prior to a qualifier against Wales, he had sought information from Liverpool players among his squad on how to stop Ian Rush. The players remained tight-lipped, unwilling to break a code that was almost Masonic in its intensity (which, given the origins of Liverpool Football Club, was entirely fitting I suppose). Nothing wrong with that – I would want any United player to put club over country in this way, and nothing wrong either in the practice of putting club before the press. What's a bit rich is when those who knowingly keep such a tight rein on communication with outsiders, including the media, then complain that no one pays them enough attention.

One of my earliest literary ventures in my typewriter years of 1983-86 involved the writing of a book about post-war FA Cup winning goalscorers. To this end, I was advised by someone in the know to write to all relevant clubs (ie those who'd won the cup during that time) and ask for information about the players and matches in question. This I duly did, and was pleasantly surprised by the helpful responses from the majority of clubs. Leading the way were Aston Villa and Ipswich Town, whose club statisticians provided enough information and background material on Peter McParland and Roger Osborne respectively almost to enable me to write detailed biographies of the players themselves. United weren't far behind, sending me loads of stuff on Stan Pearson, including pages of statistics and career records, with city among many other clubs who came up trumps, providing less detail but still a lot of very valuable information as well as some helpful tips on where I might find out more. From Liverpool, I received a very polite letter, wishing me all the best with my book but stating that they didn't provide such information.

Ultimately, the book remained an unfinished project, but the episode spoke volumes about the approach of the various clubs to dealing with outside agencies. Villa, Ipswich and United were clearly keen to use any opportunity, no matter how marginal and no matter how obscure the author, to get maximum information about their clubs and their histories out into the world. It's not difficult to deduce from this that they would be similarly, and perhaps understandably more, helpful to press agencies seeking the same thing. Had the book seen the light of day and become the authoritative tome on the subject I'd hoped it to be, I can imagine the reaction from Liverpool supporters: complaints about the small amount of space given over to their club, citing it as yet another example of how clubs like United were given far more attention than theirs. And if I'd wanted to write more about them, I'd have needed to rely on unofficial sources, because the club had denied themselves the opportunity to provide me with the information they'd like me to use. Quite simply, Liverpool FC never sought, in those days, to seek to engage with media or publicity outlets on anything like the scale of other clubs. I'm sure this brought about benefits, allowing the likes of Bob Paisley and Kenny Dalglish to maintain a very useful level of in-house secrecy that yielded rewards on the pitch. But then to complain of a lack of publicity smacked of double standards and only served to encourage further feelings of victim syndrome among their support.

Such issues are touched on by Alan Edge, in his *Faith Of Our Fathers*, one of the most entertaining books among those written by fans in the wake of Nick Hornby's *Fever Pitch*; so entertaining, indeed, that the fact that it's about his devotion to Liverpool FC didn't put me off enjoying it one bit. However, even the generally well-balanced Edge can't shoo the monkey off his back when it comes to feeling that his club received a raw deal from the media and the outside world in general. He devotes two whole pages to his rage at the portrayal of Tommy Smith and the allegation that he 'couldn't play' from an unidentified Arsenal fan (presumably Hornby), even going so far as to label the viewpoint 'heretical'. [1] I'm not even going to get into a discussion about whether he's right with what would appear to me the somewhat dubious claim that Smith's grace bore comparison with a ballerina (!), except to note that Bill Shankly himself hardly spoke in these terms about the man in question, preferring rather to emphasise his toughness and the uncompromising reputation of 'The Anfield Iron' in the tackle. Presumably Shankly chose to place this emphasis on his player for the purpose of putting the willies up the opposition. This was, indeed, shrewdly judged hyperbole from one of the game's masters. If the rest of us swallow whole the image presented by Liverpool FC, their manager and largely the player himself, how can that be anyone else's fault? Shankly was, as usual, emphasising what would serve the purpose of his club on the pitch and I suspect he would have viewed the resulting stereotype to be have been further grist to the mill. Unlike his successor Paisley, this was a man who certainly did play the media game, and did so very well.

And yet, in terms of using the power of the media to benefit their club, Shankly and Paisley weren't as far apart as might be presumed. If, and it's a big if, Liverpool got less attention from the media in the Paisley and post-Paisley era, this was only the result of a highly sophisticated control of information that would have given Alastair Campbell wet dreams. Not only did they manage to keep high profile transfers under wraps until the last moment in a way that the pre-Ferguson United could never dream of, they also generally managed to keep any off-field tomfoolery away from the front or back pages too. Of course, the squeaky clean image procured via this strategy also managed to convince their own fans that all representatives of Liverpool FC actually *were* squeaky clean, a fiercely protected fallacy which largely holds to this day. If you believe that there are simply no negative details in existence to be kept from the public then your assumption will, inevitably, be that all the media are actually doing are keeping still more glorious information about your club from being known. Of course, the nurse who was pissed on by Terry McDermott may beg to differ.

United under Atkinson failed, indeed barely even tried, to attain any such control over the media, but that's not to say we'd always had the kind of open door policy that traded off our image in the way our Liverpool FC cousins claimed as an incontrovertible truth of footballing life. While Busby was, in his own way, a bit of a charmer when it came to dealing with the press in the fifties, that was a more innocent time generally and one where gentlemen's agreements with reporters who rode on the team bus still meant something. [3] However, this practice was effectively ditched by the club after Munich and, by the end of the sixties, its spirit was long gone. Tommy Doc and Ron Atkinson, of course, were pretty media-friendly as managers go, but generally speaking this had a detrimental effect on United's image. Although the Doc was, by common consent, a master of the press conference, tantalisingly dangling titbits in front of eager journalists who would then go away with the kind of stories other managers would never dream of letting them loose on, this inadvertently led to a whole series of embarrassing media-induced scenarios for the club from the leaking of Denis Law's free transfer (which an astonished Law witnessed on the telly) right through to the Doc's selling of his story about his affair with Mary Brown that led to his sacking. Atkinson pissed off a whole bunch of United players by inviting a film crew on board the Wembley coach for the 1983 cup final, only realising at the last minute that there wasn't room for all the players and meaning a number of them (led by a fuming Martin Buchan) had to drive down on their own. This can't have helped team spirit or preparation and some have suggested it might explain United's rather lacklustre performance in the draw with Brighton. I can't say whether this is true or not, but it's safe to say that it can't have helped. While Dave Sexton was entirely the opposite, equally, he lacked the skill of his Liverpool counterparts in controlling the information stream to the benefit of his club and his lack of comfort in any dealings with the media was obvious.

If United's image as a glamour club has historically grated at Anfield, I'll simply leave it to some of their own to explain perhaps where it comes from. In 1975-76, United won the Fair Play League – something we picked up regularly back then – after astonishingly only receiving ten bookings throughout the whole season. Bill Shankly presented us with the award with glowing comments about United's style of play and the breath of fresh air we brought to the game.[4] Add that to other comments from honest Liverpudlians through the ages, such as John Gidman, for example, who once stood on the Kop but relayed to his wife the news that he'd signed for United with the words that he'd signed for the biggest club in the world. [5] Similarly, Peter Schmeichel claims it was his compatriot Jan Molby who urged him to sign for us, saying he informed him that, despite Liverpool's many years of success, United were the biggest team in English football. And, as if Michael Owen's switch of allegiance enough wasn't a hard enough pill to swallow for Liverpool fans, the fact that he used every opportunity to lavish glowing praise on his new club, if also perhaps to appease sceptical United fans, rubbed salt into already very raw wounds. I suspect what irks Liverpool fans most in all of this is that, stripped of the political need to pretend otherwise, even their own players and fans understand very well the unique appeal of United and their status in the game.

It's hard to imagine hardcore United fans caring about the way the rest of the world think about us in that way. No doubt Vidic can be said to be able to 'play a bit', but we love and enthusiastically sing about his uncompromising hardness so it's difficult to see anyone at United objecting about his portrayal as a hard man in the way that Edge got so indignant about the Smith stereotype. We relished it when Cantona was demonised, first by Leeds fans and then by pretty much everybody else, because it just made him more one of us. Ditto Roy Keane and his on-pitch excesses in the tackle; it's laughable for anyone to suggest that Keane couldn't play, but it didn't stop them. Let 'em. Tommy Docherty's alleged failings as a human being garnered far more media attention than did his skills as a manager – one of the few in the game to take a team from relegation through to borderline champions – but do we care? These people were United; what the rest of the world thinks of them is neither here nor there. What I've never understand about Liverpool fans is quite why they care what anyone outside their own club thinks about them or their players. It's as if their own devotion is so insecure they crave confirmation of it from everyone else in the football world. As a football fan, surely one of the first things you learn is that no one outside your club will ever understand or feel the way you do about your team. United fans, I think, not only understand this but revel in it, while Liverpool supporters never seem able to come to terms with this elementary fact of footballing life.

It's more understandable that Edge rails against some of the callous and disgraceful slurs against his fellow fans that were put about following the Hillsborough tragedy, specifically the 'Private Grief, Public Circus' article in the London Evening Standard, to which Edge responds scathingly.[6] I wouldn't disagree with a single word he writes in this attack.. It's unfortunate that he and so many Liverpool fans I meet treat these revolting examples of the gutter press at its worst as somehow representative of media presentation of the club in general. This couldn't be further from the truth, with Liverpool FC enjoying years of positive acclaim and sanitised myth-making, highlighting their many achievements and, in direct contrast to some of the writing on Hillsborough, parading an image of humble honesty and good nature enshrined by Shankly and then bequeathed to the club's fans as something they didn't have to work at all to earn and which was clearly far from accurate. [7] Greeny told me how visiting fans who naively accepted this portrayal of his club were viewed as easy prey by the thousands of Anfield boot boys who happily concealed themselves behind this helpful media-induced charade.

Edge unfortunately buries his well-judged and laudable comments on Hillsborough in a tide of self-pitying slush when the words Manchester United are mentioned , claiming, without offering any evidence, that a large proportion of the media are Manchester United supporters. [8] While hardly as malicious, such claims are just as poorly thought out as those of the Sun, Star and Evening Standard journalists who wrote such irresponsible mush about Hillsborough. Apart from the simplistic tendency to talk of 'the meejah' as if it's one homogenous body, the idea that the BBC and ITV, employing for years pundits with a Liverpool background, either with the club or the city (I cite Alan Hansen, Mark Lawrenson, Ray Stubbs, Graham Beacroft, Elton Welsby, Jim Beglin and Alan Parry as merely a few prominent representatives), ignored his club's successes is preposterous. Daily Mirror football writer Frank McGhee was often held up by Liverpool fans as a paradigm case of a sports writer completely biased towards Manchester United. I've never doubted the contention that McGhee was a United fan, but his works include a scathing attack on the club in 1981 following the transfer of Joe Jordan to AC Milan, within which he lambasted the club's dependency on big money transfers and said they'd deserved what they'd got when being forced to let Jordan go for a cut-price fee and one notorious lambasting of the image of Bobby Charlton.[9]

These are only two examples, but you can guarantee that, had McGhee's words been about, say, Dalglish, the Liverpool FC self-pity mafia would have been out in force, neglecting in their fury the simple truth that what happens to them is only what happens to everyone else and any kind of bias or favouritism is merely in the eye of the jaundiced beholder. Not that it deserves any such serious scrutiny, but if the media was so full of Manchester United supporters you'd assume this would have some effect on football writers' player of the year awards. Unlike Liverpool, no United player has ever received the award chosen by journalists other than when we've won the league or European Cup. No United player won it during the fifties, despite our three league titles and not even in the wake of the Munich tragedy was the opportunity seized by journalists to award it posthumously to one of the universally mourned babes. Instead, it went to Danny Blanchflower. It wasn't until our third premiership title that a United player – Cantona – won the prize for the first time in 28 years. Remarkably, in the year that we won the treble, the award went to David Ginola, like Blanchflower a Spurs player ,whose entire stash of honours in English football consists of a single League Cup winners' medal.

Indeed, despite the fact that the last time they won the league The Beatles were still living off cornflakes and trying to eke out a living with odd gigs at the Cavern, Spurs players have been selected by journalists for the award on six occasions in total; although United have won the Premiership on twelve occasions, only five times has a United player been selected for the award during that period, which is less than Arsenal, whose players have won it six times. If there's anything to be drawn from all this, it's perhaps that a London-based media inevitably tends to go for London-based players rather more than might seem warranted. Almost half of the winners of the last forty years played for London clubs, despite the fact that clubs in the capital only won the league eight times during that time. Anyway, whatever the reasons for all this, it's certainly hard to tie it in with the image Edge creatively weaves, which has what used to be called Fleet Street decked in United bunting and its hacks with a load of sharpened pencils at the ready, intending to put Bryan Robson's name on their nomination form but somehow misspelling and coming up with Steve Perryman instead.

That Edge, for all his merits as a writer, completely misunderstands the issues at stake when it comes to United and Liverpool, is emphasised at his railing at a single United fan (Jim

White, though he isn't named) for naming his book *Are You Watching Liverpool?*. Of course he did. Newsflash: in case Liverpool fans were too busy whining to miss it, you were top dogs in those days. Of course the focus was on you and us getting ahead of you. A back-handed compliment if ever there was one. Anyone at the United end bothered by the *Man United Ruined My Life* book title? Thought not.

It also can't seriously be ignored by any thinking human being how much time press, TV and radio all gave to covering violent incidents involving United fans in the seventies or how they fed off the off-field and on-field foibles of Best, Cantona, Giggs and Rooney to rake over their own malignant depictions of footballing celebrity or that the sexual activities of Dwight Yorke suddenly became of little interest to the press after he left United. It's not an issue here of what's true and what isn't, simply that agencies of the media will do whatever they can to gain maximum readership, listening or viewing figures, and that means that hyperbole, whether of a negative or positive shade, will be a feature of this kind of lowest common denominator reporting. What no body of fans can hope for is that agencies of the media will reflect our own feelings for our clubs, because that's special to us. It seems to me United fans in general have a more realistic angle on this and therefore, when we were on the verge of the treble and the News Of The World instead opted to go instead with a story that we 'topped the league of shame' as a result of Dwight Yorke's nocturnal activities, we turned our back on it and just kept celebrating.

Football fans in general, and certainly supporters at Anfield, tend to have a fairly superficial awareness of what the media are up to anyway. Much of United's coverage, even in our less successful periods, expressed great pleasure in watching the acknowledged glamour club of the game falling on its arse, often, as still happens today, manufacturing sensationalised transfer targets with the aim of showing that, by the end of the saga, United had missed out again, or alternatively feting successful signings (Garry Birtles, Alan Brazil, Terry Gibson etc) only to rub their hands with glee when they turned out to be 'failures'. It's true that the English press lavished enormous praise on Bryan Robson, but this was always in the context of his role as England captain, mirroring similar attitudes since to the likes of Alan Shearer and John Terry, and was more of a precursor to their post-1998 courting of David Beckham in his England and celebrity guises than anything to do with any affection for our club. And they always missed the point anyway when it came to truly understanding what was so special about Robbo.

Attitudes to football are generally underpinned by what the celebrated Paul Kahmenan has developed the useful term 'System One Thinking' to describe. Basically, Kahneman gives the name 'System Two Thinking' to the human capacity to absorb a number of facts, amass a collection of evidence, and come to a conclusion. It's something, notes Kahneman, that requires a large amount of effort and is something that humans can only go so far in doing before mental exhaustion sets in. And yet, he says, we mistakenly believe that this type of rationality is the hallmark of most human thinking, when in fact it's something we do only rarely. Instead, he notes, far more of our judgements are formed by our System One capacities: reactive, spontaneous judgements based not on evidence at all but on the kind of instantaneous reactions human beings are psychologically programmed to make. These can be on the level of innate behaviour, but more commonly are on the level of a learned experience, for example seeing a red light on a traffic light and immediately beginning to suppress the brake, or being given a set of facts about a person and immediately building a mental picture of what that person is like. Our conclusions, as in the latter case, may be incorrect and may even be subsequently corrected, but that doesn't stop us being psychologically impelled to make them.[10]

Footballing rivalry, it seems barely necessary to point out, essentially involves System One thinking. It may be supported by certain facts and sets of evidence but ultimately its responses are instantaneously reactive. If a team I don't like gets a dodgy penalty decision, my System Two Thinking may be applied in retrospect to weigh it up and understand that, in the wider scheme of things, these things happen and it's not the result of any favourable decision making on the referee's part. Yet in the instant the decision is made it takes quite an effort of psychological will not to react with outrage, our System One reaction kicking in immediately and running rampant. For some people, it runs rampant in a completely unchecked manner. For others, we can apply some subsequent logic to it and bring it under control. But our initial reaction is fundamentally the same.

With regard to the issues discussed above, the claim by Liverpool fans that their hatred of United is based on their media image is a pure example of System One thinking that they then refuse to rationalise and instead employ all evidence in the service of backing up the prejudiced opinion. This is certainly not unique to Liverpool supporters – Andy Mitten's excellent book *Mad For It* has an excellent article on the Chester/Wrexham rivalry that illustrates how far the latter will go in terms of insisting that their hatred for their English neighbours is entirely justified by socio-economic factors [11] and it's a characteristic you'll find among some supporters of whatever ilk. I do think, however, that Liverpool FC have rather institutionalised the reaction so that the myth has become established as one that has tribal significance for them – there is almost a belief that to be a true supporter of Liverpool Football Club you must buy into this idea and regard it as both credible and factual, when of course it's nothing of the sort, and that anyone who fails to go along with it somehow can't claim to be a true supporter of Liverpool FC.

It was entirely accurate to describe the late seventies and early eighties Liverpool outfit as a well-honed machine, efficient, well-prepared and professional to the point of dullness. It often pissed Liverpool supporters off that they were rarely described as having the flair of United, or as the Newcastle side of the mid-nineties (trophy count – nil) or Arsene Wenger's Arsenal would be. But the Dalglish team of the late eighties were different. At times they were breath-taking and, much as I spent every match I saw on telly desperately wanting them to lose, sometimes you just had to hold your hands up. Never before had I seen a side so utterly and consistently dominate games with a passing game that wouldn't have shamed the Brazil side of 1970 or the Holland team of 1974. Let the record state that the Liverpool team of this period were brilliant. No arguments.

This period marked the beginning of the end of the club's dominance. We couldn't have dared anticipate it at the time. When Alex Ferguson arrived at United in 1986, he seemed just the latest in a succession of managerial appointments to appear on the surface to have the pedigree to sort things out but who, bitter experience told us, wouldn't upset the footballing order to any significant degree. Now, of course, we can see the rooting out of the club's drinking culture and renewed emphasis on self-discipline, hard work and training, whereas then it just looked like unsophisticated management techniques were resulting in, among other things, the senseless and acrimonious departure of crowd favourites like McGrath and Whiteside. Now, we can see the policy of introducing players with higher standards of professionalism (the teetotaller Viv Anderson, for example, or the cultured, intelligent McClair) when at the time it just looked like the usual combination of ordinary, mediocre buys and players who'd done well at other clubs but surely weren't anything better than what we already had, and worse than those we were getting rid of. Now, we see Ferguson's uncompromising stance accompanied by a willingness to accept and dismiss the bad publicity that was the inevitable result of his upheavals – then, we just saw the articles published under the names of McGrath and Graeme Hogg and accusations that he didn't know what he was doing and, given our recent history, could be forgiven for believing them.

And we saw Liverpool forging onwards and everything turning to gold under Dalglish. He bought mediocre players like Kevin McDonald, Mike Robinson, Jimmy Carter and David Speedie, and yet they still seemed to keep winning; whereas we now understand that such uninformed signings were symptoms of Dalglish veering dangerously from the club's well-established and successful transfer policy. We saw the signing of Glenn Hysen from under the noses of United as another example of players going to Anfield rather than us in the way the mercurial John Barnes, one of the prime architects of that fabulous Dalglish side, had; when in truth this turned out to be one of a number of a series of hapless centre back signings that would become a major debilitating factor for the club. We celebrated their defeat in the FA Cup Final by Wimbledon and, dramatically, in the last game of the league season by Arsenal as scraps from a table from which all too few scraps fell. They were, we suspected, memorable but fleeting events that posterity would record in the same manner as our defeat of them in the FA Cup Final of 1977, brief interruptions of an onwards march rather than symptoms of the end of the empire. Hindsight is a wonderful thing, and in this case even more wonderful, but at the time we could only pray that our hopes were more than the vain flickers of optimism we secretly assumed them to be.

Yet through it all, despite the scintillating artistry of that last great Liverpool side, the Kop were growing ever quieter. The roaring terrace of the sixties and seventies had been replaced by a nervy, embittered atmosphere that, again, began to seem more obsessed with United than with their own team. It wasn't just the appalling Munich chants and banners; it was also this gradually descending heavy, loaded quietness, as if the whole spirit of the club had stopped generating the aura it had created over more than a decade. Liverpool fans stopped creating their original Kop anthems as they had always done in the past, when the stealing of other fans' chants had been a complete no-go area; the Kop ceased to be this seething, passionate mass that almost seemed to suck the ball towards its goal. It now seemed more likely to suck in and swallow its own false teeth in its state of permanent indignation. Like my Rainhill friend had implied, it was almost as if they'd forgotten how to enjoy themselves, or as if they didn't even like enjoying themselves, masochistically gorging themselves instead on the self-generated conception of a world unfairly dominated by Manchester United. Little did they know how close they were to this nightmare vision transforming into reality.

The ultimate self-generated indignity – and a shame they didn't even appear to notice – occurred as a result of the emergence of a successful Everton side in the mid-eighties. Everton should have been seen as a threat to Anfield's dominance, consisting as their impressive haul did of two championships, an FA Cup and a Cup Winners Cup during one three year period. Logic would certainly have dictated this, given the reaction among Liverpool fans to Everton's League Cup final appearance in 1977; Liverpool supporters began referring to the competition routinely as 'the Mickey Mouse cup' following Everton's impudent stab at a moment in the big time, only to reverse their response to it when they reached the final themselves a year later (a loss to Nottingham Forest, after which Phil Thompson brought the euphemistic phrase 'professional foul' into the footballing vocabulary, an example of how Liverpool's footballing pragmatism could even elevate tripping a player on the edge of the area to the level of professional sophistication should it serve the interests of their own club) and then won it four times in succession in the early eighties, the last a victory against Everton, the first of three such Wembley encounters during which it became ritualistic for supporters to celebrate the ascendancy of both Merseyside clubs, at least at Anfield. As Everton began to emerge as a serious rival on more important fronts, this co-opted celebration and mood of victory by proxy grew as Liverpool fans somehow managed to take the credit for their ancient rivals' successes by claiming it was really all about victory for Merseyside. Contrast this with Manchester Council's misguided plans to host a joint celebration in 1999 for both United's treble winners and city's jubilant side from the, er, second division play-offs. When it became apparent that a Merseyside-like mood of mutual celebration and civic self-congratulation didn't pervade the city and that the rest was going to be acrimonious chaos, the plans were wisely dropped.

Though it has since become clear – if it was ever in doubt - that the vast majority of Everton fans don't feel anything like as warmly towards their neighbours, and indeed Liverpool fans themselves quickly ceased to find their incestuous affair attractive when first Everton, then they themselves, stopped bringing the trophies home to their love nest, the time was marked by a mainly Anfield-inspired tendency to declare Merseyside footballing dominance particularly for the benefit of 'the Mancs' at the other end of the East Lancs Road. During this time city were pretty much ignored and the phrase 'Mancs' was used to refer almost exclusively to Manchester United. Though our rivals nowadays indulge themselves with the self-delusion that United fans live only outside the metropolis that overshadows them to the east, it was generally proclaimed by Liverpool fans in those days that the idea that United were really big enough to have fans *outside* Manchester was part of the media-inspired mythology attached to our club. As part of the cult-like drive to attempt to get me to join the accumulated hordes of Liverpool fans at school, and indeed long after that time, I was informed with absolute conviction that United were really a small team with no history whatsoever, any claims to significance only inflated by a fawning media. No one knew United outside England, I was told. The idea that foreign nationals used the words 'Bobby Charlton' as a kind of universal greeting was a piece of media-devised nonsense, they squeaked in protest. Foreigners knew Liverpool, and only Liverpool, because Liverpool were the only truly successful and important team in England, they protested shrilly. When I pointed to the heaving attendances at Old Trafford week after week, they told me they were fabricated, their apparent bulk reinforced by generous camera angles from a complicit Match of the Day. It was Liverpool, they insisted, who had fans all over the world, the only English club big and famous enough to do so: United were a small club with an inflated reputation based on nothing but lies. Thus was the spurious logic that penetrated the playground and continued to prevail well into my early adulthood as the Merseyside clubs seemed to be moving inexorably to a shared trophy room and United, unfortunately, increasingly gave the impression of not even needing one.

Liverpool fans did not, at that time, walk completely alone. It was Everton-supporting Radio Merseyside/Radio City DJ Billy Butler who led the charge in the local media, rounding up his audience in wholesale displays of paranoia that both reinforced feelings of persecution among the locals and gave the above mythology the backing of Merseyside-perpetrated conventional wisdom. Butler's central stance in those times was, as far as I could make out, not based on a commercially-motivated desire to drag in extra audience numbers, but something that stemmed purely from an utterly unreasoned bias. Amazingly, the unintended effect of his prejudice was to demean the achievements of his beloved Everton. A period of history that should by all rights be recorded as one of the most glorious for Evertonians was instead locally labelled a 'Merseyside dominance' period that allowed Liverpool fans to take unwarranted credit for their blue neighbours' successes.

On one memorable occasion Butler suffered from his failure to get his research done when inviting John Motson onto his show to face his barrage of questions related to the pro-Manchester United bias that, as he saw it, any right-thinking person would know Motson held. I'm no great fan of Motson but, in any argument based on football facts, he's a pretty formidable adversary, and Butler's confidence was quickly crushed. His opening salvo, during which he accused Motson of the heinous crime of labelling Manchester United 'the most famous club in the world' was quickly and easily despatched by the former BBC commentator. 'Well it's just a fact,' he pointed out, 'that Manchester United have more supporters clubs around the world than any other club.' Butler, who clearly had no answer to this, sought refuge in a series of further lame accusations. Faced not, on this occasion, with a similarly biased footie fan on the other end of a Radio Merseyside phone, his envy-raddled and unsubstantiated twaddle was completely demolished by a comfortably informed and completely unruffled Motson. Butler's endearing Liverpool-supporting sidekick Wally Scott kept wheezing with laughter – 'he's got you there Bill! He's got an answer for everything, this fella!' It was actually pretty good radio; not that it could ever hope to put into reverse Butler's anti-United stance.

To be fair, the aforementioned Wally Scott, while a ready foil for the Butler ravings, rarely joined in with any passion, and came across largely as a committed Liverpool fan but one without any trace of envy or malice anywhere in his make-up; and it would in any case be ludicrous to suggest that all Merseysiders shared such beliefs. Indeed, one of the unfortunate results of Butler's rants was to give the impression to the outside world that scousers really were all this unreasonable and paranoid, just as his weekly Sunday morning show 'Hold Yer Plums' routinely featured a load of phone call participants just too dim to be real, parading as entertainment the dangerous stereotype that Merseysiders really were that thick. Had fellow scouser Elton Welsby or anyone else dabbled in this sort of thing in a Wednesday night footie show, you can guarantee he'd have been hauled across the coals by an affronted Butler the following morning.

But the attitude clearly resonated with a whole load of Liverpudlians, recalling the local ire at the Manchester Ship Canal going up around a hundred years earlier and similarly fruitless attempts to stop it, not through reasoned argument, but through self-serving finger-pointing, falsehoods and ridicule. The DJ – and he wasn't anything like alone in this – simply saw Everton, and, at the time, to an extent Tranmere, becoming successful as a means of proclaiming the dominance of Merseyside in the wake of the perceived threat from Manchester, this time in the shape of a supposed media bias towards United that was uncritically accepted by his audience. Like the Ship Canal, what was really ushered in was a steady decline in Merseyside fortunes. Tranmere Rovers would make the First Division (formerly the Second Division) play-offs in three consecutive seasons before returning home to the lower leagues. Everton, a club with historical wealth and support levels that were by now equally largely buried in history, have declined on both these fronts and only won one trophy since securing the league in 1987, when they beat us in the FA Cup in 1995. Liverpool have won intermittent trophies in that period, but have never come close to recapturing their glory years and have still not won the league since 1990.

Which was, of course, the year in which Alex Ferguson won his first trophy for Manchester United.

[1] Edge, A. *Faith of our Fathers,* p193

[2] http://www.lfchistory.net/Articles/Article/853

[3] Dewhurst, K. op cit pp 12-13

[4] Egan, S. op cit p340

[5] Mitten, A. *We're The Famous Man Utd*, p131

[6] Edge, A. op cit, pp196-197

[7] Hill, D. op cit, p107

[8] Edge, A. op cit, p216

[9] McKinstry, L. op cit, p285

[10] Khaneman, D. *Thinking Fast and Slow*, pp21-26

[11] Mitten, A. *Mad For It*, pp154-155

Chapter Twelve: I Am The Resurrection

Old Trafford, 1 January 1989. Manchester United 3 Liverpool 1

'There was only one good bit of football in the whole game and that was Liverpool's goal' said Brian.

In fact, the goal of which he spoke, which involved a simple pass from Beardsley finding Barnes, who scored after a slight stumble, doesn't stand out at all, and came very much against the run of play against a United side who were under strength and included some kids barely out of the youth team. These were the real Fergie's Fledglings, a name which has since been attached to the famous class of 92/93 but actually referred originally to a group of young players who were their forerunners, and of whom none ultimately made the grade at United with the exception of Lee Sharpe, who wasn't a genuine United prodigy anyway, having been procured from Torquay United at seventeen. Barnes' goal put Liverpool in front after 70 minutes, but there was still time for these young lads, led by the admirable Russell Beardsmore, who looked every inch a star of the future in that game, to respond in style.

The kid set up McClair for our equaliser. Another youngster, Mark Robins (who would go on to achieve semi-legendary status for allegedly saving Ferguson's job with his goal at Forest twelve months later) was involved in the build-up for the second, executed with characteristic ferocity by Mark Hughes. Fittingly, it was Beardsmore who got the third following a cross from Sharpe.

'Great passing football played at pace,' was my verdict.

'A hundred miles an hour rubbish,' said Brian.

It seemed foolish to make too much out of it. At the end of this season United would finish in 11th place, one place below Millwall and, although in retrospect some of the pieces of a great team had fallen into place – Sharpe, McClair, the returning Hughes – many of them were still clearly the wrong size and belonged to a different jigsaw or, in the case of Ralph Milne playing, just needed to be thrown in the bin. I've long argued, whenever anyone takes up the seasoned mantra about Robins saving Ferguson's job that following season, that the real mystery was why the manager wasn't sacked in summer '89. We were, after all, in a far worse state than in the final seasons of either Atkinson or Sexton. And the size of our crowds had, admittedly in a bad time generally for football attendances, reached a post-war low and even allowed Liverpool, for a couple of seasons anyway, to lay claim to the title of England's best supported team.

Characteristically for United, looking back on it, it might have gone either way – enormous success or apocalyptic disaster. Ultimately, Beardsmore and Robins (and even Sharpe, eventually) didn't fulfil their early promise and 1988-89 generally felt like a series of false dawns. You can criticise them now for their lack of faith, but those lads who raised the 'tara Fergie' banner back then were voicing the thoughts of the vast majority of supporters. The board, to their credit, weren't prepared to listen. Had they taken the axe to Fergie that summer, we'd be looking back now on a reign so disastrous it dwarfed the follies of Atkinson and Sexton and United might, even now, be searching for the key to that magic locker wherein lay domestic and European success.

Perhaps in the end it was performances like the above that made the difference. It certainly made a difference in the league title race that season because, had we not come back so strongly after losing that late goal, Arsenal's heroics on the last day of the season might well have been seen as no more than the flogging of a horse so dead it had maggots crawling around in it: as it turned out, the maggots all had red shirts on with 'Candy' across the front.

Revolutions never happen overnight. Like the slow march of political progress in the wake of Peterloo, they are the result of an accumulation of events over years, decades even, and it's impossible to identify with any certainty the precise source of the momentum, the point where that momentum became unstoppable and even when the revolution was complete. In retrospect, however, we can identify key events that gave the revolution its shape. Such is the case of the transference of the balance of power between Manchester United and Liverpool that transformed my life and the lives of so many others; a transformation our memories might recall as almost an overnight affair but which really revealed itself gradually over a period as long as nine years.

Although we didn't realise it, it was happening even as Billy Butler rounded up the troops in the perceived battle against the great United-obsessed media. He even played a small and indirect part in it, rapturously receive Everton's capture of Norman Whiteside from United in 1989. United fans of the time viewed it ominously as another hero following McGrath and Strachan out of the club. In retrospect it was the soon to become familiar stamp of a manager who was prepared to do whatever it took, however difficult and unpopular, to ensure the revolution was both successful and non-reversible.

Liverpool supporters weren't even aware the end was close, and indeed many are still in denial now. How many of them, when they won the league in 1990, could have predicted that over two decades later they would still be waiting for the next one? And how many Manchester United fans could have dared hope that twenty-one years later we would have secured our nineteenth title, to become officially the most successful domestic side of all time, when as recently as 1990 the tally stood Liverpool 18 United 7? None, I suspect. Take Alan Edge's word for it, who wrote confidently even as late as 1997 about the unlikely prospect of United even coming close to the successful legacy of Liverpool. [1] No longer unlikely; and, as early as 1991, no longer successful.

In retrospect, for Liverpool the peak was 13 April 1988 where no less a judge than an awestruck Tom Finney pronounced their 5-0 demolition of a strong Nottingham Forest side the greatest footballing performance he'd ever seen. That night I was at Telford United's ground, watching Runcorn FC losing their only game of their fine run-in that season, following left-back Peter Densmore's sending-off and the strange search for Steve Nelson's boot initiated by Ken McKenna picking it up when it came off in the penalty area and depositing it in the centre circle while a bemused Nelson looked around for it in the goalmouth. I had a limited word count to work within, but such an incident had to go into the report. After writing it for the sports editor to pick up the next morning I watched the highlights of the Liverpool game and it was hard to disagree with Finney. 'Liverpool are better than Brazil now,' Brian told me. 'If it wasn't for the Europe ban we'd be doing that to teams in European Cup finals every year,' another Liverpool supporter scoffed.

But Liverpool never again reached such heights. It's incredible to reflect on just how quickly the decline set in following that Forest match. Just over a year later, on 15 April 1989, they again lined up against Forest at Hillsborough for an FA Cup Semi-Final and it was this game, rather than the former, that, sadly, could be said to have changed English football forever. Although he would hang on for almost another two years, Kenny Dalglish would spend much of the early months of that period attending funerals and seeing football matches put into perspective like never before. Unlike the departure of previous Liverpool managers, this one came out of the blue and there was no succession plan, which seems perverse for, at the time, this most well-organised of all football clubs. The club's board surely would have seen the immense emotional pressure on Dalglish and you'd have thought they might have been better prepared for his resignation. After all, Shankly's retirement had not exactly come with plenty of notice and they managed that seamlessly enough. But they weren't.

By the time Dalglish resigned as Liverpool boss, in the same academic year during which the Berlin Wall came down and Thatcher was forced out of office, I was living in Liverpool. I'd started a degree in English Literature and Communication Studies there just as the Madchester music phenomenon was beginning to swarm out from Manchester, going global in no time at all and in the process drawing in my home town of Widnes as a willing satellite. Even aside from its musical merits, Madchester was an interesting phenomenon. Generally speaking, homogenous 'scenes' are for Liverpool and its more compact city centre, while important musical entities from East Lancashire tend to operate as highly proficient rogue snipers whose influence is of a scale that belies their initial isolation. Yet it can scarcely be disputed that Madchester, however mythologised, existed as a definitive scene. Its two major players – Happy Mondays and Stone Roses – knew each other well and knowingly inhabited common musical ground and, despite Tony Wilson's claims that the former (signed to his Factory label) changed music while the latter didn't, the very significant changes that came about were unquestionably to a large degree a joint effort. A flurry of bands formed under the influence of these protagonists, including very good ones like New Fast Automatic Daffodils and Paris Angels as well as a host of lesser imitators, and other, older bands were absorbed as forefathers without any artistic or style concessions, among them New Order and James, the latter of whom appeared musically to have very little to do with much of it but who happened at that time to be crafting communal anthems like 'Come Home' and 'Sit Down' that captured its spirit perfectly.

It was while running one of my weekly music nights at the Derby Arms in Widnes that the guitarist from Runcorn band The Nice Party came in to say that he'd seen The Stone Roses and that what he'd seen was life-changing, that after this the music he made and that everyone made was going to change, had to change. It seemed somewhat hyperbolic to put it mildly, but he wasn't wrong. The Roses would soon bring their runaway train of a bandwagon to Widnes but, by that point, with the 24 hour party going on every day in Manchester, I wasn't around. Predictably, on the mean streets of Liverpool One, responses to the phenomenon and the national prominence of Manchester music – easily the biggest provincial scene since Merseybeat - were anything but warm. 'Are you frum fuccccggghhhing Manchester, lah?' the teenage skinhead who lived around the corner asked me.

I refused to humour him with a straight answer. 'What do you reckon?'

'Yerzzzz all sound the fucccccccccgggggghhhhhing same ter me, lah,' came his response. It was a dangerous time to possess any kind of Lancastrian accent in Liverpool. Those of us at the university who came from designated 'woolyback' territories and our Mancunian and Salfordian brethren inevitably stood out in this most insular of all cities; we were carrying the double stereotype of student and, however inaccurately, Manc, and thus experienced conflict that ranged from the inhospitable to the downright antagonistic. Most of it was mundane and fairly non-threatening. 'There ye go, yer twat,' the guy on the door to the Mardi Gras – at the time Liverpool's foremost club for the indie set – would routinely say when taking the money from anyone with the wrong sort of accent, and at pubs like The Vines you'd always have to wait to get served until the scouse clientele had got their noses into the bucket first. Whilst it's fair to point out that other pubs and venues were far more welcoming (the excellent Kavanagh's on the edge of Toxteth, The Swan and the Cracke, as well as the Planet X and Pink Parrot clubs) while others were safe enough (McMillans), frequent looks over your shoulder were always advisable.

One day, I sat in a state of high intoxication in The Flying Picket with a fellow student called Jo, from Salford, as well as Graham, whose Canadian drawl and the fact that by then he'd been working among the kids in Toxteth for a couple of years tended to keep him out of danger. The idea of us sitting there in a pub full of scousers, especially with Jo's broad Salfordian accent, just got funnier and funnier as we got drunker and drunker, and at one point a bunch of really hard-looking scouse blokes at the next table gave us a really tough collective stare.

'What are you looking at?' I said, not in a confrontational way. In fact, given the amount I'd had to drink, it probably came out more like, 'sppllgyyyyyooouhhhgh'.

'You,' a scouse skinhead built like a brick shithouse among them said. 'I'm fugggghinning lookin' at you, lahhh.'

Given the state I was in, the only response I had in my locker was to laugh uncontrollably and I start shouting 'It's the Mersey mafia! What did Tom O'Connor do with the bodies? What happened to Ray Clemence's finger nails?' and other inanities. I can now think of a million things I might have said that would have amounted to more devastating repartee but I'm afraid at the time that was the best I could manage.

Fortunately, they seemed to regard us, unsurprisingly, as morons rather than potential adversaries but we decided it was a good time to leave anyway. Not being especially handy I was looking to make a quick move to the other end of the town centre but Graham found a girl sitting down being sick on the pavement outside and insisted on checking she was OK, claiming she was 'the mother of my children'. Anyway, no one followed. Probably lucky we were in the brotherly socialist arms of The Flying Picket and not The Vines or one of the many city centre clubs we'd never have been seen dead in whatever the atmosphere at the time. A popular tactic among scouse drug dealers in the wrong sort of pub or club back then was to target anyone with even a vaguely Mancunian accent as a potential Ecstasy dealer and physically prevent them from leaving their seat, to venture to bar, bog or anywhere else. One of them would position himself close by and push down on the shoulder. 'Sit down, fer fuck's sake. Yer've gorran arse, aven't yer? Sit on it.' And there they'd stay, until the often innocent lad at the wrong end of their attentions pissed himself or worse.

Despite this, there were many of Greater Manchester origin perfectly willing to stick their necks out. Gibby, a 'Mancunian' from Stockport walked around pretty much everywhere with his floppy city hat on and organised coach trips to the Hacienda, the buzzing centre of the Madchester scene, and of everywhere else. He personified the party-going Manchester vibe of the time. When the Berlin Wall came down, he jumped on a bus to the airport while the rest of us were heading to lectures and disappeared for several days with the words, 'Must be a 'ell of a party goin' on there. I'm 'avin' some of it.' He returned several days later un-chastened by a forceful rebuke from his personal tutor who responded to his impertinence by refusing to have him back in his group. Another tutor was more liberal in his attitude over Gibby's 'disappearance'. 'Ah, he has an interesting social life,' he remarked with a smile.

The worst feature of life at Liverpool University were by far the mock-Scousers who made pilgrimages to Anfield a part of the student lifestyle and donned their pretend accents in a ludicrous attempt to fit in. They were the sort of middle class students parodied by Pulp in 'Common People' a few years down the line. It's something that, if you're from a working class background and at a major university, you can scarcely fail to notice – the number of posh bastards who think putting on a regional accent and pretending to be impoverished, many of them living in local properties 'bought' by family members with the aim of selling them on at a profit a few years later, is cool. Instead, I took the opportunity myself on a few occasions to visit the less salubrious environs of South Liverpool FC who played in the Northern Premier League in front of gates of no more than a few hundred and whose Holly Park ground was regularly trashed by locals to the extent that, in the end, they were forced to close down. That legendary scouse community spirit, eh? No one remarked on my accent there. I think they were happy to get fans in wherever they came from. But if anyone was more likely to get a pasting even than those of us of Lancastrian extraction, it was those posh twats who loved to sit under the giant portrait of George Orwell in the Cambridge and talk in mock-scouse accents that they found hilarious when it was evident none of the locals did.

Meanwhile, back in Manchester, in spite of the looming gangster problems that would one day sound the death knell for the Hacienda and other clubs, Madchester was signalling a distinct change in youth cultural attitudes, away from the violent subcultures that had permeated football grounds since the late sixties, and towards partying, fun and positive highs. While the media and the authorities fretted about the debilitating social impact of Ecstasy, the acid house revolution and its Mancunian incubator, few were, at the time, prepared to admit that a general peace-loving vibe among young people was a welcome side-effect. In football, long before all-seater stadia would emerge to take the credit for it, incidents of terrace violence had become far less frequent. [2] While it didn't stop Liverpool fans tipping cups of piss on the heads of United fans in the Anfield Road end, the chance of a repeat of some of the animosity that accompanied Ron Atkinson and his team's visits to the ground seemed increasingly unlikely, even though to Liverpudlians the rise of Madchester had been about as welcome as an Ecstasy tab in your kid's tube of Smarties.

Footballing and musical culture had rarely seemed so intimately related. It was as if all of those Mancunian cultural influences spearheaded by Buzzcocks, Joy Division/New Order, The Smiths and others all came together, interbred, in some cases re-assembled themselves and emerged as one great big all-inclusive party spirit that made it all right to dance, go to the game without the prospect of getting the shit kicked clean out of you and also, if you wished, made it equally OK just to go off on your own and do your own thing. And if those bedroom loners wanted to change all that, they could just drop an E and attain for themselves a ticket to the self-selected elite of the 24 Hour Party People. The spirit of Manchester night life quickly infused the entire nation and not long afterwards began to intrude on other cultural fronts also.

Football needed it an infusion of these vibes just as much, and perhaps more, than the rest of society. It was the Madchester vibe, long before Gazza's tears, that began to drag football out of the hangover of its post-Hillsborough bad trip. One day in the summer of 1990, I made sure I finished an exam early so that I could get over to Graham's place on Upper Parliament Street (in an area that, almost a decade later, still bore the scars of the Toxteth riots) for the start of the Cameroon v Argentina World Cup match. After it, we headed into Liverpool City Centre. It was a night of varied pleasures, taking in the opulence of the Philharmonic pub, the art students' stronghold of Ye Olde Cracke, the backstreet biker's den that was The Swan and then on to a night of pissed-up silly dancing and the possibility of a sub-gothic snog to the great sounds of Planet X. Remarkably, in every pub or club we entered – regardless of its particular ambience or clientele – we heard New Order's 'World In Motion' blaring out either from DJ deck, jukebox or tape behind the bar, its new footballing message that footballing allegiances were OK but there was room for brotherly love too encompassing what, only a few years earlier, had seemed an impossibly wide demographic. E is for England, proclaimed New

Order, and they put their finger right on the pulse: one nation under the Manchester-inspired groove.

That football became drawn into this spirit so quickly is no accident: perverse as it may sound, football hooliganism is one of its key antecedents. The Madchester hordes were direct descendants of the Perrys of the football terraces, or Scallies in the Liverpudlian vernacular; it was just that, as the fashions came together, they'd dropped their penchant for mass violence in favour of narcotics and hedonism. [3] It's the only time in my memory that city regalia has become remotely fashionable, with many ravers adopting it as a style accessory of choice, including those with no interest in football whatsoever. Of course, being city there was a complete failure to recognise the opportunity this gave their club on the eve of sales of football merchandise taking off big time, and it was United, as always, who were alert enough to reap the rewards of Manchester becoming the country's youth culture capital. The Stone Roses, United fans to a man, were highly proficient voices of the new nation and, despite the record label problems that bedevilled their every move in subsequent years preventing them from capitalising on it, at one stage they looked more likely than anyone since The Beatles to permeate all levels of British culture. The Melody Maker saw them as nothing less than figureheads for a new pop religion and noted the germinating influence of their background on the United terraces in bringing this about: the heroes of this new movement needed to have a secure footing in both cultural worlds in order to be true standard bearers, it seemed, and the Roses were it. [4] Although Wilson's point that the Mondays changed music and the Roses didn't is understood – it was the Mondays who more effectively incorporated dance music grooves and the new hedonism into their sounds and live performances, which came to have more of an atmosphere of a rave, while the Roses remained anchored in a traditional band format - it looked for a time that the latter may go even further and change the whole damn civilized world.

As I moved away from Widnes, well-meaning amateurs like me lost our grip on the town's music promotions (the regular clientele for my music nights was pretty much made up of A Level students anyway, the bulk of whom left to pursue their own university adventures at the same time), for a time yielding to an unproductive spell presided over by a professional promoter from Salford and then a bloody brilliant and transformational link-up with Manchester International which saw some major players take the stage at Widnes' now demolished Queens Hall. I found myself making regular visits back to my home town as the new religion's trinity of Stone Roses, Happy Mondays and Inspiral Carpets, along with other great bands of the time, performed at the venue. In fact I recall walking down to the place one pleasant summer evening to see the Roses and just getting in on the door; within months they were selling out in no time at all every venue they performed at. The Roses then played their legendary gig at Spike Island. There can be few better examples of the commonality that exists between Mancunian and what passes for Widnesian culture than this event. References to this gig rarely mention that Spike Island is in the West Bank area of Widnes. Most appear to assume that it exists somewhere much further east up the M62, though they're not exactly sure where; even Dave Haslam can only hazard that it's 'near' Widnes. [5] It's also another example of how fluent and far-reaching the perceived Manchester borders are, particularly so in comparison with the entrenched Liverpudlian boundaries I experienced, so rigid that even a female student from Bootle had her obvious affinity with the place, not to mention an accent that should have given her no trouble whatsoever getting served at The Vines, regularly questioned.

The influx of Mancunian celebrities into the town was a challenge the Widnes hard men weren't going to pass up. It's rumoured that one day the Mondays were recording at Pentagon Studios – close the Queens Hall – and they nipped into The Sun Inn for a pint. The pub has long since closed, revived as an Irish bar of dubious authenticity, but then it was a distinctly scabby fleapit of a Widnes boozer whose only feature of note was a better than average jukebox. The Mondays sat down at one of the pub's rickety circular tables with their pints, only for a regular of the pub to march over, accuse Shaun Ryder in time-honoured fashion of 'thinking he was hard', call him a 'soft twat', pick up the entire table loaded with drinks and take it over to the other side of the room, where he and his mates got stuck into the spoils.

Despite this, even in a filthy post-industrial backwater like Widnes the staple of violence that was the legacy of the seventies was fading from working class street life as fast as Mark IV Ford Cortinas. It wasn't unusual in those days to be walking the mean streets of Ditton or the town centre and find three snarling lads coming the other way, knowing it was 50-50 that something would kick off. One day in 1990, I was walking alone through the austere surroundings of Derwent Road and saw two particularly mean-looking bastards walking towards me. The worst thing you could do in such a scenario was cross the road – the urban equivalent of pulling out of a tackle, and just as likely to get you a nasty injury – so the only thing for it was to carry on in a straight line, hope you didn't have to dodge round them and try not to look too much of a tit. As I approached them, however, it became apparent that the bigger of the two was hell-bent on walking full-on towards me. As he approached it struck me how thugs like him were wearing more colourful attire these days and that he had those impossibly wide baggy jeans on, things that no one would have been seen dead in even a year ago but were now the height of style, along with, even more remarkably, the occasional poncho or even kaftan. As we made to collide and I braced myself for the consequences, he suddenly pulled out his hand in a 'shake' gesture, gave me a sincere clasp and advised me to 'Give a little love back to the world,' after which he walked on, humming to himself.. I didn't know whether I was more surprised by the failure of violence to ensue, or the fact that he'd just announced the title of the UK's Eurovision Song Contest entry in broad daylight.

It represented a deep move in working class culture away from a violence that had always been so much a part of my immediate surroundings, sparked by drugs and music as Ecstasy scare stories littered the press and yet another folk devil emerged to scare conservative British society, but one that seemed able to take on all the others and win, purely through a universal spirit of Ed Sanders-like passive resistance that emerged so quickly that no one – not the hooligans, nor the omnipresent smellies nor those who (like me, I admit) had never had any truck with so-called dance music in the past – had any time to resist it. What quickly became clear was that the drug of choice for the new love generation was far less inclined to result in someone punching your lights out than was my own favourite, alcohol. Something that began in Manchester inevitably wasn't going to stay there. Another chapter of the city's vibrant legacy was being written in front of my eyes. Stone Roses fans would chant 'Manchester, nah nah nah' at gigs whether they came from the city or not. And the Manc standard-bearers were very clued up about the outward-looking heritage they represented. I was there when Ian Brown gave his 'it's not where you're from, it's where you're at' response to the chanting Mancunians (if they *were* Mancunians – I'm sure I saw some Widnes kids joining in) in the front rows. Brown says this remark was made at the famous Spike Island gig [6] and it may well have been, but I'm sure he also said it at the earlier Widnes Queens Hall gig because I was there, along with a whole new generation of kids from my area who were discovering new and deep connections with Mancunian culture.

With both Spike Island and the International link-up, Manchester had stretched its tentacles across to West Lancashire in a way that Merseyside – with even its 'woolyback' mentality weakening in the face of the inclusive vibes emanating out of the east Lancashire metropolis – had always found it alien to its cultural identity to do. 'Madchester', characteristically, easily absorbed those from the fringes of the Greater Manchester conurbation. Inspiral Carpets, a band from Oldham, never saw the Manchester scene as anything other than home. The Charlatans, a band fronted by a Mancophile from Northwich, were keenly embraced as one of their own by Mancunians. [7]

It's only with hindsight that you can tie all of this in with the decline of Liverpool and the re-birth of Manchester United under Ferguson, although it's a temptingly neat fit. Yet, during the emerging Anfield crisis that, as yet, still wasn't even apparent, other clubs do deserve a mention, particularly Arsenal who, under George Graham, emerged as genuine rivals to Liverpool in the period. And, for a time, we appreciated them for it because, for a time, that's all we had. I've never celebrated a goal that wasn't scored by a Manchester United player with the voracity with which I greeted Michael Thomas's winner for Arsenal at Anfield to steal the league, famously, at the culmination of the 1989 season, and I'm sure I'm not alone. And nor were Arsenal alone in providing moments to savour, however indirectly. it wasn't until Schmeichel's last minute penalty save from Bergkamp in 1999 that I found anything that usurped my delight at Dave Beasant's when the so-called Crazy Gang defeated the so-called Culture Club (well, they played like 11 Boy Georges that day anyway. Wound up by a media-created pantomime villain like Vinnie Jones? For shame) in the cup; another event that indicated a growing weakness in the Liverpool make-up, were we able to see it.

I'd bet Brian before the Arsenal game that they'd do it, more out of bravado than anything else, if I'm honest. Adding to the entertainment was the case of Brian's mate from Wrexham who'd convinced himself, with the kind of conspiracy mentality only a Liverpool supporter could embrace, that the entire media and the FA had got it wrong and that Arsenal had to win by four goals, not two, to pip them because he knew there was a four-goal deficit to make up and couldn't do the maths. I imagine him in the Kop that day, waving his scarf around his head at the end and wondering why it was only the Arsenal fans joining in.

When Liverpool faced Crystal Palace in the FA Cup semi-final on 8 April 1990, pretty much everyone expected them to win easily and set up a tasty final against United, who'd been negotiating tricky away matches all the way through the competition and for the most part scraping through. As we waited for our own semi-final to kick off that day, the big doubt was whether we'd get past the mighty Oldham Athletic to secure our first visit to Wembley for five years. There was no doubt, surely, that Liverpool would be waiting for us there. On the night of Liverpool's win in the quarter-final, I'd foolishly mistimed my journey to the halls of residence from the White Star in the city centre to find myself on a bus full of Liverpool fans in high spirits, merrily anticipating a tie against a Crystal Palace side they'd already demolished 9-0 earlier that season.

Amazingly, and memorably, it didn't work out that way. Liverpool's defence were all over the shop as Palace kept refusing to be killed off, exposing the lack of comfort of the centre backs and eventually running out 4-3 winners. I couldn't believe it. 'They've not replaced Hansen,' I began to pronounce over and over to myself in astonishment. After all the years of seeing top Liverpool players bugger off only to be successfully and seamlessly replaced (Keegan, Toshack, Clemence, McDermott, Souness...all gone, and none apparently missed, as others as good or better filled their shorts, in a manner of speaking), suddenly the almost impossible seemed possible – that Liverpool's scouting network that had for years mined so much gold in the lower leagues and other backwaters (Hansen, Rush, Whelan, Nicol, Neal and so many more) had suddenly broken down. It looked like the first sign of a truly decisive turning point. But I stilled my beating heart, bewitched as it had been by so many false dawns.

It had been with just such caution that I'd approached an article in the University of Liverpool student magazine earlier that year, in which a female amateur journalist whose name I forget, but whose words will linger until I'm lowered into my cold, cold grave, predicted that Liverpool, although on the way to winning the league yet again, would become a spent force in the next few years. Heard it all before, I grumbled, as I read about how Dalglish was altering the fabric of the club to an extent that would inevitably lead to its decline, how the famous scouting network was being senselessly ripped apart, the boot room no longer the successful war office it had always been, how the youth set-up was now pretty much non-existent and how those shrewd transfers were a thing of the past. That game against Palace gave the first indication that she may just have a point. The signings of Jimmy Carter and David Speedie the following season, when Arsenal cantered to another league title despite having a couple of points deducted for perhaps the greatest of all 21-man brawls, against us (it's *always* 21 men who are involved. Never 22, or twenty), having only been defeated once in the league all season, seemed strangely ill-judged for a club with Liverpool's hitherto faultless transfer market efficacy. Pleasantly, it was Ian Woan, who'd been the best player I ever saw playing for Runcorn and had subsequently been signed by Brian Clough for Nottingham Forest, who scored the goal against Liverpool that assured Arsenal of the title, just three years and a bit on from that famous Finney-lauded performance against the same club.

And, as Liverpool began to falter, something even more unbelievable was beginning to happen. In November 1990, I watched open-mouthed alongside a flatulent Accrington Stanley fan in the TV room at Rankin Hall of Residence at the university as United beat that fine Arsenal side 6-2 in the League Cup; and this at a time when all clubs still fielded their strongest sides in the competition. I watched as Sharpe got another and another while the Accrington fan stank and sweated his way through a bag of boiled sweets, his hair and face drenched and rank. But the unpleasant stench next to me couldn't detract from my enjoyment of what I was witnessing on the screen. We'd seen great one-off performances before, but I knew this was something different. Something was going on, something unfamiliar and brilliantly intoxicating. And when, at the end of that season, Mark Hughes scored from an impossible angle to clinch victory against Barcelona and bring back the European Cup-Winners' Cup, again, I experienced feelings unlike anything I'd known before. 'Want some of this to celebrate?' my pungent co-viewer for the Arsenal game offered, pulling out a bag of something from his pocket. 'Tried MBS? It is some serious shit.' Whether this was a literal description of its contents or, as I assumed, a reference to its narcotic potency, I didn't know but I declined his offer. Then Sharpe got his hat trick and I began to allow myself to dare to dream, no other stimulation required.

And yet the revolution, while increasingly being televised, was nowhere near complete. At the time I still couldn't even say whether it *was* a revolution, or a mere respite from Liverpool's winning ways before a new manager came in for them and steadied them back on course. But when their former captain Graeme Souness returned and took up the reins, breaking with the conveyer belt efficiency of internal succession after it had served them so well over four managers, pretty much everyone saw the edifice coming down and the foundations being ripped up with it. Souness is now saddled with the reputation of destroying the club's carefully established traditions but, as my amateur journalist colleague foresaw, they were already well on the way to being demolished before he returned. Such is the veneration of Dalglish among Liverpool supporters, they can't bear to accept this truth and so Souness is loaded with a reputation he only partly deserves (he finished off the job pretty spectacularly, after all).

And we can apportion some of the blame, or in our case gratitude, higher up in the Anfield echelons, because the same board that failed to spot Dalglish's imminent departure also failed to see that bringing in an outsider (Souness' recent successes at Rangers notwithstanding) would hardly put right what had so emphatically been torn asunder. That they should eventually turn to Roy 'no one outside Merseyside remembers how great we were' Evans (who did as much as anyone to give his paranoid assumptions credence) smacked of a feeble and unsuccessful attempt to re-establish the long fractured line of succession. As that truly great scouser (actually educated in Widnes) Alan Bleasdale put it in *Boys From The Blackstuff*, 'Once you've broken something, you can't break it again.'

[1] Edge, A. op cit p218
[2] Kurt, R. *United We Stand*, p16
[3] Robb, J., *The North Will Rise Again*, p263
[4] Robb, J., *The Stone Roses*, p3
[5] Haslam, D. op cit, p254
[6] Robb, J., *The North Will Rise Again*, p311
[7] Robb, J., ibid, pp337-338

Chapter Thirteen: Hallelujah

Of course it wasn't universally accepted at the time that Liverpool *were* broken. When we experienced our all-time low of giving up the title to, let's face it, a pretty run of the mill Leeds United side in 1992 at Anfield, Liverpool fans still behaved as if they were somehow in the ascendancy, as if watching us fail to achieve our holy grail didn't just make up for their own ailing prospects, it managed to render them inadmissible. They would, it's true, go on to win the FA Cup that season, but I would remember for many years, with a grin as wide as the East Lancs Road, the comments of Liverpool fans at the end of that miserable campaign. 'United are an alehouse side who will never win the league,' I read one letter writer scoffing in my mum and dad's Liverpool Daily Post, and the mantra 'you'll never win the league' was repeated to me over and over that summer. Having grown so familiar with disappointment over the years I was, I have to confess, worried that they might be right. One FA Cup, followed by a European trophy when we'd finished half a dozen places down the league, followed by a near miss on the championship. Why shouldn't it now just go back to normal?

It's predictable to cite the signing of Cantona the following Autumn as the turning point: I'm going to ask you to take me at my word that I saw the writing on the wall the second I heard about this most momentous transfer in Manchester United history. It felt right; completely out of the blue but completely right. I'd witnessed his hat trick in the Charity Shield that August, admired his dominant display up front against Stuttgart in Europe and it was clear the guy was class. It never once occurred to me he might one day end up wearing the red, white and black. The day he did, I sat up into the small hours drinking Canadian whisky with a fellow United supporter called Roger in his house in, of all places, Liverpool, listening to Tom Waits records, both of us pissed out of our skulls but agreeing, with utter conviction, that Cantona was the final piece we needed. We'd win it.

Winning the league in 1993 changed more than just the whole path of history for Manchester United. It also, eventually, brought about a change in attitudes to us, and certainly to me as a Manchester United fan living too close to Liverpool (I'd moved back to Widnes after getting a teaching job at my old college on completion of my degree). I say eventually because it wasn't that winning the league on that one occasion suddenly changed everything. The year we won it was also the year of my third and last visit to Wembley to watch Runcorn be well beaten by Woking in the FA Trophy final. I was doing a weekly show at that point for the Halton FM community radio station. My weekly show was called *The Diamond Mine* and went out on a Wednesday night, offering a mix of irreverent banter and edgy music, the first show of the station's more adventurous evening programming which meant that those who had stayed a little too long after the conservative fare on offer in the afternoons and 'drivetime' frequently sent in complaints at their ears suddenly being assaulted by the likes of Blood Sausage, Jawbreaker and Bikini Kill. But on this occasion I was assigned the task of phoning in a match report from Wembley Stadium. I steered clear of much of the grumbling from my fellow supporters (the usual stuff about the referee being biased and not getting any luck, accompanied by the interesting observation by one ageing woman that 'the pitch should've had a squeegee on it at half-time – it wer too fuckin' wet fer us') and offered instead the more balanced view that Runcorn were beaten by the better side, had a lot of the play, true, but only because we were chasing the game. Everyone there was gutted, I pointed out. One of the lads doing the afternoon show in the studio – their mixture of Nirvana, The Lemonheads and Pearl Jam about as left-field as any of our afternoon schedules got, and therefore not the place you'd normally stick a football report (perhaps fittingly, we interrupted 'Lithium') – said, 'yeah, we're pretty gutted too,' and then he and his co-presenter audibly fell about, guffawing with laughter.

It was during my regular Wednesday night show that news filtered in of rather more pleasing developments. I'd been kicking myself that I'd allowed myself to be shoved into the Wednesday evening slot when I'd much rather have been watching football-related events unfolding in the alehouse across the road. We had to observe a strict schedule to allow a two minute news broadcast to come in on the hour and I listened in with rather more keenness than was customary to one of those broadcasts that, on Wednesday 21 April, announced the news that United had beaten Crystal Palace 2-0 away while Villa, our closest challengers that year, had been walloped 3-0 at Blackburn. Posterity has me sitting doing my show at the time the news was broadcast, whooping with delight and proceeding to do the last hour in victorious mood, but actually I know I was already aware that Villa were 3-0 down at half-time while we were at 0-0, which already had me in a good mood before I found out the even better news in the final scores, which came through not long after my show had finished.

On the coach journey home from Wembley, my mate Brian (a different Brian, and one of those unusual characters who appeared to support Runcorn and absolutely no one else, and nor was he anti-United) shared out two types of yellow and green (Runcorn's colours) cake – one labelled 'safe' which he happily dispatched to the older supporters on the bus and one labelled 'dangerous' which had strange bits in it and was restricted to circulation among his closer social circle - offered some reflections on United's recent victorious premiership campaign. It would be a one-off, he declared. Villa were an improving side who would come back stronger next season. Blackburn had money to spend and they'd be up there challenging too. And of course Liverpool's recent decline was really just a brief hiatus before they came back as powerfully as ever. It might well be, he said, without any of the animosity of our rivals and in unusually laid-back tones (presumably something to do with the cake), that we'd have to wait another 26 years until the next one.

Such observations were by no means unusual at the time. In fact, only the comments on Blackburn's imminent though thankfully temporary rise would prove to have a semblance of truth as a Cantona-inspired United romped to the double in 1994. This side would rightly come to be regarded by United fans as one of the best ever, yet at the time it was still regarded by many Liverpool, and occasionally Everton, supporters I knew as something of an irritating blip in the normal order of things. When Alan Hansen made his infamous 'you win nothing with kids' remark at the beginning of the 1995/96 season, there was a context to these remarks that often gets forgotten now. The conventional wisdom outside United's fan base at that point had it that United had had their time in the sun, that Blackburn had come along to out-spend us, were currently in the process of overtaking us and that the miserable displays in Europe confirmed that these United sides were not anywhere near as good as the English sides who'd dominated the European Cup before the ban kicked in. Cantona had never stayed anywhere long and therefore, it was presumed, was bound to bugger off at some point in the near future and without him United were nothing, as the failure to win the league in 1994/95 during his lengthy suspension had shown, not to mention the feeble display in the FA Cup final that had seen us beaten by a stubborn but essentially ordinary Everton side. And it was taken as read that Ferguson wasn't capable of building a side in the long-term that could bring about any sustained dominance of the game, hence Hansen's smug comfort that there was no chance in hell that a side containing such unfamiliar names as Butt, Scholes and G. Neville could ever bring about such a thing.

History has pretty much erased these perspectives from our consciousness, or at least rendered them laughable, but remember that Hansen's comments were made after a close season during which we sold Paul Ince (then regarded by almost everyone whose view counted as the best midfielder in the country and possibly Europe), the legendary Mark Hughes and the searing talent that was Andrei Kanchelskis, and signed no one. In those days there were no Glaziers to blame for keeping an over-zealous grip on the purse strings, so all of this just compounded the view among rival supporters that Ferguson was showing his true, pre-1990 colours and the whole thing was falling apart: players like this wouldn't be allowed to go unless there were some major problems and dissatisfaction within the camp, or perhaps their success had gone to their heads and they were demanding the kind of wages United, having fallen behind Blackburn, weren't in a position to cough up. The future was Jack Walker's and the whole experience of seeing a Manchester United side regularly winning trophies would shortly pass away like so many bad nightmares and a new order would establish itself, led by Dalglish at the helm at Blackburn and therefore – by proxy – Liverpool inspired. Sadly, even a number of United fans appeared to agree. In a Manchester Evening News survey that summer, a majority of those who responded said that Ferguson should go. Even allowing for the fact that the survey was almost certainly contaminated by mischievous, pissed off city fans, many among us clearly subscribed to the general perception that United were now embarking on a period of decline.

So when Hansen made those remarks, they weren't considered anything like as rash or provocative as they've been classed in retrospect. Indeed, the former Liverpool captain no doubt felt he was on safe ground, and certainly that he had the weight of public opinion on his side. No one outside Ferguson and his coaching team could really have known what a hell of a crop of players was graduating from the youth set up at that point. Later we'd know all about Beckham, Scholes and Gary Neville, with a fine supporting cast that included his brother Phil and Nicky Butt joining the already lauded Giggs, but then only those United fans who kept a close eye on the youth and reserve sides had any inkling of what was to come, and even precious few of them would have been hard put to predict the legends that were in the process of being created. After all, hadn't the emergent Fergie's Fledglings now fled the nest and migrated to lower climes? Why should this promising bunch be any different?

Even though he would have known very well what he had coming through, there are few (and perhaps no) managers who would have done what Alex Ferguson did and pressed ahead with his plans without leaving a safety net/public relations sap of buying in a few more experienced players to allow him some sort of Plan B if his reliance on youth failed. This kind of advanced perception and skilled risk taking is a characteristic of great managers, but a characteristic all too rare among managers in football. Understandably afraid of making decisions that might cost them their jobs, many managers play it safe in such situations. Constantly in the glare of a media who know sod all about football and pronounce their views with the untainted convictions of the ignorant, few football managers have enough about them to fly in the face of the received wisdom of those who, unlike the managers themselves, are free to make whatever judgements they like and not be required to answer for them later.

All of which went into the pot in the pivotal 1995-96 season, and much else too. It was United's fascinating overhaul of the 12 point lead Newcastle held on New Year's Day 1996, that confirmed we were here to stay and that a true dynasty of success really was being established. We also got to be reviled by other clubs on a hitherto unknown scale (we were always kind of disliked anyway, but this was cranked up to new levels of hysteria and whingeing) and, with a spirit true to Manchester and to United, established among ourselves that we didn't much care about any of that. It was a watershed year in many ways, but most of all in our everyday lives as United fans because it brought to full fruition that mood of constant opposition that ever since has been part of the life of every true red. We didn't take the Liverpool way and start squawking about how the world didn't understand us; we revelled in our isolation. The sense of never walking alone that the Kop had proclaimed since the early days of Shankly's dynasty says much about their club, the insecurities of their fans and their psychological needs. United rejected all that just like we rejected the anthem back in '58. United walk alone, and we're happy to do so.

Liverpool weren't in the mix anymore and Blackburn were fading fast: another standard-bearer for the ABUs was required. Step forward Kevin Keegan, manager of a Newcastle United side that played admittedly good football, and of a club who, while somehow clinging to a sepia-tinged view of themselves as a big club, had not won a trophy since 1969. Their Achilles heel? 'The Messiah' himself. Keegan had been a hugely successful player in the seventies and eighties, firstly for Liverpool and later for Hamburg and then, um, Southampton and Newcastle, and had a frequent and annoying tendency to express utter loyalty to whatever cause he was involved with before suddenly deciding to bugger off somewhere else. Nonetheless, he'd been England's top player for years, talked with the enthusiasm of a fan and sought and gained popularity in the media via the simple mechanism of saying the kind of things he knew people wanted to hear. All of which endeared him to the kind of people who'd enjoyed the performances of Eddie the Eagle. And of course Newcastle, very recently in the second tier of English football and only just clinging on before rising to the top of the Premiership almost overnight, endeared themselves to those in the game who most of all wanted to see the really big clubs (United) getting a bloody nose.

But there was a problem in all this, one waiting to leap on Keegan and his squad in the early months of 1996. The people who held these kinds of opinions were 'build you up, knock you down' types led by a tabloid press who were only too willing to kick over the statues they'd created in pursuit of another good story. So inevitably, when Newcastle endured the kind of temporary bad spell that all clubs have at some point during a season, the press began to hype up the prospect of them blowing it. They knew their readers and, however much delight there was among them at this upstart club playing great footie and preventing the mighty Manchester United from winning the league, they weren't going to sacrifice the considerable levels of satisfaction they always gained at the thought of someone else's glorious expectations going down the pan. In the same situation Ferguson would shrug his shoulders, wind the media up some more and get on with the business of winning trophies. Keegan, though, needed to be loved and now it seemed his every move was being presented as a further banana skin en route to falling arse over tit completely. The anxieties of those who'd been relying on Newcastle to put one over on United were starting to cause friction in the relationship. And the recipient of a love who relies essentially on a very thin and insecure thread of trust to sustain him is likely to feel the strain when times become more testing.

Thus, the signing of the precociously talented Faustino Asprilla, while a textbook move to strengthen the late season squad in the days before the introduction of transfer windows, was seized on as a desperation signing by Keegan. In the days before large squads and rotation became fashionable, suggestions were voiced that he didn't think his current squad was good enough to see the through the task in hand. Rumours about Asprilla's personal life were added into the mix by a tabloid press for whom such a tactic was second nature and, without the protection from the media that a Ferguson figure would have offered, it was almost inevitable that such over the top targeting of the player by crowds of tabloid reporters at every move to and from a football ground would affect his game. Which it duly did. Keegan was put into that quandary that Fergusons's bloody-mindedness would always keep him aloof from: if he left Asprilla in the side his under-performance would inevitably be blamed for Newcastle's poor form; if he left him out he was, in the eyes of the media, admitting he'd been wrong. And where Ferguson would simply have made the decision and damned their eyes, Keegan's courting of the media left him exposed to their suddenly unwanted attentions.

These were highly significant times. For Keegan, read Atkinson's failure to pull the title out of the bag for United in the early eighties. Both men suffered from a high media profile and a revealing tendency to call their players by nicknames or first names (defending Asprilla, Keegan repeatedly referred to him as 'Tino'), as if unable to assert their authority or even want to, as if in awe of simply being in the presence of eleven daft lads who could play a bit. Keegan's failure did more than just present United with an opportunity to win the league we shouldn't have had. The case of Keegan and the pressure exerted by Ferguson's side also illuminated how far United had come since the Atkinson days, and suddenly put the fear of God into those who'd been kidding themselves that our recent period of superiority would shortly come to an end.

As United closed in on the title that year, you could see Keegan crumbling a bit more in every interview, it becoming more and more inevitable that this would nurture still more fear in his panicking team; and so the enthralling drama unfolded, sparked by the tragic flaw in Keegan's management: a self-defeating desire to be loved. Ferguson, it was now evident to anyone who had doubted it, lacked any such needs, driven instead by a simple desire for footballing glory. Much has been made of Keegan losing his head in front of the Sky Sports cameras, and much has been said about Ferguson pushing his psychological advantage to inspire those remarks. Ferguson, in his autobiography, is adamant that, while he has frequently played mind games with other managers, this wasn't his intention on this occasion, and I believe him. [1] The truth is he didn't need to do it – Keegan and Newcastle were already falling apart. I'm willing to believe, as I did at the time, that his remarks about Leeds, following their impressive resistance in the game against United in the run-in, were as much about his much publicised subsequent concerns about how one of his closest managerial friends was being treated. Howard Wilkinson was already vilified by the embittered Leeds faithful for letting us have Cantona so easily, and Ferguson's comment along the lines of, 'they're cheating their manager...we'll see if they play like that against Newcastle,' I still take to be more of a reflection on how an ailing Leeds had suddenly raised their game against their rivals and showed what they could do for Wilkinson if they really put their minds to it. While I'm happy to give Ferguson much credit for his management of United and particularly the rigours of that premiership run-in, I think some people regard every move of his as strictly calculated and devious and credit him with an almost supernatural psychological control over events. And I think Ferguson is more than happy for them to think that, because even when he makes a mistake the media pick it apart and look for some sign of a plan in it. Even during what Gary Neville has labelled the Djemba-Djemba years [2], you still felt some people were asking, 'what's he *really* up to?'

I watched the final game away to Middlesborough in the Tut & Shive pub in Warrington. It remains, for me, the most memorable of all our premiership wins, the icing on the cake provided by defeat for city at Liverpool on the same day, sending them down. But sweet too for the manner of its achievement, and the fact that it so firmly announced we were here to stay. The pub was packed with United fans (and two Liverpool fans wearing Newcastle tops, who were pretty decent guys for all that and added to the atmosphere, even shaking the hands of every United fan as we left the boozer at the end). As the end of the match neared, one guy ripped a Newcastle Brown poster from the wall, put it up against one of the telly screens and shouted, 'Suck on that, you fat Geordie bastards'. By that point I was completely shitfaced and I remember saying to my mate Carl as we emerged into the early evening Warrington sunlight that I owned all of this, embracing with lifted arms the town centre from the top of the hill, the rich pastures of Greater Manchester to the east and the former badlands to the west a heaven and hell now firmly in their rightful places.

[1] Ferguson, A., *Managing My Life,* pp373-374
[2] Neville, G., *Red*, p214

Bibliography

Books

Andrews, D.L.(ed) (2004) *Manchester United: A Thematic Study* Routledge

Aristotle (1955) *Ethics* Penguin Classics

Ayer, A.J. (1956) *The Problem Of Knowledge* Penguin

Belton, B. (2009) *Red Dawn* Pennant Books

Blundell, J. (2006) *Back From The Brink* Empire Publications

Brown, A. & Walsh, A. (1999) *Not For Sale: Manchester United, Murdoch and the Defeat of BSkyB* Mainstream

Burke, T, (1910) *Catholic History of Liverpool* C. Tinling Accessed at: http://archive.org/stream/catholichistoryo00burkuoft/catholichisto ryo00burkuoft_djvu.txt

Burn, G. (2006) *Best & Edwards* Faber & Faber

Burns, J. (1996) *Maradona: The Hand of God* Bloomsbury

Burns, J. (2009), *Barca*, Bloomsbury

Bush, M.L. (2005) *The Casualties of Peterloo* Carnegie Publishing

Charlton, Sir B. (2007), *The Autobiography – My Manchester United Years* Headline

Collin, M. (1997) *Altered State: The Story of Ecstasy Culture and Acid House* Serpent's Tail

Conn, D. (1997) *The Football Business* Mainstream

Conn, D. (2005) *The Beautiful Game?* Yellow Jersey Press

Crick, M. & Smith, D. (1989) *Manchester United: The Betrayal of a Legend* Pelham Books

Crosby, A. (2000) *The Lancashire Dictionary of Dialect, Tradition & Folklore* Smith Settle

Curtis, D. (1995) *Touching From A Distance* Faber & Faber

Dewhurst, K. (2009) *When You Put On A Red Shirt* Vintage

Dunphy, E. (2007) *A Strange Kind of Glory* Aurum

Edge, A. (1997) *Faith Of Our Fathers* Two Heads

Egan, S. (2010) *The Doc's Devils: Manchester United 1972-1977* Cherry Red Books

Ferguson, A, (1999) *Managing My Life* Hodder & Stoughton

Foot, P. (1990) Introduction, *Shelley's Revolutionary Year* Redwords

Glanville, B. (ed) (1986) *The Joy of Football* Todder & Houghton

Hill, D. (2001) *Out Of His Skin* When Saturday Comes

Hill, T. (1999) *The Kids Are United* Gollancz

Hornby, N. (1992) *Fever Pitch* Gollancz

Kent, N. (2010) *Apathy For The Devil* Faber & Faber

Kahneman, D. (2011), *Thinking Fast and Slow* Penguin

Klein, N. (2001) *No Logo* Flamingo

Klein, N. (2007) *The Shock Doctrine* Penguin

Kurt, R. (1998) *Red Devils: A History of Man. United's Rogues and Villains* Prion

Kurt, R. (1994) *United We Stood* Sigma Leisure

Lichtenstein, C. & Shregenberger, T. (2001) *As Found: The Discovery of the Ordinary,* Springer

Martel, Y.(2004) *The Facts Behind the Helsinki Roccamatios* BCA

Middles, M. (2002) *From Joy Division To New Order: The True Story of Anthony H. Wilson & Factory Records* Virgin Books

Milton, J. (2003) *Paradise Lost* Penguin Classics

Mitten, A. (2008) *Mad For It* Harper Sport

Mitten, A. (2011) *We're The Famous Man Utd* Vision Sports

Muir, R. (1907), *History of Liverpool* Williams & Northgate

Neville, G. (2011) *Red: My Autobiography* Bantam Press

Poole, R. (2002) *The Lancashire Witches: Histories and Stories,* Manchester University Press

Robb, J. (2001) *The Stone Roses* Random House

Robb, J. (2009) *The North Will Rise Again: Manchester Music City: 1977-1996* Aurum

Salewicz, C. (2006) *Redemption Song: The Definitive Biography Of Joe Strummer* Harper Collins

Sudbury, J. (1998) *Other Kinds of Dreams: black women's organisations and the politics of transformation* Routledge

White, J.(2008) *Manchester United: The Biography* Sphere

Wilson, J. (2009) *Inverting The Pyramid: The History of Football Tactics* Orion
Worrall, F. (2007) *Celtic United* Mainstream

Other Publications

Brown, A. (2002) *Do You Come From Manchester?* Manchester University Press
Daily Telegraph
The Guardian
Labour History Review
Liverpool Echo
Manchester Evening News
National Fan Survey – Summary Report 2007/08
Red Issue
Red News
United We Stand

Websites/pages/blogs

Includes sites used for research purposes plus a selection of useful and informative United sites and blogs.

http://a-kick-in-the-grass.blogspot.co.uk
http://alfiesantics.wordpress.com
http://www.bbc.co.uk
http://www.blogunited.co.uk
http://www.chartists.net
http://epltalk.com
http://www.knowhere.co.uk/St-Helens/Merseyside/Northern-England
http://thekop.liverpoolfc.tv
http://www.liverpoolfc.com

http://www.manchesterunited-mad.co.uk
http://manutd24.co.uk
http://www.manutd-blog.com
http://manutdfootballblog.co.uk
http://www.manunitedonly.com
http://www.merseyreporter.com
http://oldtraffordfaithful.com
http://radicalmanchester.wordpress.com
http://redflagflyinghigh.com
http://redrants.com
http://redmancunian.com
http://stretford-end.com
http://stretfordendarising.com
http://strettynews.com
http://thebusbybabe.com
http://thebusbyway.com
http://www.toffeeweb.com
http://thechriswhitingshow.wordpress.com
http://thefaithfulmufc.com
http://therepublikofmancunia.com
http://www.theunitedreligon.com
http://www.trulyreds.com
http://www.writtenoffside.com

Selected Manchester/Salford Discography 1977-1990

What follows is not an exhaustive list of all music that came out of Manchester and Salford during the period between punk and Alex Ferguson's first trophy with United, because you could probably fill a book with that all on its own. What I've attempted is to include as many notable releases during the period as I can think of, and even that means leaving out several important releases from The Fall and The Smiths, for example. The assumption is that you can check out more releases by the bands listed if you wish, and a quick internet search should be enough to track down pretty much every band/artist listed below.

1977
Alberto Y Los Trios Paranoias – *Snuff Rock* 7" EP (Stiff)
Alberto Y Los Trios Paranoias – *Italians From Outer Space* LP (Transatlantic)
Buzzcocks – *Spiral Scratch* 7" EP (New Hormones)
Buzzcocks – *Orgasm Addict*, 7" single (United Artists)
The Nosebleeds – *Ain't Bin To No Music School* 7" single (Rabid)
Slaughter & The Dogs – *Cranked Up Really High* 7" single (Rabid)
Slaughter & The Dogs - *Where Have All The Boot Boys Gone?* 7" single (Decca)

1978
Alberto Y Los Trios Paranoias – *Heads Down No Nonsense Mindless Boogie* 7" single (Logo)
Buzzcocks – *What Do I Get* 7" single (United Artists)
Buzzcocks – *Another Music in a Different Kitchen* LP (United Artists)
Buzzcocks – *Love Bites* LP (United Artists)
Buzzcocks – *Promises*, 7" single (United Artists)
The Fall – *Bingo Master's Break Out!* 7" single (Step Forward)
The Freshies – *The Freshies EP* 7" EP (Razz)
Jon The Postman – *Jon The Postman's Peurile* LP (Bent)

Jon The Postman's Psychedelic Rock 'n' Roll Five Skinners – *Steppin' Out (of Holt's Brewery)* LP (Bent)
Magazine – *Real Life* LP (Virgin)
Magazine – *Shot By Both Sides* 7" single (Virgin)
Slaughter & The Dogs – *Do It Dog Style* LP (Decca)
The Smirks – *OK-UK* 7" single (Beserkley Records)

1979
A Certain Ratio – *The Graveyard & The Ballroom* Cassette (Factory)
Buzzcocks – *A Different Kind of Tension* LP (United Artists)
The Fall – *Dragnet* LP (Step Forward)
The Fall – *Live At The Witch Trials* LP (Step Forward)
The Frantic Elevators – *Voice in the Dark* 7" single (TJM)
Joy Division, *Transmission*, 7" single (Factory)
Joy Division, *Unknown Pleasures* LP (Factory)
Magazine – *Secondhand Daylight* LP (Virgin)
The Mothmen – *Does It Matter Irene* 7" single (Absurd)

1980
Crispy Ambulance – *From the Cradle to the Grave* 7" single (Aural Assault)
The Distractions – *Nobody's Perfect* LP (Island)
Durutti Column – *The Return of the Durutti Column* LP (Factory)
The Fall – *Groteseque* LP (Rough Trade)
The Fall – *How I Wrote (Elastic Man)* 7" single (Rough Trade)
The Fall – *Totally Wired* 7" single (Rough Trade)
The Freshies – *I'm In Love With the Girl on the Manchester Virgin Megastore Checkout Desk* 7" single (Razz)
Joy Division, *Closer* LP (Factory)
Joy Division – *Love Will Tear Us Apart*, 7" single (Factory)
Ludus – *The Visit* 7" EP (New Hormones)

1981
A Certain Ratio – *To Each...* LP (Factory)
Durutti Column – *LC* LP (Factory)
The Fall *Slates* Mini-LP (Rough Trade)

The Freshies – *Virgin Megastore* 7" EP (Razz)
The Freshies – *Wrap Up The Rockets* 7" single (MCA)
Ludus – *Pickpocket* cassette (New Hormones)
Stockholm Monsters – *Fairy Tales* 7" single (Factory)

1982
The Chameleons – *In Shreds* 7" single (Epic)
Crispy Ambulance – *Unsightly & Serene*, 7" single (Factory)
Crispy Ambulance – *The Plateau Please*, LP (Factory)
The Fall – *Hex Enduction Hour* LP (Kamera)
The Fall – *Lie Dream of a Casino Soul* 7" single (Kamera)
Ludus – *The Seduction* 2xEP (New Hormones)
New Order – *Ceremony* 7" single (Factory)
Quando Quango – *Go Exciting* 7" single (Factory)
The Passage *XOYO* 7" single (Cherry Red)

1983
The Chameleons – *A Person Isn't Safe Anywhere These Days* 7"
single (Statik)
The Chameleons – *As High As You Can Go* 7" single (Statik)
The Chameleons – *Script of the Bridge* LP (Statik)
Howard Devoto – *Jerky Versions of the Dream* LP (Virgin)
Howard Devoto – *Rainy Season* 7" single (Virgin)
The Fall - *Kicker Conspiracy*, 7" single (Rough Trade)
The Fall – *The Man Whose Head Expanded* 7" single (Rough Trade)
New Order – *Blue Monday*, 12" single (Factory)
New Order – *Power, Corruption & Lies* LP (Factory)
Quando Quango – *Love Tempo* 7" single (Factory
The Smiths – *Hand In Glove* 7" single (Rough Trade)
The Smiths – *This Charming Man* 7" single (Rough Trade)
Tools You Can Trust – *Working & Shopping* 7" single (Red Energy
Dynamo)

1984
The Fall – *The Wonderful & Frightening World of the* Fall LP (Beggars
Banquet)

Inca Babies – *Grunt Cadillac* 7" single (Black Lagoon)
Inca Babies – *Big Jugular* 7" EP (Black Lagoon)
Inca Babies – *The Judge* 7" single (Black Lagoon)
The Smiths – *Hatful of Hollow* LP (Rough Trade)
The Smiths – *The Smiths* LP (Rough Trade)
The Smiths – *William, It Was Really Nothing/Please Please Please, Let Me Get What I Want/How Soon Is Now*? 12" single (Rough Trade)
Stockholm Monsters – *Alma Mater* LP (Factory)
Stockholm Monsters – *How Corrupt Is Rough Trade?* 7" single (Factory Benelux)

1985
Big Flame – *Rigour* 7" EP (Ron Johnson)
Big Flame –*Tough* 7"EP (Ron Johnson)
The Chameleons – *Singing Rule Britannia (While the Walls Close In)* 7" single (Statik)
The Chameleons – *What Does Anything Mean? Basically* (Statik)
The Fall – *This Nation's Saving Grace* LP (Beggar's Banquet)
Happy Mondays – *Forty Five EP* 7" EP (Factory)
Inca Babies – *Rumble* LP (Black Lagoon)
James – *James II: Hymn From A Village* 7" single (Factory)
New Order – *Low-Life* LP (Factory)
Quando Quango – *Pigs & Battleships* LP (Factory)
The Smiths – *Meat Is Murder* LP (Rough Trade)

1986
A Witness – *I Am John's Pancreas* LP (Ron Johnson)
Big Flame – *Cubist Pop Manifesto* 7" EP (Ron Johnson)
The Chameleons – *Strange Times* (Geffen)
Easterhouse – *Contenders* LP (Rough Trade)
Easterhouse – *Whistling in the Dark* 7" single (Rough Trade)
The Fall – *Bend Sinister* LP (Beggars Banquet)
The Fall – *Living Too Late* 7" single (Beggars Banquet)
The Fall – *Mr Pharmacist/Lucifer Over Lancashire/Auto Tech Pilot* 7" single (Beggars Banquet)

Happy Mondays – *Freaky Dancin'* (Factory)
The Smiths – *Panic* 7" single (Rough Trade)
The Smiths – *The Queen is Dead* LP (Rough Trade)

1987
Dub Sex, *Push!* Mini-LP (Ugly Man)
Eskimos & Egypt – *The Cold EP* 7" EP (Village)
The Fall – *Hit The North* 7" single (Beggars Banquet)
Happy Mondays – *24 Hour Party People*, 7" single (Factory)
Happy Mondays – *Squirrel & G-Man Twenty Four Hour Party People Plastic Face Carnt Smile (White Out)* LP (Factory)
Miaow – *When It All Comes Down* 7" single (Factory)
Mock Turtles – *Pomona* 12" single (Imaginary)
The Smiths – *Sheila Take A Bow* 7" single (Rough Trade)
The Smiths – *Strangeways Here We Come* LP (Rough Trade)
Stone Roses – *Sally Cinnamon* 12" single (FM Revolver)
Twang – *Sharp* 7" single (Stet/Ron Johnson)

1988
808 State – *Newbuild*, LP (Creed)
A Guy Called Gerald *Voodoo Ray* 12" EP (Rham!)
Barry Adamson – *Moss Side Story* LP (Mute)
The Fall – *The Frenz Experiment* LP (Beggars Banquet)
The Fall *I Am Kurious Oranj* LP (Beggars Banquet)
Happy Mondays – *Bummed* LP (Factory)
Happy Mondays – *Wrote For Luck* 7" single (Factory)
Inspiral Carpets – *Planecrash* 12" EP (Cow/Playtime)
Luxuria – *Unanswerable Lust* LP (Beggar's Banquet)
Man From Delmonte – *Will Nobody Save Louise* 7" single (Ugly Man)
Morrissey – *Suedehead* 7" single (HMV)
Morrissey – *Everyday Is Like Sunday* (HMV)
Morrissey – *Viva Hate* LP (HMV)
Stone Roses – *Elephant Stone* 7" single (Silvertone)

1989
808 State – *Ninety* LP (ZTT)

808 State – *Pacific State* 12" EP (ZTT)
808 State – *Quadrastate* 12" EP (Creed)
A Guy Called Gerald – *Hot Lemonade* LP (Rham!)
Dub Sex – *Swerve* 12" single (Cut Deep)
Electronic – *Getting Away With* It 12" single (Factory)
Happy Mondays – *Madchester Rave On* 12" EP (Factory)
Happy Mondays – *WFL* 12" single (Factory)
Humanoid – *Stakker Humanoid* 12" single (Westside)
Inspiral Carpets – *Dung 4* Cassette (Cow)
Inspiral Carpets – *Find Out Why* 7" single (Cow)
Inspiral Carpets – *Joe* 12" single (Cow)
Inspiral Carpets – *Move* 7" single (Cow)
Inspiral Carpets – *Trainsurfing* 12" EP (Cow)
James – *Come Home* 7" single (Rough Trade)
James – *Sit Down* 7" single (Rough Trade)
King of the Slums – *Barbarous English Fayre* LP (Play Hard)
King of the Slums – *England's Finest Hopes* 12" EP (Play Hard)
King of the Slums – *Vicious British Boyfriend* 12" EP (Play Hard)
Mock Turtles – And then She *Smiles 12" single (Imaginary)*
New Order – *Technique* LP (Factory)
Stone Roses – *Fools Gold* – 7" single (Silvertone)
Stone Roses – *Made of Stone* 7" single (Silvertone)
Stone Roses – *She Bangs the Drums* 7" single (Silvertone)
Stone Roses – *The Stone Roses* LP (Silvertone)

1990
808 State – *Cubik/Olympic* 12" single
A Certain Ratio – *acr:mcr* (A&M)
A Guy Called Gerald – *Automanikk* LP (Columbia)
The Fall – *Extricate* LP (Fontana)
The Fall – *Telephone Thing* 7" single (Fontana)
Happy Mondays – *Kinky Afro* 7" single (Factory)
Happy Mondays – *Pills 'n' Thrills and Bellyaches* LP (Factory)
Happy Mondays – *Step On* 7" single (Factory)
The High – *Somewhere Soon* LP (London)
Inspiral Carpets – *Life* LP (Mute)

Inspiral Carpets – *This Is How It Feels* 7" single (Mute)
Inspiral Carpets – *She Comes In The Fall* 7" single (Mute)
James – *Gold Mother* LP (Fontana)
Krispy 3 – Comin Thru Clear 12" single (K3)
MC Tunes – *The North at its Heights* LP (ZTT)
MC Tunes vs 808 State – *The Only Rhyme That Bites* 12" single (ZTT)
MC Tunes vs 808 State – *Tunes Splits the Atom* 12" single (ZTT)
Mock Turtles – *Turtle Soup* LP (Imaginary)
New Order – *World In Motion* 7" single (Factory)
Northside – *Shall We Take A Trip* 7" single (Factory)
Paris Angels – *Scope* 12" single (Sheer Joy)
Paris Angels – *Perfume/All On You* 12" single (Sheer Joy)
Ruthless Rap Assassins – And It Wasn't A Dream 12" single (EMI)
Ruthless Rap Assassins – Just Mellow 12" single (EMI)
Ruthless Rap Assassins – The Killer Album LP (EMI)
Stone Roses – *One Love* 7" single (Silvertone)

Connect with me Online

http://adeepershadeofred.blogspot.co.uk
www.facebook.com/mark.nevin.988
Twitter: @DeepredMark

Printed in Great Britain
by Amazon.co.uk, Ltd.,
Marston Gate.